Cambridge Studies in French

CLAUDE SIMON
WRITING THE VISIBLE

Cambridge Studies in French
General editor: MALCOLM BOWIE

For a list of other titles in this series,
see pp. 233—4

CLAUDE SIMON

WRITING THE VISIBLE

CELIA BRITTON

Lecturer in French Studies,
University of Reading

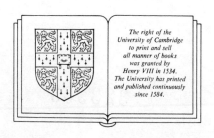

The right of the
University of Cambridge
to print and sell
all manner of books
was granted by
Henry VIII in 1534.
The University has printed
and published continuously
since 1584.

CAMBRIDGE UNIVERSITY PRESS

CAMBRIDGE

NEW YORK   NEW ROCHELLE

MELBOURNE   SYDNEY

Published by the Press Syndicate of the University of Cambridge
The Pitt Building, Trumpington Street, Cambridge CB2 1RP
32 East 57th Street, New York, NY 10022, USA
10 Stamford Road, Oakleigh, Melbourne 3166, Australia

First published 1987

Printed in Great Britain at
the University Press, Cambridge

British Library cataloguing in publication data
Britton, Celia
Claude Simon: writing the visible. –
(Cambridge studies in French).
1. Simon, Claude – Criticism and
interpretation
I. Title
843.914   PQ2637.I547Z/

Library of Congress cataloguing in publication data
Britton, Celia.
Claude Simon: writing the visible.
Bibliography.
Includes index.
1. Simon, Claude – Criticism and interpretation.
I. Title.
PQ2637.I547Z6   1987   843'.914   87–10267

ISBN 0 521 33077 7

WS

CONTENTS

v

ACKNOWLEDGEMENTS

Some of the material of this book originally appeared in articles in *French Studies*, *Degré Second*, *The Review of Contemporary Fiction*, and *Claude Simon: New Directions* (edited by Alastair B. Duncan); I would like to thank the respective editors for their permission to use parts of those articles. I am also grateful to the University of Reading for allowing me to take three months' leave of absence in order to finish the book. In writing it I have benefited from help and advice generously offered by a number of people. Above all I would like to express my gratitude to the following: Malcolm Bowie, for his constant encouragement and guidance; Giulio Lepschy, whose comments on the first chapter have clarified many issues; Lorraine Standing and Lorna Scott for their help in preparing the manuscript; and Lyle Conquest for providing moral support – this book is dedicated to him.

The following English translations of Simon's works may be consulted:

The Flanders Road, tr. R. Howard, John Calder, London, 1961
The Grass, tr. R. Howard, George Braziller, New York, 1961
Histoire, tr. R. Howard, George Braziller, New York, 1968
The Battle of Pharsalus, tr. R. Howard, George Braziller, New York, 1971
Conducting Bodies, tr. H.R. Lane, Calder & Boyars, London, 1975
Triptych, tr. H.R. Lane, John Calder, London, 1977
The World About Us (*Leçon de choses*), tr. D. Weissbort, Ontario, Review Press Translation Series, 1983
The Wind, tr. R. Howard, George Braziller, New York, 1986

INTRODUCTION

Claude Simon is unquestionably one of the most powerful and innovative novelists of the post-war period in France; and this is a period in which literary innovation has meant above all the challenging and undermining of realism. The Nouveau Roman group, of which Simon has always been considered a central member, has been in the forefront of the attack on representational writing since the mid 1950s. To attempt, thirty years later, to discuss his novels in their relation to, precisely, the representation of the *visible* may therefore seem a reactionary move, or simply a perverse one. But what this book sets out to do is not in any sense to reclaim Simon for realism, or return to earlier critical positions; it is rather to uncover in his writing certain tensions and contradictions which seem to me to be connected with the issue of visual representation – an issue which, as I hope to show, remains less resolved in textual practice than it is in literary theory. It is also, in Simon's case, an extraordinarily potent issue, precisely because of the ambiguities and polarities that it generates: his texts are written through, and derive a peculiar energy from, these internal tensions.

A more external tension, however, becomes apparent as soon as the chronological development of Simon's novels is compared with that of his fellow *nouveaux romanciers* Michel Butor and Alain Robbe-Grillet. This shows how much longer Simon remained within a humanist framework of psychological representation – i.e. of experiences and images perceived, remembered or imagined. Thus Robbe-Grillet's *La Jalousie* and Butor's *La Modification*, which both came out in 1957, are far more 'structuralist' texts than Simon's *L'Herbe* which appeared the following year; similarly, Robbe-Grillet's *Dans le Labyrinthe* of 1959 – an even more radical undermining of the 'readability' of realist fiction – predates by a year Simon's best-known and perhaps most *emotionally* forceful novel *La Route des Flandres*; this latter is in turn contemporaneous with the extremely complex and almost mathematical structures of Butor's

1

Degrés; and 1962 saw the publication of, on the one hand, Butor's *Mobile* which can no longer be called a novel at all, and, on the other, Simon's *Le Palace* which still retains a basis in psychological realism – a central consciousness remembering its past experiences.

There is thus a considerable discrepancy, at least up to the mid 1960s, between the representational discourse of Simon's novels and the conscious subversion of representation pursued by the other principal members of the Nouveau Roman group. In fact as late as 1975, Robbe-Grillet points out that Simon's continuing attachment to *referents* (i.e. objects of representation) sets him apart from the rest of them; in a discussion at the 'Nouveau Roman: hier, aujourd'hui' conference at Cerisy, 1971, he said: 'Il n'en reste pas moins que Claude Simon nous donne constamment ces référents ... Donc il faut bien croire que Simon accorde aux référents une importance supérieure à celle que font les autres romanciers de cette réunion' (vol. 1: 33).[1]

There is of course no particular reason why Simon *should* write against representation and reference; but given the very overt and systematic problematization of representation that his colleagues were engaged on, his own involvement in it nevertheless seems slightly strange. It has usually been assumed, if not very explicitly, that this can be explained in terms of a simple logic of development: that Simon moves from conventionally realist novels to, firstly, a modified 'phenomenological' kind of psychological realism based on the perceiving consciousness, and then to the 'formalist' novels of the 1970s (with the two points of transition, in so far as these can be pinpointed, usually taken to be *Le Vent* in 1957 and *La Bataille de Pharsale* in 1969). From this point of view there is of course no *contradiction*; in relation to the rest of the Nouveau Roman, Simon is merely a late developer. And the explanation is, indeed, supported by the fact that it is only when he 'catches up' with the others that Simon starts to theorize his own writing: all his conference papers and articles were produced in the 1970s, at the same time as he was writing his formalist novels.

Some such evolution in his writing – i.e. a gradual and fairly consistent movement away from realism – has undoubtedly taken place. But it is not at all clear that this can serve as an adequate explanation of the status of representation in his work. In other words, the question of representation is still, precisely, a *question* and even a problem, for several reasons which I will briefly outline. Exact definitions of what counts as representation will be discussed in the next chapter; but in so far as one of its possible forms is a concern

2

with the visible, however fragmentary, it can be found throughout *all* of the novels, including the three 'formalist' ones, in which – as I shall argue later – the relation between the visible and the text has been transformed, but the two poles of that relation are still present. Above all, however, the idea that Simon's writing follows the path of an in some sense natural or automatic development away from realism, culminating in *Leçon de choses*, becomes completely untenable with the appearance in 1981 of *Les Géorgiques*, which marks a very definite return to the discourse of the 1960s.[2]

Thirdly, Simon himself, in retrospective comment – made from the vantage point of the 1970s – on his earlier novels, tends to assimilate them to his current position by simply denying any representational elements in them: as though what is at issue here is less a rational appraisal of his development than a certain need to 'repress' representation. He is particularly emphatic on the question of *visual* representation: at the Cerisy conference devoted to his work, a question to him about the description of a door in *La Route des Flandres* provokes the reply: 'vous ne pouvez pas "voir", de quelque façon que ce soit, la porte dont vous parlez. Jean Ricardou a très justement fait observer que, contrairement au cliché répandu, on ne "voit" rien quand on lit (sauf des caractères imprimés ou calligraphiés). Comme il a dit, il n'y a pas vision, mais intellection, ce qui est tout autre chose' (Ricardou 1975: 408).[3] Leaving aside for the moment one's impression of a certain amount of coaching from Ricardou, it is still hard to reconcile the theoretical position which Simon adopts here with most readings of *La Route des Flandres*.

Moreover, a similar inconsistency can also be found operating in the reverse direction; that is, even the most forceful of Simon's theoretical contestations of representation contain a peculiar undercurrent of resistance to 'pure textual production'. In a paper entitled 'La fiction mot à mot', given at the 1971 Colloque de Cerisy on the Nouveau Roman, he criticizes realist texts for their reliance on a logic of fictional events which remains completely extraneous to the text (Simon 1972: 77), and proposes instead 'une certaine logique interne du texte, propre au texte, découlant à la fois de sa musique (rythme, assonances, cadence de la phrase) et de son matériau (vocabulaire, "figures", tropes – car notre langage ne s'est pas formé au hasard)' which he sees as 'fécondante et, par elle-même, engendrante de fiction' (78).[4] But this turns out not to be, strictly speaking, a purely textual logic in the sense of a logic based on the play of signifiers, the specific qualities of *words*; because when he goes on to illustrate it with examples from *Les Corps conducteurs*, it is noticeable that they are all, without exception, based on the visual properties of the signified as much as the links between signifiers: they are all *shapes*. The sequence *croix — crucifix — cruciforme* (ibid.: 78–9) is in any case hardly very adventurous as word-play; but it is also sanctioned by, and does not go beyond, the *visual* similarity of the objects referred to; and the same is true of the various different characters who are brought into relation by all being 'courbés', and of the S-shaped curves of the river 'snaking' through the forest, the string on the pavement, and the feather 'boa' on the carpet (79).

Thus at various points in the article, the visible creeps back — as when Simon uses a quotation from Leonardo da Vinci talking about painting in order to allow him to say: 'Et, le livre refermé, le lecteur peut tout de même … "saisir tout le champ visuel d'un seul coup"' (86).[5] The fact that even when he is ostensibly writing a systematic attack on representation and hence, by implication, on the visual, the latter refuses to go away suggests strongly that throughout the 1970s Simon is caught up in a certain *misrecognition* of the presence of the visible in his writing, and that this prevents his rejection of representation from being entirely rational and straightforward. It also suggests that the visible is a more insistent and troubling force than has hitherto been assumed, and one that cannot be contained within the boundaries allocated to it by a simple evolutionary explanation.

It seems, in other words, that the status of the visible — ambivalent, persistent and in some degree unacknowledged — is in need of further investigation. The emphases of recent literary theory, and its application to Simon's work, have tended to obscure the very obvious fact that his novels are actually obsessed with vision, and with visual representations (pictures, sculptures), and with the problems involved in textual description of visual reality and visual representations. As Serge Doubrovsky has put it: 'This work may be read as a metaphorical epic of the *eye* … Seeing, for Simon, is the driving force behind saying; vision is the awareness of the absolute distance (from words) to things, but inversely, it is the fascination of the language-master with reality' (1981: 15). There seems, in fact, to be an investment of *desire* in seeing, in the visible as such, which undercuts the explicit theoretical stance on representation and which is, conversely, repressed by the theory.

The elements of representation to be found in his novels, and the significant force that they exert in his work as a whole, will be discussed in more detail in subsequent chapters. My initial point is that Simon's texts cannot be ascribed unambiguously either to representation or to textual production. Karin Holter concludes her paper on

Triptyque with a *general* statement of the text as a tension between co-existing forces: 'ce passage montre assez que toute lecture aussi bien que toute écriture doit accepter et essayer de penser, pour chaque texte, la tension contradictoire entre le référentiel et le littéral' (1975: 375),[6] providing a nicely balanced formulation within which individual texts can be analysed. What seems to me the distinctive feature of Simon's work, though, is that the 'tension' is not merely an issue of theoretical interest but results in a very particular power and fascination in the novels themselves. They are a mixture of representational and 'productive' discourses; and this mixture, moreover, is not homogenized; there is a perceptible alternating movement in the texts between one discourse and the other, an *oscillation* whereby fragments of representation − 'which, though vivid in detail, blur and fade into one another at the edges'[7] − emerge, appear to establish themselves, and then dissolve again into the play of textual relations. The oscillation sets up a rhythm of appearance and disappearance, of illusion and aporia, which both structures the entire text and, in its hesitation, evokes a fragility and a lightness which also become objects of fascination.

I shall thus be arguing that significant elements of representational discourse are to be found throughout Simon's novels; that they are above all concerned with vision and indicate a certain specific desire for the visible; that they are in contradiction with other elements in the texts, with his theoretical statements and with much of the more recent criticism of his novels; and that the terms of this contradictory co-existence need to be explored. Moving outside the dominant formalist discourse on Simon does not mean returning to a realist perspective: it means in the first place *revealing* the question of the persistence − and simultaneously the subversion − of visual representation in his writing.

Critical writing on Simon in fact falls into two fairly distinct periods.[8] The early criticism takes a broadly phenomenological line, stressing the themes of perception, imagination and memory; the novels are seen as breaking away from traditional realism, but as still remaining within a kind of psychological realism updated, as it were, by an injection of phenomenology. This approach was also applied to the other *nouveaux romanciers* (notably in Olga Bernal's book on Robbe-Grillet, 1964), but in Simon's case it had the added sanction of Merleau-Ponty's own considerable interest in Simon.[9] The transition from this to the later type is motivated in part by a change in Simon's own work, but also by the impact of structuralist theory on literary analysis in general.

5

In order to bring out the problems which seem to me to be associated with each of these two approaches, I shall discuss in some detail one representative piece of work from each period. The early phenomenological criticism is well exemplified by Michel Deguy's excellent article on *Le Palace*: 'Claude Simon et la représentation' (1962). This focuses on the predominance of visual perception in the novel; Deguy argues that Simon sets up a particular 'cinematic' mode of vision which creates a subject as pure spectator, as 'un homme au monde comme pur regard fasciné par images' (1015), and which in so doing reduces the whole of reality to (pictorial) representation: 'Tout est transparence à cet art; il a réduit l'être de ce qui est à cette transparence à la représentation, à cette "représentabilité"' (ibid.). Simon's writing, in other words, is governed by 'une perception qui atteint le réel *comme* illustration ou dessin' (1014, author's italics),[10] and so effects a derealization of reality.

Deguy's discussion of 'le regard' and its objects is penetrating and profound; it is close to my own concern with the visible in Simon's novels, and I have found many of his insights extremely helpful, as will be evident from subsequent chapters of this book. The overall theoretical context of his article, however, seems to me rather less illuminating. His position is more or less explicitly phenomenological: he remarks on 'le parallélisme du discours romanesque ici avec le discours phénoménologique de Merleau-Ponty', cites Merleau-Ponty's remarks on perspective, and asks 'Peut-on parler, à propos du discours romanesque, d'une phénoménologie de la perception spontanée, sauvage et tragique?' (1010, note 1). From this point of view, the derealizing effect of representation is a form of alienation – 'Les rapports entre choses et êtres ... comme dépourvus de tout autre sens que celui d'être régis par une nécessité qui échappe aux *acteurs*' (1028, author's italics) – and hence 'tragique': later in the article, he distinguishes between the classic 'conscience phénoménologique auprès d'un monde *plein* découvert par *profils*' (1020, author's italics),[11] and the 'anéantissement' (annihilation) of Simon's world, which thus appears as a *degenerate* variant of the phenomenological view. This moral emphasis emerges more clearly towards the end of the article when he claims 'nous croyons ensuite que cette manière de voir qui commande cette manière de faire voir, est commandée très profondément par l'intuition éthique, qui vient elle-même de l'expérience; ou plutôt les deux ici ne font qu'un' (1026).[12] The connection that he goes on to make between the 'manière de voir' and Simon's attitude to history is certainly convincing: but the implication that it is primarily a moral question is less so.

More centrally, to explain the conjunction of the visible and the unreal solely as a form of alienation is to overlook the strong element of desire that is bound up with vision — although Deguy himself does in fact describe the perceiving consciousness as 'fascinée donc et frustrée à la fois, et de telle sorte que la fascination et la frustration s'exaspèrent réciproquement' (1016–17),[13] which, surely, exactly formulates the structure of desire. The derealization of the visible thus seems more likely to be an effect of phantasy, as I will argue later, rather than of alienation.

But the principal difficulty in Deguy's conception of the novel — and one that is common to all the early criticism of Simon — lies in his treatment of the actual writing. In seeing language simply as expression ('Pourtant le roman ne cherche à dire rien d'autre qu'une manière de dire les choses comme elles sont, c'est-à-dire comme elles apparaissent', 1009),[14] he forecloses any consideration of the text as text, and of its capacity for generating meanings through the play of language itself. Tying writing down to the expression of an existing meaning also results in a short-circuiting of its relation to vision: words are the direct unmediated trace of the look: 'Les déplacements du regard composent un édifice de lignes dont les phrases sont comme les traces écrites, l'ombre projetée sur le papier, lignes de force du discours, architecture à plat ... Au regard qui parle ici s'appliquerait littéralement la formule de "caméra-stylo"' (1014).[15] The explosion of metaphors here is powerfully suggestive, but in assimilating writing successively to shadow, magnetic field, building and camera, it also has the effect of cancelling out its specificity as writing. The mechanisms whereby vision is translated into text are surely more complex and problematic — more prosaic, also — than this.

Deguy's article illustrates both the strengths and the weaknesses of the loosely 'phenomenological' type of criticism of Simon, and in so doing indicates also the direction that later treatments of his work were to take. The question of the relative autonomy of language is central to the debate: what comes to challenge positions like Deguy's, and rapidly assumes dominance, is the emphasis on the text as 'l'aventure d'une écriture' (adventure of a piece of writing), to use the phrase coined by Ricardou, and as fundamentally anti-representational. It is in fact Ricardou who is mainly responsible for this critical revolution. He is a crucial figure, not just in relation to Simon but to the Nouveau Roman in general; and although his influence has now declined considerably, the impact he made on critical theory is irreversible, in the sense that it is now virtually impossible to go back to the type of work that was being done in the 1960s.

7

His book *Le Nouveau Roman* will be discussed in Chapter 1 in a wider context. As for his analyses of Simon in particular, his articles on *La Route des Flandres*, *La Bataille de Pharsale*, and later *Les Corps conducteurs* and *Triptyque* were immensely influential in the 1970s, and inspired a great deal of similar work by other people (including, some would say, Simon himself); they remain of importance. Their main characteristics are an extremely detailed attention to the micro-structures of the texts (metaphors, puns, anagrams, alliteration and rhyme, pastiche, etc.) and the organization of these verbal strategies into an almost equally detailed classificatory system. He maintains a vigorous stance against realist expressive discourse; his article 'La Bataille de la phrase' – which may be taken as typical of his approach – prefaces its analysis of Simon's novel of nearly the same name with a general section entitled 'Système d'une subversion de l'expression', setting out the mechanisms whereby 'les traditionnelles procédures expressives' are transformed by 'le texte moderne' into *generative* 'moyens de production' (1971: 119) – giving 'métaphore productrice', 'calembour producteur', 'fragment producteur', and 'vocable producteur'.[16] He then discusses *La Bataille de Pharsale* under the general headings 'Génération' (124), 'Transitions' (137), 'Relations' (146), and a short concluding section called 'Ecriture/lecture' (155). Each section views the novel as a construction of language, producing and produced by its own 'laws' of generation and structure. Metaphors, for instance, function like railway points, as a kind of switching system to change the direction of the text; he says of one example: 'En cet aiguillage, la métaphore est aussi bien *structurelle* (elle ordonne les cellules du texte) que *transitaire* (comme un sas, elle autorise le passage de l'une a l'autre)' (120, author's italics). And within this textual transportation system, 'le calembour peut aussi fonctionner comme un aiguillage. Il suffit que l'analogie de certains de leurs signifiés permette la jonction de deux cellules fictives eloignées' (121).[17] Fictional incident, from this perspective, is merely an epiphenomenal spin-off of the productivity of the text.

The method results in an analysis of the text which is often perspicacious and revealing: in the first section, perhaps the most impressive, he demonstrates brilliantly how the initial section of the novel is generated by the Valéry stanza placed *en exergue*. But overall the insights are to some extent submerged by his fondness for taxonomical proliferation: the fact that he needs thirty-two categories (and two diagrams) to account for the 'moyens de production' of a single novel reduces the explanatory value of all of them, and seems to have less to do with Simon's writing than with Ricardou's overruling desire for order combined with complication.

This kind of formalism also makes it impossible to look at the position of the subject in the text; in rejecting the humanist subject of expressive language, he posits the text as — in some unexamined sense — self-generating, and the subject is simply excluded. What Ricardou is ultimately engaged in is the fetishization of a conception of the text which is too technocratic to be really revolutionary ('productivity', after all, is a concept of management, used *against* the workers).

There is a further way in which, I would argue, his approach is seriously reductive. In the same article, he attacks '[les] fanatiques de l'expression qui réduisent le langage à un presque rien instrumental' (131), and remarks scathingly that he has chosen *La Bataille de Pharsale* to illustrate his theory precisely because 'il est semble-t-il de bon ton, aujourd'hui encore, de restreindre les travaux de Claude Simon au libertaire foisonnement du lyrique et du sensoriel' (118).[18] He, in contrast, makes the opposite assumption, not only that Simon's novels are completely non-representational, but that *all* 'modern texts' are: the starting point for his theoretical work is that 'À peine *abolis*, en leur complicité, les rassurants schémas de l'expression et de la représentation, il faut faire face à un immense afflux de possibles' (118, my italics).[19] The normative bias of this position is obvious: representation and expression are reactionary, therefore they no longer exist. This is clearly open to criticism on simple logical grounds; in relation to Simon specifically, it has the effect of suppressing another whole dimension of his writing. It is not just that attention to linguistic devices *need not* exclude consideration of the diegetic level of the writing; it is rather that this level *has to* be taken into account, because it cannot be eliminated as easily as Ricardou thinks; as David Carroll points out in his book on Simon, 'By emphasizing technique and instrumentality ... problems of sense and representation do not simply disappear' (1982: 166).

That is, a critical account of Simon's novels is in my view bound to start from the proposition that they are, as texts, an interplay of representational and anti-representational elements. This point has of course already been made in previous work on Simon,[20] but usually restricted to the 'central period' novels, and sometimes in a rather partisan spirit: there is a tendency to assume that representation is, simply, a bad thing. Thus, for instance, Gérard Roubichou's rather loaded characterization of *Histoire*:

The 'newness' of *Histoire* originates above all from the fact that here the Simonian novel appears more completely than in the past as a site for textual production at every level ... [but] *Histoire* still demonstrates the effects of an inheritance or tradition proper to Simon's novels: that is, the dialectic at work between the textual and the representative (*sic*) since *The Wind*. However, *Histoire* takes Simon a step forward, although the work still must be emptied of its psychological content   (1981: 182)

– is typical of a pervasive implicit denigration of representational writing which, while it ultimately derives from a coherent critique of bourgeois ideology (see Chapter 1, note 25), often in practice becomes both moralistic and simplistic. Thus Lucien Dällenbach's description of the later novel *Triptyque* implies the same normative logic of the 'step forward', and adds to it the rhetoric of a promised land of pure textuality: 'Avec *Triptyque*, le roman simonien fait un nouveau pas en avant et accède, pourrait-on dire, au lieu que les œuvres précédentes n'avaient cessé de convoiter et d'approcher sans parvenir à l'atteindre. Eliminant les "scories" qui subsistaient dans *Histoire* et *Les Corps conducteurs*, il assure mieux encore sa continuité scripturale et opte sans repentir cette fois pour la discontinuité référentielle' (1975: 162).[21]

More importantly, the co-existence of these antagonistic elements is usually, as in the cases of Roubichou and Dällenbach, explained away simply as a transitional stage in a process of development – and this, as I have already argued, is inadequate. There has not, to my knowledge, been any serious questioning as to *why* the tension persists throughout virtually all of Simon's work. What is needed is not to privilege either side but to explore their interaction and the conditions which produce it.

An approach somewhat different from Ricardou's is represented by a minority current in the Cerisy conferences – Sylvère Lotringer, Irène Tschinka – and, in a more developed form, by work such as Stephen Heath's book on the Nouveau Roman, and David Carroll's recent juxtaposition of Simon's novels with a range of different critical theories. Dällenbach's more recent writing on Simon (for instance, 'Le tissu de mémoire' in the 1982 paperback edition of *La Route des Flandres*), and Antony C. Pugh's articles, also fall into this category. Despite important divergences, these can all be characterized as poststructuralist, as opposed to the basically structuralist orientation of Ricardou and his disciples. This means, above all, that instead of a conception of the literary work which simply represses the question of the subject, they are committed (as the title of Carroll's book,

The Subject in Question, suggests) to a subversion of the traditional humanist conception of the subject – including its phenomenological version – in favour of what can loosely be called a post-structuralist one, arrived at either on the basis of psychoanalysis, as Heath does for the most part, or, in Carroll's case, according to the Derridean concept of deconstruction.

They are all, however, to some extent influenced by, or at least involved in the debate over the status of, psychoanalysis, particularly in its Lacanian form. Much has been written over the last few years on the validity or otherwise of 'applying psychoanalysis to literature', and on the validity of formulating the relationship between them in that rather bald way. Thus Shoshana Felman, in her introduction to the issue of *Yale French Studies* (55/56, 1977) devoted to psychoanalysis and literature, prefers the term 'implication' to application: literature and psychoanalysis meet on equal terms, in a relationship of reciprocal implication, rather than the hierarchical application of a superior psychoanalytic theory to an inferior literary object. It is not quite clear how much weight the distinction between implication and application can be made to bear: given that psychoanalytic concepts can be 'applied' either subtly and cogently or crudely and unconvincingly, one wonders whether it really amounts in practice to much more than a distinction between good and bad critical analysis. If it does, then it is because 'implication' means something more than just using psychoanalytic ideas with the understated elegance that current fashion requires; it involves treating psychoanalytic discourse as also in a sense literary – the position adopted by Barthes when, in *Le Plaisir du texte*, he writes: 'Le monument psychanalytique doit être traversé – non contourné, comme les voies admirables d'une très grande ville, voies à travers lesquelles on peut jouer, rêver, etc.: c'est une fiction' (92).[22] Literature, as Carroll points out, has after all been intimately involved in the development of psychoanalysis: 'literature played an important role in the formation of many of the major Freudian concepts, and thus psychoanalysis was never really an "outside" threatening the "specificity of literature" (assuming this concept has meaning) because it was from the start "literary" in many ways, "inside" as much as "outside"' (1982: 28).

That the relation has to be one of intertextuality, between two *texts*, rather than application of a theory to an object, becomes particularly clear anyway when the theorist in question is Lacan; the deliberately polysemic and metaphorical nature of his discourse works to resist any attempt on the part of the reader to reduce it to a manageable and straightforwardly 'applicable' set of ideas. Hence the metaphors ('point de capiton', 'lamelle', etc.), the notorious ambiguity of such key terms as 'l'Autre' and 'objet a', the punning play on 'hommelette' ('the little man, the feminized man and the scrambled man', Bowie 1979: 143) and 'séparer'.[23] Lacan's theory is, as the title of his main collection suggests, above all *writing*; that is, it demands a response as text.[24] Malcolm Bowie argues that the force of Lacan's theorization of the unconscious itself prevents the reification of the discourse into any kind of system: Lacan aims 'to allow the energies of the unconscious to become palpable in the wayward rhythm of his sentences, to discourage the reader from building premature theoretical constructions upon the text and to compel him to collaborate fully in the inventive work of language' (1979: 121).

This of course raises some important issues regarding the status of psychoanalysis as theory: the more it begins to look like literature, the less plausible are its claims to any kind of scientific truth. In fact the debate between Lacan and Derrida centres on precisely this question.[25] We need to ask, therefore, in precisely what sense is psychoanalysis 'literary', to what extent does this make it different from other sciences, and, finally, how relevant is any 'scientific' status it may have to any insights it may offer into literature?

In the first place, it is clear that psychoanalysis cannot simply be equated with literature (or fiction, in Barthes's formulation), because it is interdependent with a clinical practice which has no equivalent in literature. It *is* 'literary', however, in so far as Lacan's — and indeed Freud's — views on the human psyche are inseparable from their textual formulation; that is, the language of psychoanalysis is not merely a neutral instrument of communication, but exerts a determining influence on the whole enterprise. And yet this is a feature which it shares with science in general; the insight that all theory is invisibly constrained by the discourse it supposedly 'uses' — and that its access to absolute truth is therefore effectively cut off — is of course central to Derrida's critique of Western epistemology, but has also long been recognized from within the scientific community itself: as early as 1962, the theoretical physicist Thomas Kuhn, for instance, comes reluctantly to the conclusion that scientific data are to some extent the product of theory rather than the other way round, and links this explicitly to the fact that, as soon as one departs from the pure abstractions of mathematics, a neutral scientific language is impossible.[26]

But this does not mean that scientific research and the construction of theories is a worthless enterprise; Kuhn argues convincingly (p. 65) that there is a kind of dynamic in scientific research whereby the very rigidity of the 'paradigm' precipitates its eventual breakdown and the transition to a different paradigm which, while not 'better' overall, at least allows new problems to be addressed and even solved; he concludes that it is possible for science to progress, in a non-teleological fashion, on the basis of the relative validity of the theory in question. Thus it would seem to follow that, while there may be other reasons for doubting the scientificity of psychoanalysis, the fact of its implication in a non-neutral language should not disqualify it from theoretical status.

But what does distinguish it from physics, for instance, is its insistence on recognizing and reflecting upon its own rhetorical nature. It thus offers a discourse which is both significantly different from that of literature and yet at the same time equally complex and equally aware of the difficulties inherent in, precisely, its discursive status; and it is this aspect – the 'literary' rather than the 'scientific' aspect of psychoanalysis – that is arguably the more illuminating as a perspective from which to observe fiction. It will also, of course, prove more illuminating in relation to some novelists than to others; I would claim that Simon's texts are deeply implicated in psycho-analytic concepts of phantasy and unconscious desire, and are thus particularly open to – and opened up by – consideration in relation to various Freudian and Lacanian texts. In bringing Lacan's theor-etical writing into contact with elements of Simon's novels, I have tried not to be reductive of either.

A very different type of problem involved in writing this book has been the more practical question of how best to organize discussion of such a substantial body of work. Simon has written a lot, and has been writing for a long time: thirteen novels over forty years (as well as several short pieces and the autobiographical *La Corde raide*, none of which will be discussed here). Since the first two novels, *Le Tricheur* (1945) and *Gulliver* (1947), are in so many ways atypical of his work,[27] I have excluded them from consideration. The next two, *Le Sacre du printemps* (1954) and *Le Vent* (1957), will be referred to occasionally, but I shall concentrate mainly on what are sometimes known as Simon's 'middle' and 'late' periods, because it is in these that, it seems to me, his writing assumes its most characteristic and interesting forms.

In some respects these novels form a very unified corpus. A disparate collection of themes – war, the natural cycle, sexual failure and jealousy, families, old age, pictures – acquires a certain coherence simply by recurring from book to book. Moreover, certain characters figure in more than one novel: thus from being an important secondary character in *L'Herbe*, Georges moves into the central position in *La Route des Flandres*, which introduces Corinne who in turn reappears in *Histoire*, and Charles is prominent in *Histoire, La Bataille de Pharsale* and *Les Géorgiques*: while the student of *Le Palace* can (more ambiguously perhaps) be identified with the nameless narrator of *Histoire*, who is also carried over into *La Bataille de Pharsale* and *Les Géorgiques*. On a more purely textual level, also, there is a whole repertoire of images and phrases which echo from one novel to the next. The intertextual dimension of the corpus is thus extremely active; it perhaps reaches a climax in *Les Géorgiques*, which re-writes parts of *La Route des Flandres* and *Le Palace* – even to the extent of mixing diegetic levels so that the 'author' of *La Route des Flandres* becomes a character in *Les Géorgiques* – but is present in numerous links, overlaps and resonances between *all* the novels considered here. For this reason, to treat each one separately would be both limiting and repetitive; rather than analysing the corpus chronologically, novel by novel, I have chosen to structure it according to the different manifestations of the central conflictual relationship between the visual and the textual.

This approach, however, does risk obliterating the diachronic dimension, which is obviously an important factor in Simon's work. The most significant changes between one novel and the next concern various aspects of the representational level of the texts: the degree and type of characterization, particularly of the central figure or narrator, the consistency of the diegetic situation, and eventually even the status of the narrative itself. There seems to be general agreement that Simon's novels become progressively less realist up to and including *Leçon de choses*, and that *Les Géorgiques* then marks a return to the 'middle period' novels of the 60s.

Within this overall move away from, and then back to, representational writing, many critics tend to divide the corpus into a series of distinct stages; as Renato Barilli says in the discussion which followed Simon's paper at the 1971 Cerisy conference: 'Nous avons assisté à un intéressant phénomène de dialectique entre continuité et discontinuité. Le producteur a raisonné en termes de continuité, il n'a pas noté de rupture à son évolution ... Les critiques adopteraient plutôt un point de vue de discontinuité' (Simon 1972: 115).[28] The main dividing line between (relatively) psycho-realist and (relatively) anti-representational novels is usually drawn somewhere in the middle of *La Bataille de Pharsale* – as Barilli goes on to say: 'Après une première phase d'un réalisme très ouvert qui employait la technique du point de vue, la technique du flash back, etc., avec déjà des éléments formels, mais qui n'étaient pas encore tellement développés, on tend, à partir de *La Bataille de Pharsale*, vers une formalisation de plus en plus poussée' (ibid.)[29] – and this kind of formulation is widely accepted.[30]

Reading *La Bataille de Pharsale* one has, certainly, the sense of a radical break at the point where 'O' is introduced in Part III. But I would argue that what happens in the middle of the novel is above all a change of *style* (which will be discussed in more detail in Chapter 1) and that it does not necessarily involve the total redefinition of Simon's project that is sometimes assumed. *Leçon de choses* is clearly a very different kind of text from *Le Vent*, and what separates them is indeed a transition from realism to formalization, to use Barilli's terms. The problem is, though, that there are several different possible criteria whereby the *point* of transition could be defined; and exactly where the break occurs depends on which parameter is taken as relevant. If it is the existence of a consistent objective diegetic situation, then the break comes as early as *La Route des Flandres*, since here the reader is never sure of the point from which the events are narrated, whereas in the preceding *L'Herbe* the present time and place of the narrative are established, and the various flashbacks (to Marie's arrival at the house, Georges's childhood, etc.) unambiguously located in relation to this. But if the parameter is taken to be the existence of a consistent and identifiable narrative subject or point of view, then the crucial change occurs between *Histoire* and *La Bataille de Pharsale*; if, finally, it is defined on the basis of whether or not there is any evidence of *any* kind of subject in the text, then it comes between *Les Corps conducteurs* and *Triptyque* – but in this case the break is subsequently negated by the reappearance in *Leçon de choses* of long sequences of almost exaggeratedly oral, and hence 'subjective', narrative.

Rather than categorizing his writing in terms of one monolithic 'period' after another, then, it seems more appropriate to see its development as a series of partial transitions each occurring on a specific parameter of the work. There are, in other words, few clear breaks in the progression of Simon's work, and the movement away from a representational discourse is a gradual and complex one. Nevertheless it would be true to say that from the introduction of 'O' half-way through *La Bataille de Pharsale*, through *Les Corps conducteurs*, *Triptyque* and *Leçon de choses*, there is an increasingly free play of textual generation, less and less anchored in the representation of a psychologically coherent subject's perceptions, memories or imagination of a diegetically coherent world. But it is still less a question of two separate stages than of the particular balance struck between two opposing forces; with reference to *Triptyque*, for example, Sylvère Lotringer speaks of 'cet état de trouble ... où la représentation s'altérant, se décompose et pose avec le sujet la question de son altérité' (1975: 314).[31]

The position of Simon's latest novel, *Les Géorgiques*, is especially ambiguous and so worth considering in some detail. *Leçon de choses* seems to form some kind of limit in the viability of non-representational writing. After a gap of six years − usually long for Simon − the appearance of *Les Géorgiques* was hailed by many critics as a triumphal return to realism[32] (and also, somewhat vindictively, as signalling Simon's deliverance from the Rasputin-like influence of Ricardou). It is certainly true that *Les Géorgiques* is a far more realist text, in terms of characters and narrative, than the three preceding novels. It is also to some extent a return to the thematic concerns, and the characters, of the earlier novels, many of which appear here; the cavalryman's narrative is very close to *La Route des Flandres*, and, more abstractly, the psychological status of this discourse is roughly the same: the narrator remembering his past. Equally, the LSM narrative, based largely on the narrator imagining what might have happened, has the same tentative status as the hypothetical reconstructions which form the narratives of *Le Vent* or *Histoire*. But *Les Géorgiques* is an extremely *mixed* text, and to see it as merely marking a continuation from *La Bataille de Pharsale*, after the intervening aberration of the three formalist novels, is far too simple. Its basic structure − the interweaving of three narratives − is after all carried over from *Triptyque*; as is, particularly in the case of LSM, the monotonous repetition of verbs of seeing (e.g. pp.28−9). *Les Géorgiques* as a whole is best seen as amalgamating a combination of elements from *all* the preceding novels, although weighted more towards the central period from *La Route des Flandres* to *Histoire*.

Quite apart from this recapitulation of past work, however, it also contains an entirely new element in O's narrative − 'O' here standing no longer for some purely relational locus of perception and discourse as it did in *La Bataille de Pharsale*, but for a fictional version of George Orwell (and this contrast is itself indicative of a 'return to realism'). O's narrative, as I have argued elsewhere,[33] is in a sense more realist than any of Simon's previous work because it constructs 'O' as a subject who *knows*, and whose certainty contrasts stridently with the hesitant and exploratory nature of most of Simon's writing.

The text produces a discourse of knowledge, fulfilling the traditional didactic function of realism; and the visible at this point becomes an object of knowledge rather than desire. O attempts to eliminate all traces of emotion − of desire − from his account of the events in Spain, reducing it to 'la sécheresse d'un simple compte rendu' (314), and using the visible solely as a guarantee of objective knowledge: 'lui conférant plus de persuasion, plus de crédibilité, par plusieurs notations de ces détails, de ces "choses vues" dont tout bon journaliste sait qu'elles constituent les meilleurs certificats d'authenticité d'un reportage' (314).[34] The ironic tone in this description is evident, but Simon himself in fact makes a similar use of the visible in other parts of the novel: alongside the purely evocative description of Barcelona, for instance (p. 321−3), which does not *assert* anything but simply accumulates and juxtaposes isolated details, there are other passages where vision becomes *revelation* of the truth. But this section of *Les Géorgiques* is something of an anomaly in Simon's work.

I have tried not to neglect the diachronic changes within the series of texts. They are, however, only one aspect of my concern − namely, the question of language and visual representation as this is posed, implicitly, in and by Simon's novels. Chapter 1 situates it within a general theoretical debate, and Chapter 2 explores the basic relation between the text and the visual in the novels. The next three chapters are each centred on a more specific aspect of this: the position of the subject, the role of other representations − pictorial and verbal − in the text, and the negative side of the relation, that is, what is constructed by the text as unseen or unsaid. Chapter 6, in contrast, looks at what lies completely outside the whole issue of writing the visible, and shows how history operates in the text as marking out the 'space' of the unrepresentable. The final chapter draws some general conclusions.

1

THE THEORETICAL CONTEXT

Simon is working in the general context of a literary avant-garde whose main project is to interrogate and undermine what is seen as 'traditional realism'; and yet his own writing in many ways relies upon the conventions and techniques of realist representation. If this claim is to be pursued further, then the theoretical debate within which his novels are so ambiguously positioned must be examined.

The concepts of representation and realism are distinct, but overlapping. The term 'realism' covers a large, complex and often rather confused area: it is basically a literary category, but one which extends into the domains of philosophy, psychology, linguistics, pragmatics and theories of ideology. To follow up all these implications would of course go far beyond the limits of the present study, which aims simply to construct a kind of minimal definition of realism for the purposes of elucidating certain aspects of Simon's novels. Such a minimal definition also needs to be distinguished from a description of all the various forms that realism has taken historically; this amounts to a distinction between the features *essential* to a particular discourse, and those which are in a loose sense typical of, for instance, the nineteenth-century novel (e.g. realism 'usually' involves precise specification of a character's social status, etc.). That such a definition is possible is not of course self-evident; it presupposes a universally consistent *concept* of realism, over and above the historical occurrences of literary texts that have been, for one reason or another, perceived as realist. This question is raised by Jakobson,[1] and Genette points to something similar when he stresses the historical and cultural relativity of the 'illusion de mimésis' — 'dépendant comme toute illusion d'une relation éminemment variable entre l'émetteur et le récepteur ... L'évolution historique joue ici un rôle décisif ... il faut faire la part de cette relation variable selon les individus, les groupes et les époques, et qui ne dépend donc pas exclusivement du texte narratif' (1972: 186–7).[2]

But even if one accepts that 'realism' is a historically and socially variable phenomenon (after all, most things are), one can still attempt a definition of it that will be valid at least for contemporary readers of Simon's novels while remaining sufficiently general to be more — and less — than just a description of these novels. It will, in fact, be significantly more general than the many definitions of realist fiction that are based on the 'canonical' texts of the nineteenth-century novel — Zola, Balzac, Flaubert — and that define them in opposition to other genres such as melodrama or romance. There is a basic difference between this kind of characterization of 'the realist novel' which excludes other less worthy genres, and a minimal concept of realism based solely on the criterion of the 'effet de réel', to use the term which Barthes (1982) popularized.

In fact one could argue that critics and theorists of literature often define the necessary conditions for the 'reality effect' too strictly; the formal conditions for this are normally taken to include, for instance, a consistent point of view, a coherent chronological organization, and so on — but in fact many of the classic realist novels exhibit major inconsistencies on these axes (as is amply demonstrated in Genette's analysis of Proust, for instance)[3] without this apparently endangering the illusion of reality at all. Most readers hardly notice them. It seems, in fact, to be quite difficult to undercut the effects of realist representation; and its peculiar tenacity, its ability to survive what in rational terms are serious flaws and contradictions, suggests the existence in the reader of a *desire* to believe in it that goes deeper than conscious judgement. Representation is almost indestructible, perhaps because it provides a channel for unconscious desire.

Before looking at the relation between representation and desire, however, we have to establish more exactly what is meant by representation, and by realism. For a 'minimal' definition of realism, two concepts are necessary: *representation* and *reference*. A representation can be a purely mental phenomenon, or it can have some kind of material form: pictorial, for instance, or — as in the case of literature — linguistic. In other words, language can be used to represent reality. The terms of this rather bland statement need to be interrogated more closely, however: what exactly is, or can be, the relation between language and objects in the real world?

Numerous writers have talked about the novel as 'mirror' of reality. This implies, firstly, that representation is essentially a two-dimensional space[4] — Foucault's 'espace du tableau' — and, secondly, the concomitant notion of language as 'pane of glass', as an immediate and transparent vehicle for the object.[5] But these metaphors collapse under closer scrutiny; novels are made of language — they are linguistic objects – and language cannot, in any rigorous sense, 'mirror' or 'show' or imitate reality. As Genette remarks in his critique of the Jamesian distinction between 'telling' and 'showing', 'la notion même de *showing*, comme celle d'imitation ou de représentation narrative (et davantage encore, à cause de son caractère naïvement visuel) est parfaitement illusoire ... aucun récit ne peut ''montrer'' ou ''imiter'' l'histoire qu'il raconte. Il ne peut que la raconter ...' (1972: 185).[6]

Language, he concludes firmly, does not imitate, it *signifies*. (This contrast between a visual and a discursive mode reproduces, on the level of literary theory, the opposition which runs through Simon's novels, and which is the main concern of this book.) Literary representation is a matter not of mimesis or direct imitation, but of diegesis, or 'telling'. It does not, therefore, have *per se* any particular connection with the visual; the fact that in Simon's novels the objects of representation are overwhelmingly visual is a distinguishing characteristic of his writing.

If words do not mirror the real world, they can, alternatively, be thought to *refer* to it. A preferable and more influential explanation of literary representation takes as its starting point the notion of reference. This is of course itself a notoriously problematical concept; but for the purposes of this argument one can set aside, at least temporarily, most of the philosophical difficulties involved in it, and simply – and crudely – say that 'reference' means that when we use language in real-life situations, we talk *about* things in the real world, and that there is some kind of demonstrable relation between word and thing. What *fiction* does, then, is exploit the referential properties of language by *pretending to refer* in order to create an illusion of reality. This position is adopted notably by John Searle.[7] Fictional discourse acts exactly as though it were talking about real objects in the world, but invokes a special set of conventions 'which suspend the normal operation of the rules relating illocutionary acts and the world' (Searle, 1979: 66). We thus arrive at a possible definition of realism in terms of its discursive features: a realist discourse is one which produces a fictional representation of reality by imitating the linguistic operations of reference.

Searle is characteristically confident that he has solved this whole problem, saying:

Theorists of literature are prone to make vague remarks about how the author creates a fictional world, a world of the novel, or some such. I think we are now in a position to make sense of those remarks. By pretending to refer to people and recount events about them, the author creates fictional characters and events ... (73)

20

However − and despite the somewhat lofty tone of this announcement − his definition in fact raises several further problems. The first of these is almost a practical one: the trouble with saying that fiction imitates reference is that while in abstract terms this defines the logical status of the discourse, the textual *models* that the discourse must necessarily be supposed to imitate have at best a rather precarious existence. Factual narrative does occur in a wide range of contexts (historiography, journalism, etc.) − but how often does one read, for instance, a past-tense description of a house, or a verbatim account of a conversation, that is *not* fictional? Searle claims that 'there is no textual property that will identify a discourse as a work of fiction' (68); and it is true that someone reading the following extract out of context:

Ce système, pratiqué pendant quarante ans à Rome comme à Paris, avait porté ses fruits. Après avoir dépensé, depuis son retour de Rome, environ deux mille francs par an, Pons cachait à tous les regards une collection de chefs d'œuvre en tout genre dont le catalogue atteignit au fabuleux numéro 1907   (Balzac: *Le Cousin Pons*, 29)[8]

has no way of telling that this is a novel. But it is surely extremely unlikely that he or she could read:

L'escalier, éclairé sur une petite cour par des fenêtres à coulisse, annonçait qu'excepté le propriétaire et le sieur Fraisier, les autres locataires exerçaient des professions mécaniques. Les marches boueuses portaient l'enseigne de chaque métier en offrant aux regards des découpures de cuivre, des boutons cassés, des brimborions de gaze, de sparterie   (ibid: 204−5)[9]

without knowing immediately that this is fiction.

On a more theoretical level, also, the concept of fictional pseudo-reference needs some qualification in so far as it begs the question of reference itself. It tends to imply − as when Searle talks about 'rules correlating words (or sentences) to the world' (66) − that, *except* in literature, we are, as language-using subjects, in some kind of direct contact with reality. In fact, though, it does not matter very much, as far as a characterization of realist fiction is concerned, whether or not language is 'really' wired up to reality like this − as long as it *appears* to be. As long as we act on the common-sense assumption (or ideological illusion, in Marxist terms) that our every-day discourse is effectively in contact with the real world, i.e. that relations of reference are fixed and reliable, then a fictional discourse which imitates everyday discourse will still produce in us as readers the required effect of reality. To put it another way, the referential illusion can work even if reference *itself* is an illusion, because fiction can mimic the illusion. To say that literary representation 'works' — produces an effect — is not necessarily to say anything about its epistemological status, its relation to truth values, and so on.[10]

Similarly, the way in which one chooses to theorize reference in general is unlikely to affect the fact that the illusion produced by fiction is not total. That is, we believe in it *less* than we do in statements about reality: either because we know that one is, simply, 'true' and the other is not, or alternatively, if one argues that all discourse is pseudo-referential, then because fiction is a kind of second-degree illusion, created by the imitation of a pre-existing illusion, and as such is distinguished from everyday discourse by a difference in the relative degree of its efficacy — the difference, in Marxist terms, between an ideological illusion and a literary one.[11] This leads to another difficulty with Searle's model. While more naïve theories of representation sometimes assume a rather literal belief on the part of the reader (as the term 'illusion' indeed suggests), Searle is careful to say that this use of 'pretend' is not meant to imply that the reader is actually taken in by it; it is simply an agreed and transparent convention between author and reader. In that case, since he also denies fiction any special formal properties of its own — i.e. fiction is just like true discourse except that we know it is not true — one might well ask why we bother to read fiction at all. Searle in fact does ask this. But his answer curiously by-passes the whole issue: he says that we read fiction for the non-fictional 'messages' which it conveys, 'the serious speech-acts which it is the point (or the main point) of the fictional text to convey' (74). If, though — to rehearse a well-worn argument — we read simply in order to discover the author's ideas about life, the initial question remains unanswered: why bother to read *fiction*?

It would seem to be impossible to answer this question from within the conceptual framework of Searle's speech-act theory, or indeed that of classical narratology. The simple and obvious answer to it is, of course, for *pleasure*.[12] What is needed is a theory which can take account of two notions: a state intermediate between belief and disbelief, and pleasure, or, more precisely, the investment of desire in representation. It is here that psychoanalytic theory, and in particular the Freudian account of phantasy, become a relevant and, I would claim, necessary explanation. The argument that phantasy is a necessary part of all literary representation is presented by Freud in his paper 'Creative Writers and Day-dreaming' (vol. 9: 143–53). Fiction embodies the author's day-dreams or conscious phantasies. The day-dream differs from other conscious manifestations of unconscious wishes in that the route it takes to consciousness, the way it gets round censorship, is not by means of rationalization or supposedly logical justification for actions, but entirely by means of its *narrativization*; day-dreams are stories – as of course is the 'family romance' (vol. 9: 235–44), which can be considered as a special case of this – and this is their fundamental link with literary representation.

On this basis the allure of literary representation can perhaps be explained by a connection with the pleasure afforded by phantasy: pleasure, that is, which is rooted in an unconscious wish ('every single phantasy is the fulfilment of a wish', vol. 9: 146). The phantasy and the pleasure are of course in the first place the author's, and the question then is how the reader is made to share them: the barrier which normally separates us from and 'neutralizes' other people's phantasies is, Freud says, removed by an aesthetic pleasure derived from the formal properties of the work (more specifically, one might guess, the formal devices whereby the reader is made to identify with the narrator or protagonist in the text). But this is merely a kind of *'fore-pleasure* ... which is offered to us so as to make possible the release of still greater pleasure arising from deeper psychical sources ... our actual enjoyment of an imaginative work proceeds from a liberation of tensions in our minds' (153, author's italics). In other words, a literary representation is a conscious phantasy which has the specific feature of enabling its reader to adopt the position of subject in it, that is, to appropriate it as his or her phantasy and thus derive pleasure from it.[13]

The other main issue is that of degrees of belief. Here too the day-dream provides a model for that ambivalent state in which the reader knows that he or she is reading fiction and yet at the same time in some sense believes in the illusion of reality.[14] Unlike the true dream, in which the dreamer does not know he is dreaming, the day-dreamer does know that he is day-dreaming; the day-dream is not taken for reality, but does interpose itself between the subject and his real surroundings and thus serves to cut him off from them.[15]

If we thus conclude that fiction, however realist, is always in collusion with conscious phantasy, this has important consequences for the status of the subject in relation to representation. A representation necessarily has a subject, who *produces* it, and an object, i.e. whatever it is a representation 'of'; and both of these are separate from it.[16] Where the representation is a text, its subject is the author *qua* author. But the characters who are represented in it may be, and usually are, subjects of their own representations, which may take the form of memories, phantasies, and so on (or texts, if they are represented as writers). It is characteristic of realist representations that they efface any sign of the author-function from the texts, in order to appear more real − because less obviously representation: as Genette says, it is a 'façon de raconter [qui] ... consiste à la fois à *en dire* le plus possible, et à *le dire* le moins possible' (1972: 187).[17] This has led to realist fiction sometimes being equated with 'objectivity'. In fact, however, it is equally typical for it to validate itself as *subjective*, by as it were co-opting the representation of one of its *characters* and promoting that to the apparent level of 'the' representation. The character as represented subject perceives, remembers, imagines, etc., and the objects of his or her representation are offered as the principal objects of the author's representation.

In other words, the represented subject is the equivalent of Genette's 'internal focalization' − the point of view, or 'instance narrative' which governs the text: 'En focalisation interne, le foyer coïncide avec un personnage, qui devient alors le "sujet" fictif de toutes les perceptions' (1983: 49−50).[18] It is only in this sense that one can say that the realist text typically 'originates in a subject'. This is a kind of shorthand − which will be used here − for the proposition that the representation *represents itself* as originating in a character who is represented in it as a subject engaging in activities such as remembering, perceiving, etc. If the text can perform this sleight of hand − conflating the two levels of the author's textual representation and the character's psychological representation − then it can present itself as the *real* experiences and perceptions of a psychologically real subject. Even this last necessary condition is largely fulfilled, in a circular fashion, by the very narratological function that makes it necessary: the fact that the character is perceiving, remembering, etc., simultaneously requires him to be, and constitutes him as, psychologically real (or, more exactly, the subject of the discourse of psychological realism: what I shall term a 'psycho-realist subject').

Genette himself, while in *Discours du récit* he stresses the 'objectivity' of realism (and thus considers Proust to be an exceptional case, 1972: 188), elsewhere attaches equal importance to 'subjective' and 'objective' realism.[19] Moshe Ron, similarly, says that psycho-realist subjects (in my terms − he calls them focalizers) 'are somehow felt to be particularly convincing' (1981: 21).

They are also particularly convenient, in so far as they allow the author to dispense with all the other conditions that are usually necessary to realist representation: above all, consistency of time and place, but also the stable identity of other characters, and of objects, and the maintenance of distinctions between real and imaginary, the exclusion of the supernatural, and so on. If the text is supposed to be representing a character's representation of the world, then *any* incoherences, *any* transgressions of the above rules, can be rationalized in terms of the mental processes of the psycho-realist subject — whose mind can be flitting about from one memory to another, free-associating, dreaming, hallucinating, and so on. Ricardou refers to this as 'la mise en fantaisie', by means of which 'la topologie conflictuelle des variantes égales se dissout en atopique confortable: aucune des variantes ne prétend plus lutter avec telle autre, aucune ne brigue plus le réel ainsi soustrait et préservé' (1973: 92).[20] The text can still be read as a realist representation of the workings of someone's mind.[21] Thus the constraints governing the psycho-realist subject — i.e. he must have a consistent, even if minimally specified, identity, and a possible position in time and space — are ultimately the only essential ones. The device of 'subjectivizing' realism is therefore very powerful, providing much greater freedom as regards the content of the representation than would otherwise be possible.

Representation, however, is not invincible, and there are a number of different strategies which texts adopt in order to attack the reality effect. Indeed, in so far as the Nouveau Roman has a coherent collective policy on the novel, it is precisely one of *anti*-representation. Writers as diverse as Simon, Robbe-Grillet and Sarraute, for instance, are united in viewing realism as at least a problem if not an actual enemy. The Nouveau Roman came into being in order to oppose representation — although its individual practitioners carry out their attacks in very different ways and are not always in agreement on what actually constitutes an attack. But as well as its considerable diversity of textual practice, the Nouveau Roman is also important in reshaping the relation of that practice to literary *theory*. A conscious effort was made to set up an interaction of theory and practice: Ricardou, for instance, wrote a great deal of both, and it was not long before all the *nouveaux romanciers* (including Simon, although he has consistently claimed not to be a theorist) seem to have felt more or less obliged to produce some theoretical articles as well as novels.

However, the close relationship between theory and practice was due not only to this overlap in personnel, but also to the specific nature of the ideas held about representation. On one level, the contesting of representation is a theoretical position affecting the analysis of *all* literature: opening up new ways of reading old texts, as Barthes did for Balzac, for instance, in *S/Z*; and Umberto Eco had very early on made the point that 'openness' is to some extent a property of all artistic works (p. 17 in the French translation, 1965). But it is at the same time a *programme* for the production of new texts which will be consciously and systematically anti-representational. The border-line between these two activities is inevitably rather blurred: both are seen by writers of the 1960s − such as Barthes, Kristéva, Jean Ricardou and other members of the *Tel Quel* group − in vaguely political terms; and as fiction becomes more self-conscious and critical discourse less 'academic', they tend to lose their distinct characteristics as discourses.

On the level of theory, representation is contrasted with a conception of the text which, emerging as it did within the general framework of structuralism, makes language the dominant and determining factor; the text is a space of language, a space in which language is produced and transformed rather than being used to represent or express anything outside itself. The question of meaning, the relation between signifier and signified, is redefined as a set of operations which are *internal* to the text. *Tel Quel*'s *Théorie d'ensemble*, published in 1968, is perhaps the most representative and forceful presentation of this position: as for instance in the following formulation by Jean-Louis Baudry:

Dans l'espace ainsi défini, le signifié en tant qu'il soutiendrait un signifiant disparaît, l'effet de signification ne relevant que des rapports qui se créent entre les éléments signifiants distribués sur la même surface, de leurs combinaisons plus ou moins apparentes et en tous cas non dénombrables. Tout écrit, tout texte, ne peut plus être pensé comme expression d'un spectacle, d'un champ de réalité extérieur à lui, mais comme partie et partie agissante de l'ensemble du texte qui n'arrête pas de s'écrire.   (1968: 136)[22]

The primacy accorded to language in this context meant that linguistics was at first seen as a more relevant theoretical source than traditional literary criticism; but increasingly linguistics itself, at least in the Saussurean version that was most influential in the development of structuralism, was criticized for its 'ideology of the sign', its dependence on precisely the notions of representation and expressivity that are being challenged.[23] The emphasis is on the 'productivity' of the text in relation to language. Kristeva, writing in 1968, says:

nous définirons le texte comme un appareil *trans-linguistique*, qui redistribue l'ordre de la langue ... Le texte est donc une *productivité* ... La sémiologie dont nous nous réclamons considérant le texte comme *une production et/ou comme une transformation*, cherchera à formaliser la *structuration* plutôt que la structure.   (1968: 300, author's italics)[24]

In similar terms, Baudry argues for a Marxist analysis of textual production based on an analogy with economic production: his notion of 'pratique scripturale' is designed to reveal what is obscured by the ideology of representation, namely, the productive work of the text (1968: 362).[25]

Much of the discussion of textual production remains on a rather abstract plane, and tends not to examine exactly how the project of the subversion of representation is implemented on the level of actual textual practice. One theorist who has, however, paid a great deal of attention to this level of work is Jean Ricardou; less inclined to philosophical reflection, he is primarily concerned with constructing a taxonomy of the many *different* procedures which may be considered to be anti-representational. In his book *Le Nouveau Roman*, which presents the most systematic version of the taxonomy, he defines six main types of strategy. The 'récit excessif' makes its presence as artefact felt by its evident structuring; the 'récit abymé' operates with the *mise en abyme*; the 'récit dégénéré' disrupts referential contiguity with textual links based on similarity and variation; the 'récit avarié' presents contradictory versions of the same sequence; the 'récit transmuté' confuses different levels of representation, having pictures come to life or apparently real events turn out to be a story within the story, and so on; and, finally, the 'récit enlisé' contests the referential chronology of narrative realism with atemporal description.

The majority of these categories can be grouped under the general heading of *reflexivity*, i.e. the text becomes 'self-conscious', designates itself as text, and thereby destroys the illusion of transparency which is a necessary condition for producing an 'effet de réel'. There is a distinction to be made between reflection on the structure of the work and reflection on its language; techniques such as the *mise en abyme* belong to the former type, as do the 'excessive' and the 'transmuted' narrative; whereas the 'degenerate' kind, which involves transitions based on different kinds of word-play – punning, semantically related words, alliteration, partial rhymes etc. – exemplifies the category of linguistic reflexivity.[26]

Ricardou's fourth type, the 'récit avarié' (and to some extent the 'récit enlisé' as well, although the argument that description *per se* is anti-representational does not seem to me very convincing), is a subversion of a very different kind, however. In general terms, anti-representational textual strategies fall into two main groups: those based on reflexivity, as above, and those which we can bring together, following Barthes, under the heading of 'le pluriel du texte' (1970: 269): different forms of *plurality* of meaning. Here the text is not self-conscious, but *open* (in the sense that Umberto Eco gives to the 'opera aperta', 1962); it is a 'surface non-clôturée' (Baudry, 1968: 135) or, to use a different terminology, 'dialogic'.[27] The 'récit avarié' activates a series of contradictions between conflicting variants of the same sequence, and so cannot be read as *a* representation of 'reality'.

On the whole, however, Ricardou tends to minimize the effects of plurality: not only quantitatively, as one type out of six, but also in picking out contradiction as the only form of 'le pluriel' that will fit within his taxonomical framework. Contradiction may be considered an *extreme* form of ambiguity — two or more meanings that are not just different but opposed and mutually exclusive — but in another sense it is rather a tame one: at least as Ricardou formulates it, it is a conflict between meanings each of which is *in itself* clear-cut and fully constituted. His extremely bellicose vocabulary — almost all the operations of the text are defined as 'guerres', 'batailles', 'luttes' — reinforces the implication: only a very solid meaning, one feels, could stand up to this kind of treatment. Moreover, the conflict arises because each of them lays claim to the 'real': he says, for instance: 'Appelons *puissance d'une variante* son aptitude à revendiquer l'accès au réel' (1973: 95, author's italics),[28] assuming, in other words, that each variant taken by itself is representational.[29]

What contradiction lacks, compared with other variants of 'le pluriel', is, precisely, *lack*. Barthes himself, in *S/Z*, is less interested in the contradictions in *Sarrasine*, and more in those points of aporia, the *indeterminacy* that can be read even in this 'classic' text: what he calls 'les sens indécidables' (1970: 269) or the 'fading' of the text:

Les blancs et les flous de l'analyse seront comme les traces qui signalent la fuite du texte; car si le texte est soumis à une forme, cette forme n'est pas unitaire, architecturée, finie: c'est la bribe, le tronçon, le réseau coupé ou effacé, ce sont tous les mouvements, toutes les inflexions d'un *fading* immense, qui assure à la fois le chevauchement et la perte des messages.

(1970: 27, author's italics)[30]

The smooth surface of representation requires a single and continuous meaning; it is disrupted both by multiple meaning — polysemy, ambiguity, contradiction — on the one hand, and by gaps in or lack of meaning on the other. Indeterminacy, in other words, implies either too much meaning or not enough. Barthes's emphasis on lack is echoed in Derrida's article 'La différance', published in the *Tel Quel* collection (1968), which constructs meaning as deferred, never fully present;[31] and in psychoanalytically based readings of texts as in principle 'lacunaire', of meaning erased by the operations of unconscious censorship.[32]

The subversion of representation is arguably more radically practised by strategies of plurality and indeterminacy than it is by reflexive
tactics, because the latter do not have to put in question the primacy
– the *originality*, in both senses – of the subject. The problem of
the subject is fundamental to the opposition between representation
and textual production. Because Ricardou's contestation is limited
largely to various forms of reflexivity, as shown above, the assumption of an original and controlling subjectivity can be seen to persist
in his treatment of texts at least as far as the reader is concerned. He
assumes that the reader's main role is to create *order* in the text.
Nothing must be left in a fragmented or unstructured state: in Simon's
Les Corps conducteurs, for instance, 'La multitude des éclats se lit
alors comme une mosaïque épars *dont il importe d'obtenir le remem-
brement*' (1973: 65, my italics),[33] and the terms in which this operation is described evoke a subject who, far from being carried along
by the productivity of the text, is very firmly in control of it:

Déterminer une mise en abyme dans un tel dispositif, c'est *découvrir* une
séquence qui puisse remplir deux conditions: d'une part, *faire preuve* d'une
cohésion suffisante pour parvenir, en dépit de la fragmentation, à une loca-
lisation *assez ferme*; d'autre part, *réunir* une *quantité probante* d'analogies
avec tels aspects *irrécusables* du livre.   (65, my italics)[34]

The contrast between this view of reading as closure and ordering
contrasts strikingly with what Barthes has to say about reading in
S/Z:

La lecture cependant ne consiste pas à arrêter la chaîne des systèmes, à fonder
une vérité, une légalité du texte ... elle consiste à embrayer ces systèmes, non
selon leur quantité finie, mais selon leur pluralité ... je passe, je traverse,
j'articule, je déclenche, je ne compte pas. L'oubli des sens ... est une valeur
affirmative, une façon d'affirmer l'irresponsabilité du texte, le pluralisme
des systèmes.   (18)[35]

The issue of subjectivity, however, involves more than just the
reader. Its most obvious and most controversial aspect is the radical
displacement of the position of the *author*. In bourgeois humanist
criticism the author is central: as subject of the representation, he is
its source and its 'authority'; he dominates, controls and 'owns' the
meanings contained in it. The theory of textual production, in contrast, replaces this conception with 'le travail productif, produisant
dialectiquement son producteur et son produit' (Baudry, 1968:
354);[36] the author is reconstructed as an *effect* of the text.[37] The
notion of a 'full' original individual subject is, Barthes suggests,
merely another aspect of the *illusion* of representation;[38] in reality

29

both writer and reader are constructed by the text as subjects in language: 'La subjectivité est une image pleine, dont on suppose que j'encombre le texte, mais dont la plénitude, truquée, n'est que le sillage de tous les codes qui me font' (1970: 17).[39]

But textual production can also (in fact, in a sense, more easily) produce a subject in the text who, rather than being read as author or reader, replaces the character or narrator of representational writing. This conception of the subject can be theorized, following Benveniste, in terms of the distinction between *sujet de l'énoncé* and *sujet de l'énonciation*, and will be discussed later in this chapter; but before exploring further the question of the subject I shall now turn to Simon's novels and attempt to situate them in the context of the opposition which has been outlined in general terms above.

Taking first the side of textual production, with which Simon allies himself most of the time,[40] we find many elements in his texts which exemplify the kind of anti-representational writing discussed earlier. Lucien Dällenbach's important work on Simon's novels[41] has demonstrated the extent of their structural reflexivity, and almost everyone who has written on Simon at all has explored his foregrounding of the signifier in the intricate trajectories of his word-play: both a form of linguistic reflexivity and also of plurality in so far as it appears inexhaustibly mobile, a way of deferring the closure of meaning. One could also cite the indeterminacy inherent in a narrative which overtly doubts its own validity, questions its 'knowledge' or else simply, and provocatively, gives up – as to which character says what in a dialogue, for instance: 'et Blum (ou Georges): "C'est fini?"' (*La Route des Flandres*: 188). Regarding also the position of the author, Simon has expressed ideas very similar to those of Barthes, Baudry and Kristeva; in an interview with Ludovic Janvier, for instance, he says: 'Le Claude Simon travaillant ... n'est pas celui de la vie quotidienne, mais ce personnage que nous suscitons par notre labeur et qui se retire de nous dès que nous nous levons de notre table' (Janvier 1972: 13).[42]

The text thus evolves, on one level, according to its own dynamic. But there is another side to his writing as well. To characterize him solely in terms of textual production is to overlook the important question of elements of representation: the fact that the text *also* at certain points produces the illusion of an origin outside itself – that is, an assumed reality which it is representing: the momentum of the writing, the interplay of textual links, sometimes results in a presence which appears to be cause rather than effect of the text. The modality of this imaginary presence is always visual, and it never lasts very long: it is a kind of *mirage*.

The mirage is the most intense and concentrated form that representation assumes in Simon's novels, but at the same time one of the least stable. As such it constitutes one pole of the alternation, one 'beat' of the scansion of the text, which hovers between throwing up images of presence and then – to use a Simonian term – 'decomposing' them. The mechanism may be observed in a passage near the beginning of *Le Palace* (32–4). The apparent basis of the mirage here is memory and the reality of past experience: the narrator is revisiting Barcelona and remembering his time there as a student in the Civil War. It is preceded by, and contrasts sharply with, a purely textual play of variation – the ways that different newspapers have of headlining the same event. This then suddenly gives way to an evocation of the men occupying the hotel. It begins:

et eux (les quatre hommes – ce qui, avec lui, faisait cinq) se tenant là, surgis de ce néant où ils devaient retourner presque aussitôt après une brève, violente et météorique existence   (32)[43]

so that only the bare fact of their presence emerges – 'se tenant là' – cut off from any kind of spatial or temporal context. Their status is therefore very fragile; they constitute an assumed existential reality which the text is describing, and yet (because they are remembered rather than perceived) they are also said to be 'légèrement incroyables, légèrement irréels' (33).[44] More specifically, there is a strange kind of uncertainty about the subject's position; he includes himself by a process of deduction: '(les quatre hommes – ce qui, avec lui, faisait cinq)' – and not as an *a priori* fact. He remembers what he sees, in other words, rather than his own presence there. In fact the text continues to talk about 'them', with 'him' reduced to a pure act of seeing: '... météorique existence pendant laquelle il les aurait vu agir et se comporter comme des êtres de chair et d'os' (32).[45] In so far as the mirage is a representation, it presupposes a subject whose point of view it represents, and this subject may or may not figure in the mirage itself.[46] Typically, he figures in a rather peripheral and problematic way, as he does here.

The point of view – the positioning of the subject – does not remain stable here either. It shifts from the present self looking back to the past self projecting forwards into the future: 'et plus tard il lui semblera les voir, immobilisés ou conservés comme sur une photographie, dans cette sorte de matière figée et grisâtre qu'est le temps passé' (33)[47] – so that the *presence* of the figures seems to be eclipsed in an interplay of past and future. Finally, they disappear into a spiralling movement of metaphors − 'des armes démantibulés ... une auto de course arrêtée ... un obus non explosé ... des canons démolis' (34).[48]

In another 'mirage' which occurs in *La Route des Flandres*, the position of the subject is similarly peripheral and anonymous, but this time because he *is* included as one of a group. Georges and Blum are arguing about what really happened at the moment of De Reixach's death, and to prove his point Georges remembers an incident when De Reixach bought his soldiers a drink. This way of introducing the mirage itself as evidence confers on it a particularly forceful effect of reality; its visibility is *unanswerable* (you can't argue with a picture). In addition, it is presented with unusual clarity and a pictorial intensity of definition:

Oui. C'était ... Ecoute: on aurait dit une de ces réclames pour une marque de bière anglaise, tu sais? La cour de la vieille auberge avec les murs de brique rouge foncé aux joints clairs ... pendant que le groupe de cavaliers se tient dans la pose classique: les reins cambrés, l'une des jambes bottées en avant, un bras replié sur la hanche avec la cravache dans le poing tandis que l'autre élève une chope de bière dorée en direction d'une fenêtre du premier étage où l'on aperçoit, entrevoit à demi derrière le rideau un visage qui a l'air de sortir d'un pastel ...   (21)[49]

The fixity of the image, both in purely visual terms and as the stereotype of a particular pastoral convention, is reassuring to the extent of being almost euphoric; it is as though the mirage fulfils a certain need for innocently representational writing. At the same time of course it is also a caricature; too good to be true, it breaks down into an alternative version as the text continues − 'Oui: avec cette différence qu'il n'y avait rien de tout cela que les murs de brique, mais sales' (21) − which is not only less pleasing and less picturesque but loses the clarity and definition, the certainty of the first version. The central element, De Reixach, becomes partially invisible ('je ne sais même pas s'il a bu, je ne le crois pas', 22) and the setting disintegrates into a series of undifferentiated possibilities: 'un type mort (ou une femme, ou un enfant), ou un camion, ou une voiture brûlée' (22).[50]

The ephemeral nature of the mirage is an exaggerated version of the main features that Simon attributes to vision in general; throughout his novels, the most characteristic form that vision takes is that of the brief glimpse − we read in *Le Palace* of 'une apparition, un instant, aussi furieusement emportée dans le néant qu'apparue' (88) − or series of brief glimpses: in the same novel, the Italian is reduced from a continuous presence to 'l'Italien (c'est-à-dire les fugitives apparitions: extrait pour de brefs instants des ténèbres par le passage des lumières qui le sculptaient ...' (98–9).[51] This last description is very close to a passage in *Le Sacre du printemps* (published eight years earlier) in which Bernard's stepfather is talking to him in the dark and lights a cigarette: Bernard hears 'la longue exhalaison des poumons recommençant à fonctionner' (266) and simultaneously sees

le craquement, la flamme jaune extirpant de l'ombre le donquichottesque profil penché sur la cigarette déjà plantée entre les lèvres, comme si la longue carcasse d'escogriffe un instant apparue, durement sculpté par la précaire lueur se tendait tout entière pour aspirer, se remplir du parfum de la fleur éphémère, vacillante et jaune dans les ténèbres.   (267)[52]

The overlap in vocabulary ('extirpant de l'ombre'/'extrait ... des ténèbres', 'un instant apparue'/'apparitions ... de brefs instants', 'sculpté par la lueur'/'des lumières qui le sculptaient') across a gap of eight years suggests that there is something obsessive about this particular instance of the mirage (it even recurs in *La Bataille de Pharsale*, 221) – possibly because in the extract from *Le Sacre du printemps* it is clearly associated with *breathing*. The stepfather looks as though he is inhaling the light from the match which is, like all Simon's mirages, 'éphémère' and 'vacillant'; in fact, he is (presumably) drawing on the cigarette. It is thus by implication breathing in – making the cigarette glow in the dark – that makes his face visible; and this places the mirage within a rhythm of appearance and disappearance that is in some sense related to the basic bodily function of respiration.[53]

The opposition between a representational and an anti-representational text also affects the status of the *subject*. The two discourses imply very different conceptions of subjectivity, as I have already indicated. In so far as Simon's novels oscillate between the two, they therefore necessarily construct *two* distinct subjects. These are not of course localizable as discrete entities or different personæ in the texts; but as theoretical instances they alternate and interact within the narrator of each text – whether this is a character (e.g. Georges in *La Route des Flandres*) or the apparently impersonal kind of narrative instance that we find in *Triptyque* or *Leçon de choses*.

We can thus distinguish between a subject of a representation and a subject produced by a text. The former is the 'psycho-realist' subject already discussed, the represented character to whom the author delegates the work of representation, and behind whom he hides.

The latter is not really definable in terms of a relation between author and character because any such relation depends on the notion of representation to situate them as respectively subject and object; it is less an entity than a function of the discourse, existing only by implication, in so far as language requires a subject: it is the *implication* of the discourse. It will be referred to here as the subject-in-language.

The psycho-realist subject pre-exists and supports the representational dimension of the text; it is, as I argued earlier, the only essential condition for representation to take place. From its position as origin, it encloses the text within its point of view: everything which appears in the text is read, even when this is not explicitly stated, as having been filtered through the perceiving consciousness of the subject. 'Point of view' is therefore a crucial notion; in fact the evolution of the psycho-realist subject through Simon's novels shows a progressive diminution of the substance of character until all that is left is, precisely, a point of view — which nevertheless still operates as a subject.

The emphasis is also, with Simon, very much on the point of *view*, literally, since representation in his novels is above all visual. This fact in itself could be taken as evidence of his realism, because realism has historically tended to privilege the visual — 'le lisible s'articule sur le visible', as Hamon remarks (1982: 139); the realist 'moi-héros-regardant', he says, 'équivaut donc exactement au *point de fuite* du tableau illusionniste et scénographique inventé par la Renaissance' (ibid.: 153, author's italics).[54] Rosemary Jackson implicitly endorses this idea when she contrasts the realist and the fantastic text in terms of their relation to vision in 'a culture which equates the "real" with the "visible"' and 'an epistemological and metaphysical system which makes "I see" synonymous with "I understand". Knowledge, comprehension, reason, are established through the power of the *look* ...' (1981: 45).

In fact, however, it is difficult to establish a simple correlation between the visual on the one hand and realist, as distinct from fantastic, literature on the other; Jackson herself reminds us that the Greek root of the word 'fantastic' means 'that which is made visible, visionary, unreal' (13); and one strong sense of the English 'vision' implies something that does not really exist: 'a vision of the future', for example. (Conversely, as will be argued in Chapter 5, the realist novel accords an important role to *hidden*, i.e. invisible, 'truths'.) Although Jackson argues cogently for the connection between fantastic literature and phantasy as desire (e.g. pp. 6–8, and Chapter 3), what she leaves out of account is the extent to which *any* representational discourse, even the most realist, is implicated in phantasy.

The psycho-realist subject presupposes, then, a conception of original subjectivity; it operates in Simon's novels as an originating point of view which anchors and contains the elements of representation. This in turn theoretically involves a further presupposition: namely, that the language of the text is *subordinated* to the subject and its representation; but objections (from e.g. Ricardou or Kristeva) to this reduction of language to 'instrumentality' and 'transparency' lose some of their force when what the language is representing is not an objective reality but the mental activities of the subject, since in this case it becomes an interior monologue, whose stylistic richness and freedom – as numerous texts, from Joyce onwards, bear witness – can appear just as 'productive' as if it were not attached to a subject. The difference between representation and textual production is not situated on the level of *style*.

The other subject is one which, far from supporting realist discourse, actively contests it by showing the referential illusion – the 'reality' apparently called into being by the referential capacity of language – to be, precisely, an illusion. This second subject does not found or subtend a discourse, but is itself founded by language. Its existence, its efficacy, derives only from the subjective properties peculiar to language; it is a subject in as much as the very structure and operations of language require, and invoke as it were *en creux* the place of, a subject whose *trace* is thus evident in the materiality of discourse. The subject is constructed in language.

The subject-in-language is, in both theory and practice, a more problematic concept than the psycho-realist subject, and requires further theoretical justification. A possible basis for it is available in Benveniste's seminal articles 'Les relations de temps dans le verbe français', 'La nature des pronoms' and 'De la subjectivité dans le langage', which form chapters 19, 20 and 21 of his 1966 book.[55] The first of these demonstrates that French verb tenses can be explained only if one postulates the existence, within the language, of two different 'plans d'énonciation', which he labels 'histoire' and 'discours'. The next chapter then extends this idea from tenses to pronouns and deictics. What distinguishes the two 'plans' is the fact that 'histoire' is impersonal writing which appears to come from nowhere and excludes any trace of subjectivity, i.e. of its producer, whereas 'discours' manifests clearly the existence of the subject who produces it and addresses it to someone else: it covers 'tous les genres où quelqu'un s'adresse à quelqu'un, s'énonce comme locuteur et organise ce qu'il dit dans la catégorie de la personne' (242).[56] Every linguistic element whose referent is defined in relation to the speech act in which it occurs is a sign of 'discours' – primarily the first- and second-person pronouns but also present, perfect and future tenses and deictics.

The third article, 'De la subjectivité dans le langage', develops further the idea of the essentially subjective nature of language; here in fact the 'histoire'/'discours' distinction disappears, and Benveniste sees language as a whole as 'discours'.[57] His main point is the very general and fundamental one that 'C'est dans et par le langage que l'homme se constitue comme *sujet*; parce que le langage seul fonde en réalité, dans *sa* réalité qui est celle de l'être, le concept d'"ego"' (259). The site of subjectivity is language in the first instance, and the 'subjectification' of 'l'être' is solely a result of language: 'Or nous tenons que cette "subjectivité", qu'on la pose en phénoménologie ou en psychologie, comme on voudra, n'est que *l'émergence dans l'être d'une propriété fondamentale du langage*. Est "ego" qui dit "ego"' (260, my italics).[58] The fundamental property of language in question is the *je-tu* axis, described as a unique relation of polarity and reciprocity which is to be found nowhere outside language, and is an invariable feature of all languages: 'Polarité d'ailleurs très singulière en soi, et qui présente un type d'opposition dont on ne rencontre nulle part, hors du langage, l'équivalent. Cette polarité ne signifie pas égalité ni symétrie: "ego" a toujours une position de transcendance à l'égard de "tu"; néanmoins, aucun des deux termes ne se conçoit sans l'autre; ils sont complémentaires, mais selon une opposition "intérieure/extérieure", et en même temps ils sont réversibles' (260).[59]

In none of these articles does Benveniste actually introduce the terms 'sujet de l'énonciation' and 'sujet de l'énoncé' which have subsequently gained widespread currency in structuralist poetics and narratology.[60] Lacan uses them in his 'Kant avec Sade' (1963); and three years later Todorov[61] gives a clear definition of them, referring to Benveniste's 'De la subjectivité ...':

Toute parole est, on le sait, à la fois un énoncé et une énonciation. En tant qu'énoncé elle se rapporte au sujet de l'énoncé et reste donc objective. En tant qu'énonciation, elle se rapporte au sujet de l'énonciation et garde un aspect subjectif car elle représente dans chaque cas un acte accompli par ce sujet. Toute phrase présente ces deux aspects mais à des degrés différents; certaines parties du discours ont pour seule fonction de transmettre cette subjectivité (les pronoms personnels et démonstratifs, les temps du verbe, certains verbes; cf. E. Benveniste: 'De la subjectivité dans le langage', dans *Problèmes de linguistique générale*), d'autres concernent avant tout la réalité objective.   (1966: 145)[62]

In this sense, and calling on Benveniste's definition of the relation between language and subjectivity, we can equate the subject-in-language with the subject of the enunciation, seen not simply as the flesh-and-blood producer of an utterance – because it is only the utterance that confers on him the attribute of subject – but rather as the concrete manifestation in language of its producer. (If these occupy the position of grammatical subject of the sentence – e.g. as 'Je' – they will be 'sujets de l'énoncé' as well, but not otherwise.)

The relevance of Benveniste's theory to Simon's novels can be illustrated by the particular question of what happens to the subject-in-language in the later texts – those from which all overt traces of a human producer have been carefully erased. There is a marked stylistic break here; from *Le Vent* up to page 189 of *La Bataille de Pharsale*, Simon writes in long convoluted sentences, with a proliferation of comparisons and parentheses, modalizing adverbs, and a use of anaphora and deixis that constantly reminds the reader of the presence of the subject of enunciation. Although never actually ungrammatical, this style deliberately stretches the normal conventions of language, and gives an impression of hesitation and doubt, even desperation, in the attempt to articulate perceptions or speculate on things that cannot be known fully.

Then, after stating its intention to 'Repartir, reprendre à zéro (181),[63] the text switches in Part III of *La Bataille de Pharsale* to an assertive and hard-edged style: short sentences, not modalized, a flat, neutral and impersonal mode of discourse restricted almost exclusively to visual description; and this mode (which for the sake of convenience I shall refer to as the 'impersonal', in contrast to the earlier 'personal', style) is maintained with only slight variations through *Les Corps conducteurs, Triptyque*,[64] and five of the seven chapters of *Leçon de choses* (the other two are reproductions of speech). *Les Géorgiques* is a mixture of both styles, with the impersonal used mainly for LSM's narrative. With the exception of this last instance, the impersonal style thus occurs in conjunction with what can be defined on a more general level as Simon's anti-representational or formalist novels. There are connexions between these two levels,[65] but also a noticeable difference: whereas the movement from more to less diegetically realist texts is gradual, the transitions from one style to the other are very abrupt.

The impersonal style can be defined as an instance of 'histoire', in the sense that Benveniste gives it, which is above all a negative one: it lacks the linguistic features of 'discours', i.e. syntactic and lexical elements whose referent is definable only in relation to the 'instance de discours'. It therefore appears not to have a subject of enunciation. Having said this, however, we are left with various problems. Because 'histoire' is an illusion — in the obvious sense that all language is 'really' produced by a subject — there is clearly no philosophical issue at stake, but merely a stylistic one. Genette is for this reason very dismissive of Benveniste's formulation, describing 'histoire' as a 'chimère' and as 'infalsifiable' (1983: 68) and arguing that 'Dans le récit le plus sobre, quelqu'un me parle, me raconte une histoire (ibid.).[66] Within his classification, moreover, Simon's impersonal style causes no particular problem: it is simply a heterodiegetic narrative. But this definition does not tell us a great deal; a text such as *Triptyque* is far *more* impersonal than many other heterodiegetic narratives (quite apart from the question of whether it is a narrative or not), in that it excludes far more (value judgements, generalizations, and so forth). The reason why classical narratology does not allow us to gain very much purchase on the distinction between *Triptyque* and *Histoire*, for instance, is ultimately that Genette thinks that the subject pre-exists language (language and narrative are acts of communication, 1983: 68–9), and therefore not necessarily *implicated* in it. A heterodiegetic narrative will inevitably presuppose its narrator even if that narrator remains entirely aloof and detached from the discourse. (In any case, the voice Genette wishes to hear is the *author's*: 'quand j'ouvre un livre, c'est pour que l'auteur *me parle*', 69; italics in original.)[67] This means that the material traces of the subject that may or may not be observed in the text are of no particular significance for Genette; whereas they assume a crucial importance from the perspective of the subject as constructed in language.

The principal problem that arises from the conventional status of 'histoire' is not that the distinction between 'histoire' and 'discours' has to be restricted to the level of observable linguistic features; there is nothing wrong with saying that all texts have producers, but only some features of language necessarily imply their producer's existence, so the distinction is between texts that include these features and those that do not. Also, Benveniste's criterion of reference to the 'instance de discours' allows a precise determination of what the features in question are.

In practice, however, the features of *literary* style which are usually interpreted as implying the presence of a subject of enunciation are both more numerous and more vague. Phenomena such as stylistic deviation from a norm of language, or the vexed question of value judgements, are intuitively very relevant on the one hand and almost impossible to define rigorously on the other. This confusion is presumably related to the status of 'histoire': if the subject's absence from the discourse is a mere convention anyway, then the determination of which features signify its *presence* is also likely to be conventional and arbitrary. This does not mean, however, that the features are unimportant: in a given text, the presence of a particular feature is indubitably read as signifying the presence of a subject of enunciation. 'Histoire' is not a false problem, as Genette implies, but a difficult and central one − both in the evolution of Simon's writing generally, and from the particular perspective adopted here, namely that of looking at his writing in terms of its oscillation between two subjects, one of which is discernible solely as an 'instance de discours'. The question is: can one speak of a subject-in-language in relation to texts that lack any concrete discursive traces of subjectivity? I shall attempt to answer it in the next chapter.

An alternative theoretical construction of the subject-in-language can, however, be taken from psychoanalytic theory, in the Lacanian treatment of the subject as created by 'language' in the sense of the signifying chain. This account shares with Benveniste's the basic proposition that language is cause and subject is effect. There are, nevertheless, important differences between them. While on one level Benveniste's more empirical approach has the advantage of identifying the subject-in-language with a specific set of observable textual features − 'la langue comme activité manifestée dans des instances de discours qui sont caractérisées comme telles par des instances propres' (257)[68] − on a more abstract level certain theoretical problems raised by Benveniste's formulation are resolved, or at least avoided, in Lacan's.

For Benveniste, the interdependence of language and subjectivity takes the form of a universal and atemporal equivalence: subjectivity *is* linguistic, quite simply, and we are confronted not so much with a relation between two terms as with a single inseparable compound concept, subjectivity-language: 'Le langage est dans la nature de l'homme, qui ne l'a pas fabriqué ... Nous n'atteignons jamais l'homme séparé du langage ... C'est un homme parlant que nous trouvons dans le monde, et le langage enseigne la définition même de l'homme' (259).[69] This of course overlooks the obvious fact that man is not born speaking, and that the acquisition of language – even if genetically programmed – is for every individual a *process*. Even assuming that Benveniste is deliberately concentrating on human collectivities, and that language acquisition happens as it were automatically, he presents a curiously static phenomenon: there is no room in his account for any notion of process or dialectic.

Lacan, in contrast, always stresses the determining effects of the individual's *entry into* the symbolic order – saying, for instance:

Et en effet ce à quoi la découverte de Freud nous ramène, c'est à l'énormité de cet ordre où nous sommes entrés, à quoi nous sommes, si l'on peut dire, nés une seconde fois, en sortant de l'état justement dénommé *infans*, sans parole: soit l'ordre symbolique constitué par le langage, et le moment du discours universel concret et de tous les sillons par lui ouverts à cette heure, où il nous a fallu nous loger. (1966: 445)[70]

The symbolic order constitutes the subject, through the Œdipal stage, which is itself initiated by the threat of castration separating the child from the mother. The initial relation with language is thus conflictual – Lacan calls it a 'drama' – as opposed to Benveniste's harmonious integration, because it involves prohibition, repression and division: Lacan takes up Freud's concept of *Spaltung*, the splitting of the subject, and locates it at the moment of entry into the symbolic. This entry simultaneously produces the subject and his unconscious – 'C'est dans ce redoublement du sujet de la parole que l'inconscient comme tel trouve à s'articuler' (1966: 711)[71] – that is, produces the subject *as division*. Lacan defines the *Spaltung* by saying that it 's'opère de toute intervention du signifiant: nommément du sujet de l'énonciation au sujet de l'énoncé' (770);[72] the split can be thought of as the non-coincidence of 'je' as 'sujet d'énoncé' in language and as 'sujet d'énonciation'.[73]

It follows from this division that the subject's relation to language is based on a lack, on the 'manque-à-être' that founds 'le drame du sujet dans le verbe' (655).[74] Here again the contrast with Benveniste is clear: for him, language confers, precisely, 'être' – the reality of being: 'le langage seul fonde en réalité, *dans sa réalité qui est celle de l'être*, le concept d'"ego"' (259, my italics).[75] Similarly, the subjective nature of language makes it a source of power for the subject, who, in speaking, takes it over: 'le discours individuel, où chaque locuteur assume pour son compte le langage entier' (254); the relation is one of appropriation: 'Le langage est ainsi organisé qu'il permet à chaque locuteur de *s'approprier* la langue entière en se désignant comme *je*' (262, italics in original).[76]

These differences in the theoretical accounts of Benveniste and Lacan also affect the way one analyses concrete texts: they mean that the actual *linguistic* signs of the subject-in-language — what counts as 'evidence' of the subject's existence — are also different. Specifically, the introduction of the notion of the unconscious which is missing from Benveniste's account allows us to trace the subject not only in the positive signs of positionality — pronouns, performatives, etc. — but also in the wider and less well-charted areas of the activity of censorship, the breaks, gaps and incoherences in the text that are symptomatic of unconscious desires — what Lacan defines as the 'intervals' in the signifying chain.

The second major difference between Benveniste and Lacan concerns the ability or otherwise of language to represent reality. On this issue, Lacan offers a means of differentiating between the subject-in-language and the realist subject of representation — the polarity of which is basic to Simon's work — whereas Benveniste cannot, for reasons which have to do with his whole conception of language. He sees language as primarily communication — this is the framework for his work on subjectivity (see p. 258) — of a content (259); although he attacks the notion of language as instrument, he does so solely in so far as this implies a separation between man and instrument (as though man had invented language, like he invented the wheel), and not because language might be cut off from its *referent*, an idea which is not raised in any of these three chapters. The relations between language and objective reality remain straightforwardly and unproblematically those of reference, and there is no questioning of the referential dimension of language. There is therefore nothing to stop his subject-in-language from being co-extensive with a 'full', conscious, individual subject in the real world.

For the same reasons, his view of fiction is equally unproblematic: language mimics reference and in so doing creates an illusion of reality. A passage from Balzac serves just as well as two passages of historiography to illustrate his concept of 'histoire', and the three are placed alongside each other as though they were essentially the same kind of writing. In subscribing at least implicitly to a realist aesthetic, Benveniste places his 'sujet d'énonciation' in a position from which there is no way of distinguishing it from a realist subject. That is, the subject for Benveniste may well be produced by language in the first instance, but since language itself also — and just as smoothly — produces a representation of the world in fiction, there is no reason why the subject in fiction (the narrator) should not acquire all the attributes of a realist character.

Lacan's notion of the symbolic order, on the other hand, is explicitly defined in opposition to the imaginary order, and his subject as distinct from the ego; he refers to 'cette distinction fondamentale entre le sujet véritable de l'inconscient et le *moi* comme constitué en son noyau par une série d'identifications aliénantes' (1966: 417). Moreover, it is the imaginary order which governs the activity of representation, of the production of *images* to cover up the *lack* of the subject-in-language: 'C'est parce qu'elle pare à ce moment de manque qu'une image vient à la position de supporter tout le prix du désir: projection, fonction de l'imaginaire' (655).[77] The subject of representation can thus be seen to be equivalent to the imaginary ego, and distinct from − even opposed to − the subject-in-language. Since Simon's texts constantly dramatize the difference between the two subjects, and are as it were held in the tension of that difference, the concepts of imaginary and symbolic ultimately offer a more productive way of commenting on them than does Benveniste's formulation of subjectivity in language.

A further point relating to the question of representation concerns Lacan's 'symbolic' and 'real'. In defining the operations of the signifying chain, Lacan makes it clear that there is no one-to-one correlation of signifier and signified: 'c'est dans la chaîne du signifiant que le sens *insiste* mais sans qu'aucun des éléments de la chaîne ne *consiste* dans la signification dont il est capable au moment même' (1966: 502).[78] It is this 'sliding' of the signifiers that removes the possibility of language being referential in any simple sense, and hence determines a conception of language that accords at least partially with theories of textual production.

But a problem arises when Kristeva defines the text as 'un appareil trans-linguistique qui redistribue l'ordre de la langue' (1968: 300);[79] textual practices that *disrupt* the *structure* of the language system itself can less easily be seen as realizations of the symbolic order in so far as it is an *order*.[80] They may be equated with the breaks and gaps in language resulting from the operations of unconscious censorship, the emergence of desire in the intervals between signifiers, but they are somehow more systematic than this formulation suggests: Simon's continuing struggle to reconcile 'le désordre irrémédiable du vécu avec l'ordre artificiel du langage' (Doubrovsky 1972: 53)[81] is an instance of *parole* deliberately, if rather hopelessly, attempting to destructure the language system. If the Lacanian view of language is to cover this kind of textual practice, the intervals between signifiers must be made to carry a great deal of theoretical weight.

The issues raised in this chapter − principally, those of representation, language and subjectivity − are those that I consider most central to an understanding of Simon's practice as a novelist; they form both a theoretical and (because they have been actively debated, in and around the Nouveau Roman, over the past twenty years) a historical context for his writing. They are, as I have indicated, interrelated in rather complex and problematic ways on a theoretical level. But they can also be brought into relation with Simon's novels (and there is also a sense in which they are interrelated *in* the novels themselves), as I hope to show in subsequent chapters.

2

VISION AND TEXTUALITY

One of the most immediately noticeable features of Simon's novels is the amount of visual description that they contain – evidence, one supposes, of a fascination with the visible world which at times becomes almost obsessive. The first of Simon's 'hybrids' is, after all, not the 'homme–cheval' or the 'homme–fusil' but, in *Le Vent*, Montès the human camera, with his 'third eye' always hanging round his stomach (208). We may seek the roots of this obsession in Simon's early and unsuccessful attempt to be a painter, and his continuing interest in the visual arts in general, but this rather banal biographical explanation overlooks the fact that the decision to *write* the visible, rather than paint it, is a problematic and even a contradictory one.

The attempt to capture a visible object (or event, or scene) in writing is necessarily a reduction or distortion of the original. A comparison with Robbe-Grillet makes this very clear; for Robbe-Grillet, whose novels are even more obsessively visual, the function of the description is to *limit* vision, to make the object disappear;[1] and he exploits precisely the incompatibility between writing and the visible in order to produce descriptions in which the visual properties of the object, while being noted with apparent scrupulousness, are deliberately emptied of all sensuous significance – flattened out into writing.[2] Simon, on the other hand, usually does almost the opposite: his descriptions are vivid and sensuous in a way which seems to belong to an earlier tradition of realist writing. In *La Bataille de Pharsale*, for instance – often considered to be the starting point for the later, less phenomenological and more 'textual', period of novels – we find the following:

ces mauvais poids lourds plantés ou plutôt enracinés au milieu du ring montagnes de viande s'assénant des coups à tuer un bœuf l'œil stupide reniflant en
secouant la tête envoyant des gouttes de sang sur les plastrons empesés et
les visons des premiers rangs jusqu'à ce que l'un d'eux sans préavis sans avoir
fait un pas s'écroule brusquement tout d'une masse l'arbitre se précipitant
levant le bras du vainqueur dont les jambes semblent à ce moment se réveiller

pour esquisser un joyeux pas de rigodon se mouvant toutes seules semble-t-il tandis que le regard toujours vide dans le terrifiant visage martyrisé il continue à lapper paisiblement les deux traînées de morve rouge qui descendent de ses narines.

(163)[3]

This passage certainly includes the kind of generative self-reference that we associate with the theory and practice of post-modernist writing: 'montagnes de viande' echoes descriptions of another character, Van Velden; the cliché 'coups à tuer un bœuf' produces a fleeting image of a bull in 'reniflant en secouant la tête', and so on. But it is also constructed in such a way as to produce an 'effet de réel', to invite the reader to recognize a referent for its language. The formalist notion of defamiliarization that Jakobson (1965: 101) gives as one of the possible criteria for defining realism comes to mind here; by the observant and precise unexpectedness of its vocabulary – 'lapper paisiblement les deux traînées de morve rouge', for instance – the text 'evokes' visual memories of boxers we have seen in 'real life'. The other intratextual effects could have been achieved without also exhibiting this power of, and pleasure in, representational detail.

This becomes even odder, but perhaps ultimately more explicable, when set in context; the beginning of the passage just quoted is in fact: 'les guerriers de della Francesca s'assommant avec des gestes lents "téléphonés" comme on dit dans l'argot de la boxe comme ces mauvais poids lourds, etc.'[4] In other words, there are no 'real' boxers in the narrative; they are introduced purely as a comparison for warriors who are themselves represented in a painting, and via a reflection on language ('comme on dit dans l'argot de la boxe'). The description is, I have argued, realist in its internal logic, but it is not tied into any overall economy of plot or representation: it is left floating, attached to the rest of the text only by the purely verbal link of a figure of speech.

A great many of the visual descriptions in fact follow this pattern. One could almost claim that the more vivid, detailed, lush and colourful they are, the less likely they are to be part of the diegetic reality of the narrative (to the decreasing extent that this exists in Simon's work). The 'visible' is of course sometimes a matter of ocular perception, but more characteristically has the status of a mental image of some kind. Thus the descriptions are sometimes presented as very fragile and uncertain memories, providing images whose force is only intensified by their ephemerality (as in the mirage generally) and the violence of their loss. In *Histoire*, for instance, the obliteration of memories is compared to a blank cinema screen:

violente obscène indomptable s'élançant se ruant un instant seulement puis tout (les dorures les vieilles reines l'épouvantail fardé les peintures le portrait) se dissociant se désagrégeant à toute vitesse s'estompant s'effaçant absorbé bu comme par la trame de l'écran vide grisâtre   (101)[5]

— and the simile underlines the unreal quality of the images. More often, though, they are *imagined* by the narrator — Simon sometimes uses 'voir' and 'imaginer' synonymously: 'Louise pouvant la voir, l'imaginer' (*L'Herbe*: 167, and again 187) — so that their sensuous power itself takes on a hallucinatory quality, becoming more like an attribute of phantasy than of reality. Hence the recurrent formula 'il me semblait voir' which usually introduces these passages.

A typical example of this occurs when Georges's memory of De Reixach's death is interrupted by an imaginary vision of the race-course, affectively very highly charged, and striking above all for its colours:[6]

et il me semblait y être, voir cela: des ombrages verts avec des femmes en robes de couleurs imprimées ... les robes des chevaux et celles des femmes, et les cuirs fauves des bottes faisant des tâches vives (acajou, mauve, rose, jaune) sur l'épaisseur verte des frondaisons.   (19)

Three pages later he comes back to the same scene:

Et de nouveau il me semblait voir cela: se détachant sur le vert inimitable des opulents marronniers, presque noir, les jockeys passent ... leurs casaques multicolores se suivant dans les pastilles de soleil, comme ceci: Jaune, bretelles et toques bleues — le fond vert noir des marroniers — Noire, croix de Saint-André bleue et toque blanche — le mur vert noir des marronniers ...
                                                                                (22)[7]

and continues for nineteen lines with a hypnotic sequence of colours moving past against the background of foliage — with a text, in other words, that is reduced to a bare sequence of colour notations. The transition from imagination back to memory, moreover, is marked as a contrast between visible and invisible: 'Mais il n'y avait pas de tribunes, pas de public élégant *pour nous regarder*' (25, my italics).[8]

We thus find an unusual insistence on the visible combined with a distinctly unreal quality attaching to visual descriptions. Simultaneously powerful and insubstantial, the visible seems to be phantasized[9] rather than perceived: and as such it would seem to constitute an object of *desire*. If this is so, then the persistence of representational elements in Simon's novels despite the counter-claims of textual autonomy is perhaps explained by the fact that the elements are in this specifically visual form, and by this investment of desire in vision that can also, as I have already noted, be felt in his theoretical writings. If the visible is *per se* desirable, it is less surprising than it otherwise would be that visual representation is found even in fairly late novels like *La Bataille de Pharsale* and *Les Corps conducteurs*. To postulate vision as phantasized, as an object of desire, of course in itself does nothing to explain the articulation of that desire with a *text*; it returns us to the question: what does it mean to *write* the visible? A further examination of the 'vision' of the race-course will perhaps provide the beginnings of an answer to both these questions.

It is noticeable that the sequence gradually builds up to an evo-cation of Corinne, the supremely desirable woman, and that it then breaks off abruptly. It is as though she exerts an irresistible attraction on the text as soon as it moves into the mode of visual imagination and desire. At first, in this passage, she is anonymous for the reader − just a pronoun − and unseen by the characters: 'Iglésia passant sans la regarder' (23). Then she is mentioned obliquely, by describing the pink silk of Iglésia's jockey's shirt as 'comme le sillage parfumé de sa chair à elle'.[10] The text then veers away to Iglésia, his horse and the other jockeys, only to return to her, still unnamed, sitting talking to a man who is himself described at length before the text finally gives in to its desire for Corinne − naming her in a visual evocation in which, however, she appears only to disappear again: 'et à la fin Corinne se levant nonchalamment, se dirigeant sans hâte − sa vaporeuse et indécente robe rouge oscillant, se balançant au-dessus de ses jambes − vers les tribunes' (24−5).[11] Then the vision of the race-course ends abruptly. In this sense Corinne can be seen as the climax of the visible, the ultimate object of desire that the evocation of the visible leads up to by virtue of a necessary logic, but an object which is never fully attained.

The logic in question is that of desire but it is also a specifically *textual* logic. That is, Corinne is produced by the text − or, more precisely, is produced as the textual representation of a phantasized vision of an object − and the specifically textual features of the rep-resentation can be shown to contribute to its desirability. Although the text here seems in some ways to be mimicking the movements of a film camera, it is also producing effects that would be impossible in film: evoking Corinne via the metonymy of the jockey's pink silks, for instance, and also, throughout this passage, by implicit comparisons with the race-horses; but particularly by maintaining her anonymity by referring to her five times as 'elle', 'la', etc., before naming her: 'et à la fin Corinne'. Rather than an individual woman, she is thus constructed as a kind of pure female presence − as, in other words, a phantasy.

This can be taken as illustrating a more general phenomenon whereby, in various ways, it is language that produces the visible *as phantasy*. In the first place, the visible as written is, simply, not real. The reader cannot actually see 'sa vaporeuse et indécente robe rouge oscillant, se balançant au-dessus de ses jambes', for instance, so he or she *imagines* ('pictures') it, and in so doing approximately reproduces the phantasizing ascribed to the narrator. This provides a basic parallelism between phantasy or the imaginary and the visible/textual. But as well as derealizing it in this way, re-inscribing the visible within the alien structure of a text also renders it more *manipulable*. The text breaks it up, imposes on it a rhythm of emergence and disappearance, and this power of manipulation – 'processing', almost – echoes the imaginary omnipotence of the subject's control over his phantasy.

Film, of course, can and does achieve the same effects.[12] But there is a more subtle type of manipulation of the object that film cannot do very well, and that can perhaps best be defined as *modalization*. In strictly linguistic terms, mode defines the *énoncé* in its implicit relation to the speaking subject; by extension, the object of textual representation is posited as past, present or future, real or imaginary, definite or indefinite, etc., by the 'modalizing' operations of language. In the example given above modalization, in deferring the naming of Corinne, allows for a kind of *subtraction* from the unmediated fullness of the visible object, an indeterminacy (elsewhere often an ambiguity) which is not in the visible object *per se*, but the verbal description of it. In this sense, the visible object as constructed in the modalities of phantasy and desire is always already implicated in discourse. The investment of desire in the visible does not exist independently of the interaction between the visible and the textual: it is desire for the visible as constituted, mediated and limited by that interaction – desire, in short, for a discourse of the visible.

The above discussion of Corinne's appearance in the text should not be taken to imply that the fascination with the visual as a general structure is simply derived from, or reducible to, a straightforwardly erotic image of the woman. Nevertheless if the visible is desirable, it is also true that conversely the sexually desirable in Simon's texts is above all visual. Woman are above all *seen* objects. It is not just that they are described in visual terms – which is hardly unusual and does little to distinguish Simon from other writers – but that they are described *as visions*: Corinne, 'la femme la plus femme que j'avais jamais vue', is 'fabriquée ... à partir d'une brève et unique vision' (*La Route des Flandres*: 230); and the other woman whom Georges desires, the 'fille de la grange', is first presented as 'une apparition' (38) which then fades away, 'semblant s'évanouir, quoiqu'ils continuassent à la suivre des yeux ... se dissolvant' (39),[13] so that what remains, what in a sense *counts* for Georges, is not a real woman but a kind of pure visual impact:

il lui semblait toujours la voir ... ou plutôt la sentir, la percevoir comme une sorte d'empreinte persistante, irréelle, laissée moins sur sa rétine (il l'avait si peu, si mal vue) que, pour ainsi dire, en lui-même: une chose tiède, blanche ... une sorte d'apparition non pas éclairée par cette lampe mais luminescente ... non pas une femme mais l'idée même, le symbole de toute femme.

(41)[14]

It would seem also that women are desirable only in their visibility; it is striking how often women's language, conversely, appears as an object of hostility.[15] Female language seems to represent a territory from which the male narrator is excluded because he cannot understand it:

Elles continuèrent à parler mais je ne pouvais pas comprendre J'essayai mais je n'y réussis pas Je pouvais comprendre chaque mot mais je ne parvenais pas à suivre ... langage de femmes comme quand j'étais enfant ces annonces de médecine ou ces réclames maladies de femmes quelque chose de mystérieux délicat et un peu terrifiant dont je savais que je serais à jamais exclu.

(*Histoire*: 335)[16]

Women's language is a kind of sickness, and therefore frightening. It is also an obstacle to male phantasies; when Corinne speaks, in *La Route des Flandres*, it is to reject Georges's view of her: 'Tout ce que je suis pour toi c'est une fille à soldats quelque chose comme ce qu'on voit dessiné à la craie ou avec un clou sur les murs des casernes' (276)[17] – and it is significant that what she is rejecting here is precisely, in caricatural form, the idea of the woman as unreal visible object. Thus the antagonism between the male *image* of the woman and the woman's voice is made clear. Perhaps for this reason *L'Herbe*, the only novel in which the main narrative point of view belongs to a woman, contains no visual descriptions of desirable women, only a brief reference to Louise's body as she sees it herself.

In most of the other novels, however, there are images of women which are definitely erotic. There are also descriptions of sexual activity in which the subject is not, like Louise in *L'Herbe* or Georges in *La Route des Flandres*, participating but watching or, more often, trying to watch. This is especially true of *La Bataille de Pharsale* where we find repeated descriptions of Van Velden making love to the model, with the narrator looking up at the window from outside or listening at the door to the room. In *Triptyque* the two small boys are more successful voyeurs of the couple in the barn. The most enigmatic voyeur of all, though, occurs in *Les Corps conducteurs*, where what subsequently turns out to be a drawing (a reference, in fact, to an etching by Picasso) is suddenly introduced into the text as 'Le vieux roi au visage couvert de rides regarde à travers la fente d'un rideau le couple d'amants enlacés' (131).[18] But this whole sequence is caught up in an alliterative word-play – the 'vieux roi' himself is perhaps just a phonetic transformation of 'voyeur' – which undercuts its impact as a visual image. Voyeurism, in the ordinary sense, is in fact of only marginal significance in Simon's novels. The desirability of the visual is more generalized and more ramified than this, as is its genesis.

Desire, in the psychoanalytic interpretation, is to be distinguished from *need*; a need can be satisfied by a real object (e.g. hunger by food), but desire relates to an imaginary object. The original object of desire – Lacan's 'objet a' – is the lost object, the lack resulting from separation from the mother's body, and this irreparable loss generates an endless series of substitute imaginary objects, none of which can fully and permanently replace the lost object: each one is 'un objet qui ne prend sa valeur que de sa différence insaisissable d'avec un modèle perdu' (Leclaire 1966). Similarly, Anika Lemaire says 'L'objet (a) est bien alors la cause du désir, son absence ir-réparable engendre l'éternité du désir, sa fuite incessante' (1977: 266). Desire is thus characterized by its continual movement from one object to another; desire is always 'beyond' rather than 'in' its object, is always being produced in an infinite series of metonymic displace-ments: 'Et les énigmes que propose le désir à toute philosophie naturelle, sa frénésie mimant le gouffre de l'infini ... ne tiennent à nul autre dérèglement de l'instinct qu'à sa prise dans les rails – éternellement tendus vers le *désir d'autre chose* – de la métonymie' (Lacan, 1966: 518).

Returning to Simon's texts, one is struck by how very similar this description of the functioning of desire is to some of his descriptions of the act of *seeing*. In *Histoire*, for instance, there is the brick wall seen from an angle, three times near the beginning of the novel and twice near the end (45, 46, 99, 389, 415) – this repetition itself echoing the continual reproductions of desire ('qui visent plus à insister, à se répéter, énigmatiques, qu'à se saturer, se combler ou se suturer', Leclaire 1968: 53).[19] As for the content of this description, when Simon writes 'lignes de fuite ... se rencontrant à l'infini' (99), he is on one level talking about perspective in an entirely conventional way;

Vision and textuality

on another level, however, 'fuite' carries a real sense of both *loss* and *flight* (Lemaire's 'fuite incessante') because Simon has earlier used the more literal verbal form 's'enfuyant' and stressed the idea of an *imaginary* point beyond what can be seen to exist: 'le faisceau convergeant de leurs rangées parallèles s'enfuyant aspiré par la perspective vers un point imaginaire au-delà du mur en face' (45). On the next page we find a near-repetition of the image: 'les rangées de briques convergeantes aspirées là-bas par-delà le mur d'angle, par-delà les autres maisons, les faubourgs, les collines, se précipitant immobiles et vertigineuses vers le même point invisible inexistant et imaginaire' (46).[20] Vision, like desire, is constantly sucked onwards into the vacuum of what lies beyond, 'par-delà les autres maisons, etc.'. The object of vision–desire is thus the point of fusion where the parallel lines converge: an impossible fusion, in other words, just as the lost object of psychoanalysis figures an impossible fusion, equally 'invisible inexistant et imaginaire'. When the same image reappears towards the end of the novel, some of the key terms remain, but there is less emphasis on movement and more on both loss and fusion, to the point where these are identified: 'elles (les rangées de briques) se *perdaient*, s'enfonçaient, *disparaissaient* dans l'obscurité convergeant vers ce point imaginaire à l'infini où *tout se rejoint se confond s'anéantise*' (389, my italics) − whereas the final occurrence, just twenty pages from the end, reinstates the primacy of 'fuite' and this time links it explicitly to the narrator as well:

Pouvant de nouveau distinguer les lignes formées par les rangées de briques convergeant lignes de fuite

disant si je ne trouvais pas d'autre solution que de m'enfuir   (415)[21]

Perspective, for Simon, ensures the negativity of vision, inaugurates the vertiginous lack in the centre of vision which opens onto infinity and the imaginary,[22] and in so doing echoes the structure of desire.

At other times it is as though visible objects themselves contain their own lack. The opening words of *Histoire* refer to the acacia tree, which provides an initial image for this idea of the invisible at the heart of the visible: 'je pouvais la voir ou du moins ses derniers rameaux éclairés par la lampe ... des rameaux plus lointains de plus en plus faiblement éclairés de moins en moins distincts entrevus puis seulement devinés puis complètement invisibles' (11),[23] and of vision caught up in an endless pursuit of what eludes it. There is always the idea that, as Charles says when looking at his wife's grave, 'il doit bien y avoir quelque chose que je ne sais pas voir' (*Histoire*: 145).[24] Vision can never exhaust its object; again near the beginning of

Histoire, Simon refers to 'la vaste terre le monde fabuleux fastueux bigarré inépuisable' (26).[25] *L'Herbe*, also, places peculiar stress on 'quelque chose d'invisible' – on the basis of the Pasternak quotation that appears as an epigraph ('Personne ne fait l'histoire, *on ne la voit pas* ...'), the text keeps on returning to a mysterious 'something' which only Louise can see.[26]

Lacan establishes a particular relation between vision and desire in the four seminars grouped under the title 'Du regard comme objet petit a' (1973: 65–109). What is at issue here is the relationship of the look to the imaginary; the latter is based on the subject's relation to his mirror image, and therefore privileges the visual to some extent. The specular nature of the imaginary above all, however, determines it as an illusory experience of sameness, wholeness and continuity: in the imaginary, the world is 'full', and I am an integral and homogeneous part of it. In contrast to this, the *look* reveals the otherness of the world: it not only looks, Lacan says, it also *shows* (72) – shows, in other words, that it is looking – that therefore there is a break, a gap, between the subject and what it is looking at,[27] and that the visible is always relative to a particular look which is inevitably incomplete. As Simon says, the walls and ceiling 'ne sont verticaux et horizontaux que parce que l'homme n'est jamais lui-même qu'en position verticale ou horizontale' (*Histoire*: 193–4).[28] It is the look of the *other* which most clearly reveals this lack, and which is therefore fundamental to the subject's position in the world: it is 'la fonction qui se trouve au plus intime de l'institution du sujet dans le visible. Ce qui me détermine foncièrement dans le visible, c'est le regard qui est au-dehors' (1973: 98).[29] Moreover, the subject is by definition cut off from the look whereby it is instituted as object, and this is why it becomes an object of desire: it is 'evanescent', constantly elusive and elided, or, as Lacan says elsewhere, 'insaisissable': 'de tous les objets dans lesquels le sujet peut reconnaître la dépendance où il est dans le registre du désir, le regard se spécifie comme insaisissable' (79).[30]

But the look is equally, and for much the same reasons, a threatening object; it can 'kill', as the universal symbol of the evil eye suggests;[31] it is also significant that in the Holbein painting which Lacan uses to demonstrate the dependence of the visible on the look, the particular object that illustrates the argument is a human skull (86). Frightened by the lack which the look of the other reveals, the 'strange contingency',[32] the subject takes refuge in imaginary possession of what it sees (Lacan speaks of 'ce *m'appartiennent* des représentations, qui évoque la propriété', 77),[33] and in its own reflexive self-consciousness.[34] But all the time 'le regard est cet envers de la conscience' (79)[35] which escapes the closure and complementarity of a mirror-like 'seeing oneself'.

The tension between imaginary specularity and desire/fear for the look of the other is a structuring principle in certain sequences in Simon's texts. Perhaps the most obvious one is the section in *La Bataille de Pharsale* entitled 'O' (181–6): reading it, we seem to be following a series of movements between subject and object in relation to the look. Initially O is set up as 'observer': 'Soit alors O la position occupée par l'œil de l'observateur' — exactly the 'geometral point' of Lacan's self-conscious Cartesian subject (1973: 81) — 'et OF la droite qui joint ce point à la fenêtre F' (181).[36] Everything is thus organized within O's field of vision. But two pages later this is revised so that he is simultaneously subject and *object* of the look: 'Et, si l'on cherche à se faire une idée globale de l'ensemble des relations, il faut aussi considérer la droite OF dans son sens FO; soit un autre observateur (ou observatrice) O se tenant en F … et observant le premier observateur (qui, de sujet, devient ainsi objet — la lettre O pouvant donc également continuer à le désigner)' (184).[37] It is this second moment of the process, placing him as object of the look, that corresponds to the Lacanian determination of the subject by 'le regard qui est au-dehors'; the essential reversibility of the relation[38] is signalled by the coincidence of the same symbol O as both 'observateur' (and 'œil') and 'objet'.

'O' imagines himself, moreover, as object of a *ubiquitous* look: he is now 'attentif à observer non seulement la fenêtre *mais encore* à imaginer le spectacle que lui-même peut offrir à un regard extérieur, que ce soit celui de l'observatrice dissimulée derrière le reflet de la vitre ou celui de *toute autre personne* qui pourrait l'observer, soit dans le moment présent, soit dans la suite, O n'étant donc qu'un simple point compris à l'intérieur de *toute autre vision* balayant la place …' (185, my italics).[39] As Lacan puts it, 'je ne vois que d'un point, mais dans mon existence je suis regardé de partout' (1973: 69).[40] The vulnerability which this implies provokes a movement back to the imaginary appropriation of self offered by the mirror relation — Simon's text continues: 'comme il peut, par exemple, apercevoir sa propre image reflétée dans la glace d'un magasin'.[41] The appeal to the reassurance of the mirror occurs just after one of the other most disquieting features of the look has been invoked: the fact that 'l'observatrice' is 'dissimulée', concealed from his view behind the reflecting surface of the window pane (i.e., in this case, a mirror which is *not* reassuring). The look is thus posed as object of desire: in the first place because the subject's existence is dependent on it ('l'objet d'où dépend le fantasme auquel le sujet est appendu dans une vacillation essentielle, est le regard', Lacan 1973: 78–9),[42] and it is ungraspable, is there only as a lack; but also because it is the look of a particular woman – the sexually desirable woman who looks at him but whom he cannot look at and who remains 'lost', out of his reach.

Towards the end of *Histoire*, the text is suddenly interrupted by, on a separate line: 'me dit que du haut du ciel maman me regardait' (397).[43] In the boy's desire, his dead mother coalesces with a look which he cannot see because she is in heaven (i.e. like God, all-seeing, and *creating* him as object of her look). As in the above passage from *La Bataille de Pharsale*, a particular configuration of desires seems to be at work: the structure of the look is grafted onto desire for the woman who is *lost*. In this case, however, the loss and the lack are more fundamental, more original: the mother, who is always 'lost' in a series of separations (birth, weaning, threat of castration); and her death, which both makes this loss absolute, and also emphasizes in an equally absolute fashion the absent and 'unapprehensible' nature of the author's look.

La Route des Flandres offers a further *mise-en-scène* of the subject and the look in connection with death. It is not surprising that the text should constantly return to the moment of De Reixach's death in the ambush, since this is the most important incident in the novel. What is striking, however, is the way in which the scene is structured in terms of various 'looks', and emphasizes the *danger* of the other's look. In fact, the relationship between Georges and De Reixach is framed, as it traverses the whole text, by a deferred exchange of looks: the novel opens with Georges as object of De Reixach's look – 'Il tenait une lettre à la main, il leva les yeux me regarda'[44] – and closes with De Reixach as object of Georges's look in a final evocation of the ambush. But De Reixach is also the object of another look, from the opposite direction: that of the sniper who is going to kill him. A third seeing subject is thus involved, and one who remains invisible to both the others.

The development of this scene shows the visible opened up by the intervention of the look into a structure of *incompleteness*: there is no point from which we can see everything, and the look exists in relation to other looks. Georges's view is placed alongside and against what he deduces must be the killer's view – 'l'œil immobile et attentif de son assassin patient l'index sur la détente voyant pour ainsi dire l'envers de ce que je pouvais voir ou moi l'envers et lui l'endroit' (313)[45] – but this statement of division, as the text characteristically wavers between the otherness of the look and the fullness of the imaginary, is immediately followed by a very precise phantasy: if the two looks could only be amalgamated into one, the object of vision could be restored to a magical 'all-round' wholeness – what Serge Doubrovsky refers to as 'la hantise simonienne du Regard totalisant' (1972: 63)[46] – and in reunifying the divided field of vision that object would also ensure the self-possession, knowledge and mastery of the subjects:

c'est-à-dire qu'à nous deux moi le suivant et l'autre le regardant s'avancer *nous possédions la totalité de l'énigme* (l'assassin sachant ce qui allait lui arriver et moi sachant ce qui lui était arrivé, c'est-à-dire après et avant, c'est-à-dire comme les deux moitiés d'une orange partagée *et qui se raccordent parfaitement.*
(313, my italics)[47]

The first time the ambush is described – with an even greater emphasis on the lack in vision: 'mais je ne les vis pas véritablement, tout ce que je pouvais voir ... comme une sorte de point de mire, de repère, c'était ce dos osseux' (17)[48] – the definition of De Reixach as 'point de mire' reminds us that he is, equally, in the sight-line of his killer. The phrase in effect condenses *looking* and *killing* – just as the evil eye does, and the skull in the Holbein painting. The idea that being the object of the other's look is to be exposed to the possibility of death is made entirely literal by De Reixach here.

Georges's last reference to De Reixach in the novel is the distinctly odd, and oddly poignant, remark: 'il lui aurait fallu une glace à plusieurs faces, alors il aurait pu se voir lui-même'.[49] This becomes less cryptic in the context of the relation between the other, the look and the mirror: in a final twist of the phantasy, Georges comes back to the mirror in an attempt to counteract or cover over the intrusion of difference and death. But rather than just an ordinary flat mirror, Georges envisages a mirror that would allow De Reixach to see himself *from all angles*: a concave semi-circular mirror which would actually enclose him, echoing the perfect sphere of vision symbolized a few lines earlier by the orange (cited above). The phantasy is thus of a 'Regard totalisant' turned inside out: the Lacanian dichotomy whereby 'je ne vois que d'un point, mais dans mon existence je suis regardé de partout' (1973: 69) is overcome in a hyperbolic version of the specular relation where the subject can see himself 'from all sides' – and, simultaneously, in surrounding him the mirror serves to shut out any possibility of another look.

So far I have been arguing that there is a force at work in the texts that sustains the insistent presence of the visual throughout Simon's novels, and pulls them towards visual representation as a manifestation of desire. However, the very fact that the texts are *texts* also exerts a pull in the opposite direction: writing moving against representation, disrupting and fragmenting the visible as it figures in language. The tensions set up between these two forces can be seen at work throughout the novels; but one point at which they manifest themselves with particular clarity is in 'Orion aveugle'.

The whole of Simon's work is traversed by the figure of 'Orion aveugle'. As well as providing the title for one of his major theoretical works, Orion occurs in various forms in almost all the novels. He is most prominent in *Les Corps conducteurs*, where the Poussin painting is described in detail several times. Its full title is 'Orion aveugle marchant vers la lumière du soleil levant':[50] the mythical Greek giant Orion, blinded by the father of the woman he has raped, travels towards the rising sun, because he has been told by an oracle that he will regain his sight if he does. He is, in other words, a symbol of the desire to see; and in thus dramatizing the whole issue of vision and desire he plays an important part in the intertextual dynamics of this theme.

Orion's visual nature is underlined by the fact that he appears in the first place in a picture. But he is distinguished above all by the multiplicity of his modes of existence in the novels: as picture, but also as mythical figure, constellation, and, underlying all these, as a sequence of *words* – as text. Because of this diversity his significance is not in fact simply reducible to the desire to see; he is actually a rather complicated and ambiguous figure. Simon's comment on him in an interview[51] refers to the constellation Orion and focuses on the element of constantly re-enacted self-destruction: Orion moves towards the sun but as it rises the constellation is doomed to disappear in the daylight. This process is described twice in *Les Corps conducteurs*: on page 65, as the sun rises and the stars fade, and 'le corps gigantesque d'Orion qui marchait à sa rencontre s'efface, semble se dissoudre dans la lumière, et disparaît'; and again right at the end of the novel, with a slightly different emphasis – 'Un de ses bras tendus en avant, tâtonnant dans le vide, Orion avance ...' (222) – which serves to link Orion very clearly to the main subject of *Les Corps conducteurs*, the 'homme malade', who is shown a couple of pages later in a similar position, 'les paumes de ses mains tendues en avant pour se protéger' (225),[52] collapsing and apparently dying. Thus here the link with Orion is made precisely on the basis of the idea of death.

This is echoed in the rather ambiguous relation which the original myth proposes between blindness and the sun. Ostensibly, the rising sun is posited as a *cure* for blindness; but we are inevitably also reminded of the fact that looking at the sun is a *cause* of blindness; almost as though, beneath the avowed desire to see, there is another contradictory and more disturbing desire to blind oneself (which could in turn perhaps be connected with the images of castration that are also at their most numerous in *Les Corps conducteurs*).[53] The ambivalence is reinforced by the actual verbal structure of the title of the Poussin painting; 'Orion', although in fact derived etymologically from a pun on the Greek word for urine, is in French extremely close to 'orient'; and the connection materializes in *Les Corps conducteurs* when following a description of Orion we find a reference to the sun rising 'à l'orient' (59). 'Orient', moreover, is an exact semantic parallel to 'levant' (i.e. both mean 'rising' and hence, because of the rising sun, the east). Read in this way, the title of the painting becomes a chiasmus: *orient* aveugle / soleil *levant*; and in structurally equating 'soleil' and 'aveugle', this hints at a closer affinity between them than the overt contrastive relation of illness and cure.

In also equating *Orion/orient* and *levant*, presenting the subject and object of the verb as identical, the chiasmus does something more: the two halves of the title reflect each other, like a mirror image around the central 'vers', and so appear to show us Orion walking towards *himself* − but figured as a specular self with whom he can never unite, which can never be reached ('Tout indique cependant qu'il n'atteindra jamais son but', *Les Corps conducteurs*: 222)[54] because it is on the horizon − and Orion walking towards the (h)ori(z)on offers a further image of specularity. When Simon refers to the painting in *La Bataille de Pharsale*, he stresses precisely this endless 'movement into space' (162).

To arrive at these ramifications of meaning, however, one must read the painting's title as text. The figure of Orion operates within the field of the visible, but also and more fundamentally on the level of textuality. Simon in fact uses him − a pictorial image − to illustrate the position of the *writer* in relation to his text. 'That seemed to symbolize my own work: the writer advancing blindly in his language ... this allegory is all the more complete given that Orion is, as you know, a constellation and as the sun, towards which it avances, rises, the constellation disappears. The writer (the scriptor) is, in a similar manner, erased by the text which he has written and which was not the one he had projected.'[55]

Orion thus occupies a key position as a kind of *hinge* between the two orders of vision and textuality: the point of their reciprocal articulation, a figure dramatizing their conflict but also the transition from one to the other. The Poussin picture itself is in fact defined in linguistic terms, as having its own, contradictory, 'rhetoric' (*Les Corps conducteurs*: 78). Orion is one of the most fertile sources of textual generativity in Simon's writing. He appears as the naked warrior in *La Bataille de Pharsale*, the giant brandishing a sword: 'corps gigantesque et pâle qui vacillait, mal assuré, déséquilibré par les moulinets du sabre qu'il faisait tournoyer à bout de bras au-dessus de sa tête' (135)[56] – whose paleness and instability echo the fading of the constellation as the sun rises. Equally, if less obviously, he is at the root of the various scenes set in 'urinoirs' in *Le Palace* and *Les Corps conducteurs*, since in the original Greek myth Orion is magically conceived by Zeus, Hermes and Poseidon urinating on the hide of a heifer. In *Le Palace*, also, there is the neon-lit announcement in the chemist's window: 'ORINA–ESPUTOS–SANGRE' (148),[57] in which the actual word for urine in Spanish is a near-anagram of Orion. As graphic form, then, Orion undergoes various transformations. It effects an intertextual link with Proust by appearing in *La Bataille de Pharsale* as 'Oriane' (90), and between this novel (and also *Histoire*) and Apuleius in the further permutation of 'Oriane' into *L'Ane d'or* (whose alternative title is, fittingly, *Metamorphoses*) which is quoted at length just after the reference to Oriane (92–3). Again in *La Bataille de Pharsale*, the enigmatic and repeated phrase 'Oreille qui peut voir',[58] used in the context of the narrator listening outside the room in which he suspects the model is making love to the painter, can be traced back to a possible source in 'Orion aveugle', by means of a graphic transformation (Orion/oreille) and a double semantic permutation: from eye to ear, and blindness to sight ('qui peut voir').

But it is in *Les Corps conducteurs* that the textual activity of 'Orion aveugle' is greatest, both as an explicit presence, and as a more diffuse resonance throughout the text in numerous fragmentary echoes, such as: 'se mouvant dans l'*aveuglante lumière*, entourés de cette nauséeuse aura d'irréalité et d'*aubes* de carnavals' (78, my italics).[59] Alternatively, a veiled allusion triggers an appearance of Orion himself; thus, a description of dawn breaking at the writers' conference – 'il semble qu'une lueur grise commence à filtrer entre le côté de l'une des fenêtres et le bord mal joint ... du rideau de velours qui l'aveugle' – leads immediately to 'Un de ses bras tendus an avant, tâtonnant dans le vide, Orion avance toujours ...' (222).[60] The juxtaposition here provides a good example of the functioning of textual links in Simon's writing. There is in the first place the diegetic parallel of dawn breaking both in the conference and in the picture; the word 'aveugle' is common to both and provides the most obvious point of transition, but is reinforced by 'velours' which anticipates 'aveugle' and 'levant', and 'rideau'[61] which is echoed in 'dans le *vide, Orion*'.

This kind of imbrication of phonetic and semantic echoes around the phrase 'Orion aveugle' in fact pervades the whole text; one further example is the following: 'le levant' (59) gives rise a few lines later to 'le vent violent', still as part of the description of the painting, and then, running on over a diegetic switch to the view from the window of the plane, to 'l'avion s'élève'. But what seems at first to be a purely phonetic link then acquires a semantic parallel as well: the rising plane is implicitly compared to the rising sun as both appear to push back 'la ligne de l'horizon', so that — and here the text circles back to the original element of the painting — 'l'océan ... se déploie comme une *toile*' (59).[62] 'Avion' itself, of course, and hence the whole narrative sequence of flying over the jungle, can be seen as derived from a chiasmic play on the original 'Or*ion av*eugle'. The extraordinarily active function of the *words* 'Orion aveugle' thus creates throughout the novels a network of correspondences and allusions that links together such disparate themes as vision, urine, sexual jealousy, origin and absence[63] by means of a series of purely textual manipulations and transformations which foreground the materiality of language.

This is nowhere more apparent than in the sequence in *La Bataille de Pharsale* which follows the description of the Poussin painting cited above. Here, as the narrator looks out of the train window, for no discernible reason words materialize as visible objects: 'emporté immobile sur cette banquette de sorte que pourrais voir mots suite de mots s'étirant s'inscrivant sur les kilomètres de temps d'air je veux dire comme ces annonces ou dépêches dont le texte défile en lettres d'or tremblotantes sur ces écrans lumineux' (163);[64] but then the 'screen' disappears and the letters 'ORION AVEUGLE' appear superimposed on the view from the train window, interspersed with fences, meadows, rivers, etc.; then, finally, they are produced in the sky by an 'avion publicitaire'. The switch from 'lettres d'*or*' to 'avion' can be read as a further development of the chiasmus which produces 'avion' itself: here, *or/ion-av*eugle. But, more radically, the letters also constitute a kind of matrix within which the diegetic scene slides, without explanation, from the luminous screen of an advertisement to the 'real' countryside outside the train window to an aeroplane in the sky — in itself evidence of the dominance of the signifier over the effects of representation it produces and simultaneously elides. It confirms also the central importance of 'Orion aveugle' not only as imaginary figure of the desire to see, but also as a supreme instance of the 'letter', in Lacan's sense,[65] and its generative power in the text.

It is of course this duality of the visible and the textual that is at issue throughout the novels, and the concrete relations between the two must now be examined in more detail. To a considerable extent, these conform to the model defined by Ricardou as a conflict between the two dimensions of the referential and the literal (i.e. the text as pure 'letter'), which in turn correspond to the 'euphorie du récit' and the 'contestation du récit' (1973: 30−1).[66] With the important qualification that the visual is a narrower concept than the referential, this formulation seems an apt one for most of Simon's writing. Although elsewhere Ricardou comes down more heavily on the side of the literal and of contestation, here at least he gives them equal weight: 'Ainsi tout récit est-il astreint au jeu subtil, retors, byzantin quelquefois, de l'euphorique et du contestataire' (31) − and euphoria is exactly the right term for the quality of Simon's visual descriptions.

For Ricardou, however, the relation between the referential and the literal is necessarily conflictual; narrative is by definition 'le lieu d'un conflit permanent' (30). This aspect − 'la bataille de la phrase'[67] − is perhaps the dominant one, as his own detailed work on Simon's texts demonstrates. Equally, some of the examples of 'Orion aveugle' given above illustrate exactly the way in which a textual logic of the signifier is bound to disrupt the diegetic coherence of the representation. But the position is not quite as clear-cut as this implies. Firstly, I have already argued in Chapter 1 that if the text can be read as a representation of the psychological processes of an identifiable subject, then virtually any incoherences can be rationalized as those of the 'mind' at work; and while I would want to argue that this remains a rather abstract rationalization which does not concretely affect the experience of reading the texts very much (or, alternatively, produces a very reductive reading), it is applicable to Simon's novels up to *Histoire*, and does probably serve at least to cushion some of the effects of disruption and disorientation and give the more anxious reader a slightly smoother ride.

Secondly, the distinction made above between representational and visual also modifies the terms of the relation. The visual is not merely a sub-category of the referential. In Simon's novels, as I have said, it is produced as phantasy rather than as the perception of a diegetically objective reality. As such, and as the object of a desire for an already 'textualized' visible, it requires less continuity and consistency than if it were represented as diegetically real, because it is both more fragmentary and more persistent; it *survives* much more easily the disruption caused by an anti-representational, 'literal' discourse.

For these two related reasons the relation between the visual and the textual is rather more ambivalent than Ricardou's formulation allows for. The kind of 'disruptive' word-play which suddenly sets the text off in a new direction can itself also *produce* a new vision which, however ephemeral, works the euphoric magic of representation. (Indeed Simon's own description of this harmonious relation between text and vision situates the magic in language itself: 'faire surgir les images chatoyantes et lumineuses au moyen de l'éphémère, l'incantatoire magie du langage', *La Route des Flandres*: 184).[68] The clearest cases are those in which the link between word and vision is stated in psychological terms, located in a defined psycho-realist subject, as for instance in: 'Wack entra ... disant Les chiens ont mangé la boue, je n'avais jamais *entendu l'expression, il me semblait voir les chiens*, des sortes de créatures infernales mythiques' (*La Route des Flandres*: 9, my italics).[69] In a more complex example from *Histoire*:

nom (memel) qui faisait penser à Mamelle avec dans son aspect je ne sais quoi (les deux e blancs peut-être) de glacé ville noire couronnée de neige auprès d'une mer gelée livide habitée par les femmes slavonnes aux cheveux de lin aux seins lourds (les deux l de mamelle suggérant la vision de formes jumeLLes se balançant) et neigeux   (232)[70]

the proper name 'Memel' gives rise to the phonetically similar 'mamelle' and then to an imaginary *vision* motivated simultaneously by both the referent ('ville noire') and the sound ('les deux e blancs') of the first word, and both the signified ('seins lourds') and the graphic shape ('les deux l ... la vision de formes jumeLLes') of the second.

Although the productive capacity of language is demonstrated here, it is also in a sense contained and defused by the psychological justification. A more striking example of words producing vision is the glacier in *Les Corps conducteurs*; this is initially produced as a figure of language, a simile designating the passing of time, and as such invisible: 'il semble que l'on puisse entendre comme un fracas silencieux, comme l'avance d'un glacier invisible' (88). From then on, however, and without any comment or explanation, the glacier is *acted out* by the text, becoming entirely visible and entirely literal – 'Poursuivant sa lente progression la masse neigeuse et grisâtre avance irrésistiblement' (90),[71] etc. The result of this, of course, is to make *Les Corps conducteurs* as a whole less representational and less psycho-realist than the earlier novels; and in this context the effect

61

of a disruption such as the glacier, however visual, is to undercut even
further the representational dimension of the text: proof that vision
and representation are not always synonymous. But at almost all
stages of Simon's work we find a similar ambivalence in the inter-
relation of visual and textual. In *La Bataille de Pharsale*, for instance,
the occurrence of 'VESTON ET PANTALON' in the text (21) serves
to stress the visual nature of the words (the 'ideograms' replacing the
V and the As with pictures of a jacket and trousers) but is surely
generated in the first instance by the fact that the two words form
a kind of composite and approximate *anagram* of the key place name
PHARSALON. Here again, the textual link is not commented on or
attributed to any denoted subject.

Sometimes the ambivalence is very precisely materialized in the
text, as vision is simultaneously promoted and subverted – in the
following sequence from *Histoire*, for instance:

une salle représentant la basilique à trois nefs Dans les parties du bassin où
l'eau reflétait les feuillages sombres des lauriers on en voyait d'autres
accumulés dans le fond vert–noir brunes visqueuses pourrissant les plus
récentes rousses encore sépia collées ensemble par paquets minces pellicules
de temps d'été mort.   (412)[72]

Here the transition from a scene in a Greek museum to one in
the garden of the family home is made via the phonetic play on 'basilique'/'bassin'. The new scene is presented as an object of vision –
'on en voyait' – and emphasizes the visual aspect with references
to reflections, several different colours, and the photographic connotations of 'pellicule'. That is, word-play is here creating a visual
scene. But it simultaneously produces other effects which confuse
the clarity of the vision; alongside the visual, hence semantically
motivated, chain of colours ('vert–noir' – 'brunes' – 'rousses' –
'sépia') there are other chains based on the phonetic or graphic
materiality of the words: 'basilique' – 'bassin', but also 'salle' –
'basilique' – 'accumulés' – 'collées' – 'pellicules'. One of the
colours, 'rousses', is cross-linked to a semantic, and also alliterative,
sequence involving the past and death: 'pourrissant' – 'les plus
récentes rousses encore' – 'été mort'. Another colour, 'sépia', links
up with 'pellicule' to reinforce the suggestion of photographs, and
specifically old ones, again recalling the past. But there are no actual
photographs here (although we know from elsewhere in the novel that
the narrator and Corinne washed their negatives in the water tub);
'pellicule' is generated on the basis of phonetic associations and used
simply as a metaphor for past time and death. The activity of these

purely textual resonances set up a kind of interference with the level of visual diegesis: the visible at once solicits our attention and disintegrates, so to speak, before our very eyes.

The examples cited above are evidence that the relation between textual and visual elements can take diverse forms; it cannot ultimately be reduced to a simple formula of opposition, but is best conceived of as a continuum, a sliding scale of degrees of 'positive' and 'negative' interaction.

The discussion has so far concentrated mainly on the novels of the 'middle' period – *La Route des Flandres*, *Le Palace*, *Histoire* and *La Bataille de Pharsale*. It remains to trace briefly the subsequent evolution of the textual/visual relation, and in particular to look at how it is affected by the break between 'personal' and 'impersonal' styles, as I have defined these in Chapter 1. It is in fact *Histoire* which, although it belongs within the personal style, and has a consistent if rather insubstantial narrator, shows the first signs of anxiety about the viability of any connection *at all* between words and visible objects. It anticipates a kind of crisis in which the two simply come apart – a crisis which the different discursive economy of the impersonal style can perhaps be seen as resolving. *Histoire* as a whole displays, more markedly than the other novels, an acute ambivalence about the whole issue of the visually generative power of words; the generativity seems at times to peter out into irrelevance, as language comes adrift from the objects to which it refers – as in this disabused etymological musing: 'ou plutôt plissé: vieille peau de ce vieux monde ce vieux monstre Plissé pliscénien ou quoi Pliocène Sans doute rien à voir mots qui simplement se ressemblent plésiosaure' (345).[73] The associations between words no longer reflect any parallel set of associations between things in the perceptual world, and so words cannot convey any *vision* of the world: they have, quite literally, 'rien à voir'.

In *Histoire* the reader is constantly confronted with statements of the inadequacy of language as a means of representation. These are to be found in the other novels as well, of course, but perhaps never as frequently as here, with the narrator in the restaurant reflecting upon the lack of connection between the words on the menu and the actual food (151), the immeasurable distance between the word 'obus' and the reality of the shell exploding (165), the confusion over the man called Champenois who 'is not' Champenois (i.e. from Champagne) (362), and so on. The two most abstract and general formulations of this idea, moreover, both stress that the inadequation is between language and a specifically visual reality. In the first of these Simon writes: 'quand le monde visible se sépare en quelque sorte de vous ... les objets cessant de s'identifier avec les symboles verbaux par quoi nous les possédons, les faisant nous' (193),[74] and, in the second, refers to the boundary between mind and sight as 'l'esprit (ou plutôt: encore l'œil, mais plus seulement l'œil, et pas encore l'esprit: cette partie de notre cerveau où passe l'espèce de couture, le hâtif et grossier faufilage qui relie l'innommable au nommé' (297).[75]

The fact that the divorce between words and vision should be felt most intensely in *Histoire* would seem to suggest that this particular novel forms a turning point in Simon's writing. Indeed, by the beginning of the next novel, *La Bataille de Pharsale*, it is assumed that 'après tout tout savoir ne débouche jamais que sur un autre savoir et les mots sur d'autres mots' (18).[76] But it is in the novels which wholly or partially employ the impersonal style that the terms of the relation between vision, text and subject are radically altered on the level of textual practice. This question has already been raised in Chapter 1 (pp. 37–8), and the distinction made there between the gradual decline of representation in general and the break between the personal and impersonal 'styles' is relevant here. To rephrase the question: can one locate a subject produced by language in a style from which all overt traces of discursivity, in Benveniste's sense, have been erased; and can one attribute a subject of perception to a text which systematically undercuts all its representational elements?

Les Corps conducteurs has a minimal subject, in so far as the occurrences of the pronoun 'il' can be read as having a consistent fictional referent: it is the 'same man' who is ill, attends the writers' conference in Latin America, flies over the jungle, and so on. He speaks – to his conference interpreter, to the woman in the bathroom – but the text as a whole does not originate in him (as, for instance, the text of *Histoire* is supposedly produced by its narrator); there is a complete separation between him and the discourse of the novel. Rather than a subject of enunciation, he is produced as something like a pure agent of perception – but one which functions very differently from the psycho-realist subject whose perceptions subtend the representational dimension of the earlier novels. Various pictures of eyes – the diagram in the optician's window (154), the 'œil géant' adorning a carrier bag (176) – underline this textual foregrounding of vision; the eye has taken over, invaded the whole of the text – just as the magnified eye of the film star invades her whole face: 'Devant la photographie d'une vedette de cinéma une énorme loupe est disposeé de telle façon que le passant peut voir l'œil de celle-ci *démesurément agrandi, s'étendant sur presque toute la largeur du visage*, comme celui d'un cyclope' (155, my italics).[77] It thus comes as no surprise that the main function of 'il' is to receive sense impressions, and mainly visual ones. The last page of the novel, where the detailed description of an eye is followed immediately by an even more detailed description of the carpet in close-up, provides a final definition of the relation between subject and world that has governed the whole novel: 'la mince membrane de la rétine sur laquelle les images du monde viennent se plaquer, glisser, l'une prenant la place de l'autre'.[78] It is as though the terms of the representational 'equation' have been reversed: in the 'personal' style, the subject of perception is a psychological subject and as such more representational, more realist, than the subject-in-language whose implication in the scriptural activity of the text interferes with the establishment of a reality effect. Here, however, in those texts which are generally considered to be the least representational of all Simon's work, the subject-in-language has been overtaken − has been so to speak leap-frogged − by a modified, depsychologized version of the subject of perception.

Some sequences of *Les Corps conducteurs* replace 'il' with 'on'; and in *Triptyque* and *Leçon de choses* a similar 'on' is used exclusively. It too occupies and redefines the place of the subject of perception, functioning solely as an impersonal 'agent' of perception; in all three novels (but especially in *Triptyque*), the formulæ 'on peut voir', 'on aperçoit', 'on peut sentir', etc., are repeated with obsessive monotony throughout the text. It is in fact an even purer instance of perception (while also functioning on another level as an intermediate link in the chain of signifiers: 'O' − 'On' − 'Orion') than the 'il' of *Les Corps conducteurs*, because here[79] there is no subject *positioned* in the text at all. One could argue that the fictional referent of both 'il' and 'on' is nothing more than 'point of view' or 'narrative instance'; but the difference is that 'il' at least defines itself as a singular and discrete instance, whereas 'on' lacks even this specificity, remaining totally undifferentiated and diffuse.

As a result 'on' is *invisible*. In the 'personal style' novels, the moment of seeing oneself is always crucial to the constitution of the subject,[80] and even the 'il' of 'Les Corps conducteurs sees himself reflected in the shop windows (27). Here, in contrast, there is no equivalent posing of an *imaginary* instance of the subject 'seeing itself see itself'.[81] 'On' sees but cannot be seen − is, in a sense, a manifestation of Lacan's 'unapprehensible' gaze as discussed above (p. 52). As Colette Gaudin puts it in an article on *Leçon de choses*: 'Tout ce qu'on peut dire, c'est qu'il y a *du* regard' (191).[82]

This reduction of the subject-in-language in favour of an apparently absolute dominance of vision is in no sense a return to the earlier quasi-phenomenological subject of perception, because of the extreme dislocation of the level of representation in these texts and the predominance of formal principles of organization. Although the only subject left is an instance of vision, the fact that no diegetic situation is ever established means that vision itself has become an entirely *formal* structure, a kind of pretext for initiating and linking descriptions which have no referential weight or consistency. The virtual disappearance of the referential dimension thus transforms vision from a represented psychological act into a textual device,[83] a formula which is at times, through its repetition, almost parodied. At the same time, the visible itself loses the hallucinatory intensity of the earlier novels, in the first place because the psychological category of (a character's) *phantasy* as opposed to objective perception is not applicable to a non-realist discourse: there is no longer any way to distinguish fictional fact and fictional phantasy. But, quite apart from this, the stylistic presentation of the visible is also different: it becomes far more flat and neutral. The texts as a whole bear witness to this, and to pick out one example is somewhat artificial. However, the following description of the sky, from *Leçon de choses*:

Sous l'arche du pont l'ombre est complètement noire. Dans le ciel, les nuages que n'entraînent plus maintenant aucun vent virent lentement du blond au saumon, puis au rose qui ne subsiste bientôt plus qu'à l'état de traces dans le gris qui les envahit en même temps que leurs formes se modifient elles aussi avec une infinie lenteur. Le ciel un moment vert s'éteint par degrés, pervenche à la fin   (112)[84]

can usefully be contrasted with the value-loaded and far more lyrical way in which the sky is described in a 'personal' passage from *Les Géorgiques* as 'l'éblouissante et suave apothéose de l'aube diamantine' (110), 'la féerie scintillante, l'embrasement glacé, diamantin, couleur d'amandes et de roses' (118), etc.[85] The neutrality of the visible can be seen as a necessary consequence of the constraints of Simon's 'impersonal style'; or perhaps, conversely, the stylistic change is itself a result of abandoning this desperate attempt to capture in language the subjective quality of perception.

Either way, the new neutrality does not necessarily mean that the visible is no longer an object of desire; in fact the obsessive recurrence of the formula 'on peut voir' and its variants suggests that the investment in the visible, in writing the visible, remains constant. What has changed is the relation of that desire to writing: whereas in the earlier texts the language itself participates in the rhythms of a desiring vision, it now appears to be refusing desire by its impersonal exactness. But this is so self-conscious − an entirely deliberate and carefully maintained exclusion − that its effect is, arguably, to reproduce desire in a different form: that is, one that serves to dramatize the mechanisms of its repression.

One can thus trace through Simon's novels a general correlation between realism and vision − a specifically, and indeed insistently, visual representation of 'reality', whose power is ensured by its source in the desire invested in vision. On the other hand, there is a dimension of textual activity that increasingly, over the sequence of the novels, disrupts and subverts the representational elements; it also however to some extent collaborates in the phantasmatic production of the visible. If Simon's writing presents itself to the reader as structuration rather than structure, process rather than object,[86] this is because it is generated by the two conflicting principles of vision and textuality, in an interaction in which the visible is always contested but, equally, always survives.

3

THE MIRROR AND THE LETTER: MODALITIES OF THE SUBJECT

A major consequence of the fluctuating and intermittent nature of representation in Simon's novels, and the constant incursions of an anti-representational, 'productive' discourse, is the fact that it is impossible to read into the text a single homogeneous subject. Rather, the text presupposes two subjects: one represented as origin of the representation and one constructed in language – as I have already outlined in Chapter 1. In the present chapter I will examine in greater detail the way in which this conception of dual subjectivity emerges from the novels.

A useful starting point is a comparison with the status of the subject in what (with some over-simplification) has been taken as the traditional realist novel. Much critical work on realism stresses its 'informational' aspect; Philippe Hamon, for instance, claims that 'le projet réaliste s'identifie avec le désir pédagogique de transmettre une information' (1982: 134). This includes the hero/narrator's circumstances – his name, profession, where he lives, and so on – information which is particularly important, because the more loaded down he is with biographical detail, the greater the weight that can in turn be attached to his observations and judgements. Hamon argues further that 'le héros est donc un élément important de la *lisibilité* d'un récit, et son identification ne doit pas faire de doute pour le lecteur; toute une série de procédés ... viennent, en général, le souligner. Dans la mesure où il organise l'espace idéologique du récit, il l'embraye sur l'extratextuel culturel commun à l'auteur et au lecteur, et par là constitue un facteur important de désambiguisation' (152–3).[1] In typical realist texts, the narrator or hero is thus established in a consistent and informative fictional reality. As against this, one of the most commonly cited features of the Nouveau Roman is its refusal to ground its characters in circumstantial detail; a refusal which, although it is most clearly illustrated in the writing of Robbe-Grillet and Nathalie Sarraute,[2] also becomes increasingly true of Simon's work from *La Route des Flandres* onwards. The presence of

68

the subject in his novels is not primarily, and sometimes not at all, dependent on the information we are given about him.

There is, nevertheless, a psychological subject of representation, instituted as something over and above the verbal activity of the text, but the way in which this is done is not by reference to fictional circumstance. Rather, the subject 'appears' — literally — in the text purely as a visual image. He is in a sense nothing more than *visible*; his mode of existence is essentially that of the 'mirage', the illusory visual presence in the text of a reality external to it. A distinction has already been made (Chapter 1) between mirages that include an image of their subject and those that do not. I want now to concentrate on the former category as being to some extent privileged cases, in which the subject who perceives the mirage is also its object. Such cases are important because in them the mirage acquires a narcissistic function. It is solely by means of this kind of perceptual loop — *he sees himself* — that the subject's presence is established; and it is established as simultaneously a subject and an object — subject and object of 'vision', and hence of representation. His position is that of spectator of himself: 'pouvant pour ainsi dire se voir ... comme s'il avait été spectateur' (*Les Géorgiques*: 161).[3]

The positioning in the novels of these narcissistic mirages — moments at which the subject 'sees himself' — is clearly of importance. They tend to occur at key points in the overall structure. In *Le Palace*, the point is simply the beginning of the novel; after ten pages of 'inventory' of objects, the student becomes visible — a new paragraph starts: 'Puis il se vit, c'est-à-dire des années plus tard' (20). The ensuing image has the characteristic rhythm of the mirage, the sudden force of its apparition and the swiftness with which it fades away: 'faisant irruption sans même y avoir été invité ... — puis une fois de plus l'oubli, le néant ...' (20). It is also characteristic in its clarity and its perfectly intact, unreal quality: 'dérisoire personnage que l'on voit s'agiter, ridicule et présomptueux, là-bas, très loin, comme dans le petit bout de la lorgnette' (20).[4] The temporal distance between his past and present identities — seeing himself 'des années plus tard' — becomes a spatial, and hence visual, one: seeing himself 'très loin'. The difference between the two is as it were optical: a difference in the size of the image: 'regardant le double microscopique et effaré de lui-même' (21),[5] so that they are, at first, clearly separated. The present self seems to maintain its identity on the basis of a distanced image of the younger self; hence the repetition of 'l'étudiant (celui qui avait été l'étudiant)' (122, 123, 156).[6] However, by the time this appears on page 156 it is accompanied by a passage in which his identity dissolves and he *becomes* everything he perceives: 'cette partie de lui-même qui avait la forme d'un Américain dégingandé ... en train de dialoguer avec cette autre partie de lui-même qui avait la forme d'un type chauve',[7] and similar descriptions occur with increasing frequency, e.g.: 'sa peau ne constituait plus une enveloppe, une séparation entre l'univers extérieur et luis mais semblait englober indistinctement comme les inséparables parties d'un même tout, le ciel métallique ... les gens, les odeurs, et ses propres os' (216).[8]

This loss of outline, of self as a delimited entity, gradually invades the whole text; and at the same time, the shifts between past and present become far more frequent and confused. Thus as the novel proceeds the distance established between the two images begins to be eroded and the clear differentiation breaks down. (The polarization of 'old' and 'young' identities is, perhaps, projected onto the couple formed by the old man and the little boy feeding the pigeons, mentioned repeatedly in the last section.) This 'telescoping' leads up to the eventual suicide, almost as though the very existence of a subject had depended on a stable and distanced version of the mirror image.

Elsewhere the moment of seeing oneself coincides with a particularly important stage in the narrative development – in *Les Géorgiques*, the narrator's visit to the home of his ancestor (161); in *L'Herbe*, just after Louise has received from Marie the gifts which signify the transmission to her of the responsibility of looking after the rest of the family, and which precipitate in her a crisis of conscience and also to some extent of identity; we read that in the future she will remember this moment, running away from the house, '*se voyant*, pouvant voir la robe claire courant sur l'écran de la mémoire; la tache lumineuse suivie par le pinceau du projecteur dévalant la verte colline' (125, my italics).[9] The use of a film projector and screen as a metaphor for memory, and the fact that the projector is itself in turn metaphorically described as a paint brush – the eye of memory *creating* the image – focuses attention upon the actual process of seeing and also emphasizes, again, the unreality of the image.

Histoire produces, this time near the end of the novel, a 'frozen' image of the narrator parting from his wife. This is perhaps the clearest example of the subject seeing himself at a crucial, in this case tragic, moment, and one which well illustrates the peculiar combination of clarity and a precarious sense of unreality; the figures are distinct ('nets') but the image as such is not simply perceived but *deduced* via the mediation of a posited other gaze: 'tout arrêté figé le temps figé *Je suppose que si quelqu'un avait alors pris une photo on aurait pu nous voir* tous les deux nets debout face à face devant le flanc de ce wagon' (422, my italics).[10]

All these examples are based on memory, which is used in a fairly conventional fashion to legitimate the subject's 'seeing' him or herself in the past, while stressing in every case the necessary alienating intervention of an optical 'machine' − spyglass, camera, projector. There are also, however, a great many other cases of the subject, and other characters, seeing themselves quite literally and immediately in mirrors (or reflected in water, shop windows, and so on); and this raises the question of their relation to the mirage. Are all mirror images mirages, or do the categories overlap in part, or are they completely separate? The mirror image traditionally possesses the qualities of clarity, ephemerality and lack of real substance, and hence a purely visual intensity, that are associated with the mirage; and even the term 'mirage' is etymologically related to − and graphically condenses − 'mir(ror im)age' (and Lacan speaks of the Gestalt given in the mirror stage as 'un mirage', 1966: 95).

Moreover, its use in Simon's novels also seems to be closely bound up with the issue of subjectivity. For instance, in *La Route des Flandres*, the alternation between first- and third-person narration serves to foreground and problematize the status of the subject of enunciation. Specifically, the switch *into* the first-person mode is a kind of figuration, or dramatization, of the presence of the subject in the text: and the first time this happens, it does so in between two mirrors. That is, Georges in bed with Corinne in a hotel room sees the wardrobe mirror reflecting nothing but 'l'obscure lumière de la fenêtre' (42); this mirror does not retain any trace of the images which have been reflected in it − and the text moves immediately from this idea to the appearance of the first-person pronoun: 'les glauques profondeurs de la glace inaltérable, virginale et froide −, et lui se rappelant: "... Jusqu'à ce que je me rendisse compte ..."' (43).[11] Half a page later, however, we find another mirror, and this one does reflect the image of the subject (and his fellow-soldiers): 'regardant dans un bout de miroir accroché au-dessus d'un seau de toile plein d'eau glacée nos visages gris sale' − and leads into a detailed description of what they look like. The image disappears, too, with the characteristically dramatic rapidity of the mirage:

alors j'éloignai le miroir, mon ou plutôt ce visage de méduse basculant s'envolant comme aspiré par le fond ombreux marron de la grange, disparaissant avec cette foudroyante rapidité qu'imprime aux images reflétées le plus petit changement d'angle. (43)[12]

Here the mirror image does seem to function as a type of mirage. Elsewhere, however, the similarities are more ambiguous. In the second chapter of *Histoire*, the narrator gets up in the morning and sees himself in the bathroom mirror; so that this image would seem to have the same inaugural position (the first chapter being mainly devoted to his parents) for the subject as the example cited above in *Le Palace*. But here the scene lacks the visual intensity and definition that we find in the mirages, and there is no actual description of what he looks like. What is in fact described is his pyjama cord; and this rather odd emphasis is explained by the metaphorical terms in which it is presented:

S'avançant alors dans la glace, vacillant, le fantôme inglorieux du genre humain en pyjama fripé, traînant les pieds, et du nombril duquel pend le ruban de coton tressé, flasque et blanchâtre, qui retient son pantalon comme s'il conservait encore, exsangue, mal sectionné et déchiqueté en franges quelque lien viscéral, décoloré par les ténèbres, arraché au ventre blême de la nuit.

(48)[13]

The pyjama cord becomes the severed umbilical cord; waking is being torn from darkness, which is associated with the darkness of the mother's womb. The equivalence is reinforced when he returns to the same image two pages later, seeing in the mirror 'mon double encore vacillant au sortir des *ténèbres maternelles*, fragile, souillé protestant et misérable' (50, my italics).[14] What the mirror shows here, then, is not so much a visual image of the subject, as a metaphorical version of the birth trauma, of the baby torn from the mother's body.

The juxtaposition of birth trauma and mirror image which appears here as a textual figure finds an echo in Lacan's paper on 'Le stade du miroir' (1966: 89–97), where it is presented as a *causal* link: Lacan defines as the '*prématuration spécifique de la naissance* chez l'homme' (1966: 96, author's italics)[15] the fact that human beings, unlike animals, are born with their nervous systems still incomplete. It is this fact which on the one hand explains why birth is, precisely, traumatic, and on the other accounts for the *triumphant* nature of the identification, in the mirror stage, with one's visual image as a complete and separate entity: 'L'assomption jubilatoire de son image spéculaire par l'être encore plongé dans l'impuissance motrice et la dépendance du nourrissage qu'est le petit homme à ce stade *infans*' (1966: 94).[16] The child, in other words, passes from a stage in which its body is experienced solely as a collection of drives, as pleasure or non-pleasure, undifferentiated from its environment (a stage which seems to be recaptured at times by the student in *Le Palace*, as discussed above,

p. 70), to an identification with its own body seen from the outside, in the mirror, as a whole and distinct entity. Distinct, that is, from its environment, but also from the child who sees it: identification with the specular image is also alienating and in an important sense mistaken; Lacan defines the subject in the mirror stage as 'pris au leurre de l'identification spatiale (1966: 97).[17]

But while this particular combination of euphoric distinctness and alienation is also a characteristic of Simon's mirages, his textual presentation of actual mirror images is often more ambiguous and complicated.[18] Rather than simple illustrations of Lacanian theory, they are interesting precisely because they enact a number of very particularized variations on the basic theme of the mirror stage – which, as a psychoanalytic concept, is necessarily far more schematic and general. Thus Simon's mirror images are often lacking in either euphoria or distinctness. In the example from *Histoire* quoted above, for instance, Lacan's joyful baby is replaced by the new-born infant, 'fragile, souillé protestant et misérable'; and the imaginary totality of the body in the mirror is breached by the metaphor of the severed umbilical cord, representing both an *excess* and a *loss* in relation to the infant's body: it is something extra, and yet it is also the sign of the body's incompleteness and lack of self-sufficiency – 'exsangue, mal sectionné' – an index of the violence of the separation from the mother's body.[19]

L'Herbe contains another episode involving a mirror in a bathroom, remarkable both for its similar stress on the 'failure' of the mirror stage – here the failure to identify with the image – and for its elaborate and carefully realistic staging. Louise is in the bathroom that belongs to her and Georges, looking at the reflection of her face in the mirror over the washbasin. As this episode is introduced, the experience is immediately distanced and defused by the interjection into the sentence of a temporal loop: the present becomes the past seen as memory from the vantage point of the future (Cf. Chapter 1, pp. 31–2, on the mirage) – 'quittant la pièce, se retrouvant (*elle se rappellera s'être retrouvée*) l'instant d'après dans sa salle de bains' (166, my italics)[20] – so that the instantaneous, here-and-now quality of the mirror image is strangely diluted.

Moreover, the image is alienated, in the literal and precise sense that it looks back at her as though it were someone else: 'son visage (comme si c'eût été celui d'une autre, la regardant)' (166); it is a slightly menacing presence, or indeed absence: 'toujours debout dans sa solitude, face à face avec ce visage de mannequin qui la regardait sans sympathie, *absent*' (166–7, my italics).[21] Behind the mirror is the other bathroom belonging to her husband's parents, which in turn gives on to their bedroom. This gives rise to another dislocation, between what Louise sees (her own reflection) and what she hears: Sabine, her mother-in-law, talking to Pierre in the next room. When Sabine moves into *her* bathroom, and looks at herself in her mirror, the symmetry of the rooms (i.e. each bathroom has a mirror over the washbasin, so that the mirrors are 'exactement dos à dos de part et d'autre de la cloison', 182)[22] means that Sabine's voice appears to emanate from Louise's face; and when the voice accuses Louise of being unfaithful to Georges – 'Cet ingénieur des pétroles, elle est sa maîtresse, j'en suis sûre' (183)[23] – it is her own image which seems to condemn her: 'soutenant toujours ce même regard dur, froid, trop calme – le sien – qui continuait à la fixer sans ciller, sans émotion apparente, de l'autre côté de la glace, à la place même où se tenait sans doute la vieille femme' (184).[24]

The mirror stage moment *par excellence* is when the infant is held up to the mirror by its mother and the mirror shows both their images side by side; thus the mother's recognition of the child in the mirror serves to confirm his own identification. Simon's version operates both a superimposition and a displacement in relation to this. In the first place, the figure of the mother is replaced by what in English is so appropriately named the mother-in-law: the order of the symbolic *Law*, of patriarchy and exogamy, intervenes in the imaginary mother–infant dyad. The two images – of mother and 'infant', i.e. here the adult subject re-enacting the mirror stage – are no longer juxtaposed and hence both visible, but superimposed so that in a sense they cancel each other out, leaving only a hostile and anonymous 'mannequin'. And, finally, from being on the same side of the mirror as the infant and therefore able to verify its identification with its image in the mirror, the 'mother' is now behind the mirror, partially translated into the face that looks back at the subject, but also actually invisible. Rather than confirming, she is now threatening, positioned as the look that cannot be seen, and which thus undercuts the imaginary plenitude that the mirror stage is supposed to provide.

Louise is exceptional in Simon's writing because she is a female subject. Elsewhere, there seems to be a clear dichotomy between *subjects*, whose identification with their mirror images is similarly unresolved, and *women*, who, precisely in so far as they are not in the position of subjects, do achieve the 'proper' kind of capture of their image. Corinne, for instance, 'toujours fascinée par son image dans la glace ... calme attentive lointaine comme si elle s'enfermait hors d'atteinte dans le fond grisâtre de la glace' (*Histoire*: 155)[25] –

or the unnamed bride in *Triptyque* who stands in front of the mirror, takes her clothes off 'sans quitter des yeux son image' (212),[26] and whose 'contemplation' of her naked body in the mirror motivates a detailed description of it in the text.[27] But the *ambiguity* of narcissistic desire is best expressed by the man in *Les Corps conducteurs* who carries, talks to and kisses a mirror which has a photograph of a naked woman on its reverse side: 'Comme sa large main cache entièrement l'objet il est impossible de savoir s'il embrasse sa propre image réfléchie ou la femme nue' (203).[28]

Conversely, one finds everywhere in Simon's novels male narrators or protagonists who fail to recognize themselves in the mirror (e.g. *Le Sacre du printemps*: 209, *La Route des Flandres*: 112, *Les Corps conducteurs*: 45) or who, like Georges, see a mirror which is first described as being like 'celles que l'on peut voir ou plutôt dans lesquelles on peut se voir chez le coiffeur' (*La Route des Flandres*: 206).[29] This amended definition, however, is negated on the next page where it turns out that the mirror *does not reflect his image*; he nevertheless gazes drunkenly into it –

et sans doute à cause de l'ivresse, impossible d'avoir visuellement conscience d'autre chose que cela cette glace et ce qui s'y reflétait à quoi mon regard se cramponnait pour ainsi dire comme un ivrogne se cramponne à un réverbère comme au seul point fixe dans un univers vague invisible et incolore

(*La Route des Flandres*: 207)[30]

– with a desperation and intensity commensurate with the emptiness and lack of identity that the mirror offers him.[31] What the mirror reflects back to the subject is not, usually, an imaginary plenitude and totality, but various forms of *lack*.

It is relevant in this context to note that Lacan's later work significantly modifies the conception of the imaginary embodied in the original formulation of the mirror stage; Jacqueline Rose, in 'The Imaginary' (1981: 132–61), argues that 'the movement away from a stress on illusory totality and identity, to identity as a function of repeated difference, can thus be seen as representing a shift in Lacan's emphasis from the Imaginary, to the structure of linguistic insistence as already underpinning moments prior to its intervening symbolisation' (147). In other words, the specular relation is never completely sealed off from the action of the symbolic order, the intervention of the Other as locus of discourse. Commenting on a passage from the *Ecrits*:

Car l'Autre où le discours se place ... ne l'est pas tant qu'il ne s'étale jusque dans la relation spéculaire en son plus pur moment: dans le geste par quoi l'enfant au miroir, se retournant vers celui qui le porte, en appelle du regard au témoin qui décante, de la vérifier, la reconnaissance de l'image, de l'assomption jubilante, où certes *elle était déjà*   (Lacan 1966: 678)[32]

– Rose says: 'The permeation of the Other over the specular relation therefore reveals the necessity of *appeal*, and hence the structural incompleteness of that relation and then, through that, the irreducible place of desire within the original model' (149). The relation with one's image in the mirror relies, in this later formulation, on the intervention of an instance of the symbolic, opening up a *lack* in the supposed plenitude and autonomy of the imaginary. The imaginary, in other words, is revealed as a mirage held in the force field of the symbolic. It is above all this emphasis that is illuminating in the context of Simon's novels – as for instance in the example given above of Louise and Sabine, the mother-in-law and her invisible stare imagined behind the mirror, which can be read as a figuration of the implication of the symbolic in the imaginary. There is no definite boundary between the two orders on the level of the subject's actual experience or, in literary terms, of the actual construction of the text. But for the very reason that this latter does move continually between the two, the opposition in principle remains important: as theoretical concepts, the imaginary and the symbolic provide a model for the particular kind of oscillation in the textual activity of Simon's novels.

If, then, we now move across slightly more into the domain of the symbolic, of the subject constructed in language, we find further examples of the interpenetration of symbolic and imaginary, this time weighted on the side of language and the post-Oedipal phase. According to Freud, secondary identification with the father is instituted by the Oedipal phase and this for Lacan coincides with the subject's entry into the symbolic order. The relationship between father and son is, of course, a prominent theme in several of Simon's novels.

The connection between language – especially written language – and the father is made in the character of Pierre, Georges's father and an academic, who writes for a living.[33] But it is not with Pierre that Georges identifies; in fact none of Simon's protagonists ever identifies with his actual father, but always with a substitute older man instead. Lucien Dällenbach comments in his article on *La Route des Flandres*: 'Cette problématique de l'identité du sujet ... s'exprime toujours chez Simon par un rapport d'imitation fascinée et d'émulation à un "ancêtre" ou à un parent (éventuellement adoptif ou par alliance) qui joue le rôle de devancier' (1982: 308).[34] This relationship is shown between Bernard and his stepfather in *Le Sacre du printemps*, between the anonymous narrator and his uncle Charles in *Histoire* and *Les Géorgiques*, and between the same anonymous narrator and the ancestor LSM in *Les Géorgiques*. The substitute father figure is the mother's second husband in *Le Sacre du printemps*, but is a member of the mother's side of the family everywhere else. It is as though Simon's protagonists remain in some sense tied to the imaginary dual relation with the mother: even the father figure has strong maternal associations – is, in fact, a sort of male mother figure.

The figure with whom Georges identifies is De Reixach, Sabine's cousin, and so for Georges on the mother's side of the family. Although De Reixach embodies such 'masculine' virtues as military honour, courage, etc., he is structurally in a position intermediate between mother and father, and hence between imaginary and symbolic. Georges's identification with him is manifested in many different ways in the course of the novel; one of the most striking of these involves the 'narcissistic' mirage, and the importance of its placing within the narrative structure. I have already pointed to the way in which, at the beginning of *Le Palace*, for example, the student becomes a presence in the text at the moment at which he 'sees' himself: the mirage *inaugurates* him as subject. There is an exact structural parallel to this in the opening pages of *La Route des Flandres*, where we find a 'vision' which has all the characteristics of the mirage – yet it shows not Georges but De Reixach. What is inaugurated here, in other words, is not the subject in its specular relation as such but its relation to an object of secondary – i.e. post-Œdipal – identification. This is perhaps why the visual instantaneousness and static quality (cf. 'statue') proper to the mechanism of the mirage is set against a countervailing stress on duration, in the form of ancestry:

un moment j'ai pu le *voir* ainsi le bras levé brandissant cette arme inutile et dérisoire dans un geste *héréditaire* de *statue* équestre que lui avaient probablement *transmis* des *générations* de sabreurs, silhouette obscure dans le contrejour qui le décolorait comme si son cheval et lui avaient été coulés tout ensemble dans une seule et même matière, un métal gris, *le soleil miroitant un instant* sur la lame nue puis le tout – homme cheval et sabre – s'écroulant d'une pièce ...   (12, my italics)[35]

Thus the mirage, the key textual structure whereby the subject is constituted in the visual imaginary mode, is here displaced on to the figure of De Reixach and thereby establishes him as Georges's 'double'.

This in turn affects Georges's relation to language, in that he rejects Pierre both as father and as writer. Conversely, Lambert, in *Histoire*, has used *language* to free himself from his *mother* – 'Arsenal de calembours et de contrepèteries censé *l'affranchir par la magie du verbe des croyances maternelles* et des leçons du catéchisme' (49, my italics)[36] – and is thus implicitly contrasted with the narrator, who is still caught up in the maternal connotations of the mirror image discussed above: the two passages are immediately juxtaposed in the text.

In fact, however, the maternal father figure blocks any such clear separation between the maternal and the specular on the one hand and the paternal and language on the other. The imaginary and the symbolic are constantly interacting – Heath, in this context, speaks of 'the subject, thenceforth held in the ceaselessly displacing join of symbolic and imaginary, the very *drama*' (1981: 84) – and Simon's texts, in a similar fashion, almost always present the relationship with the maternal double as oscillating between the specular and the linguistic. *La Route des Flandres*, for instance, opens with a scene between Georges and De Reixach – the only time, in fact, that they are actually shown face to face. This mirror-like relation situates the encounter in the imaginary register, as does the fact that it is Georges's mother who has brought them together in the first place.

Two factors, however, work against this maternal–specular–imaginary complex. In the first place, it is not a symmetrical exchange of looks – Georges finds himself unable to look back at De Reixach, becomes purely the object of De Reixach's look and is thus positioned within a scopic field structured by the look of the other. Secondly, the encounter is based on Sabine's letter to De Reixach and is therefore mediated by language. Georges is presented to De Reixach, and to the reader, first of all by his mother's letter: the first sentence of the novel ends: '... au bout d'un moment il dit Votre mère m'a écrit' (9).[37] Thus here it is the *mother* who is associated with writing (as is the mother in *Histoire*, where her body is imagined as made of postcards and letters, as 'rien qu'un vieux sac postal', 86).[38] Moreover, this first sentence effects a curious conjunction of vision and writing in the positioning of the subject: Georges is from the outset simultaneously held in De Reixach's gaze and 'written' in the letter. De Reixach's gaze in fact makes the equation between the two as it switches from Georges's face to the letter and back again: the sentence, and hence the novel, begin 'Il tenait une lettre à la main, il leva les yeux me regarda puis de nouveau la lettre puis de nouveau moi' (9)[39] – an alternation which can be seen as re-enacting on a much smaller scale the oscillation between subject-in-language and subject of vision that is the main axis of all Simon's writing.

Other examples show the specular and the linguistic again in inter-action, but in a slightly different structure. Perhaps the most fully developed 'double' relation is that between the anonymous narrator and his uncle Charles, which occurs in *Histoire, La Bataille de Pharsale* and *Les Géorgiques*. The nephew identifies with him to the point where they fuse completely as narrators (in certain sections of *Histoire* and *La Bataille de Pharsale* the narrative point of view is ambiguously both that of Charles and that of his nephew). Here the specular relation is underlined in various ways: Charles is a maternal figure because he is the narrator's mother's brother, and also because after his wife's suicide he brings up his children on his own; and the visual schema of the mirror image is repeated in the whole chapter of *Histoire* that is devoted to describing a photograph of Charles that the narrator is looking at.

But the narrator's most frequent memories of his uncle are of Charles helping him with his Latin homework. Throughout *La Bataille de Pharsale*, in particular, fragments of this scene erupt into the text for no apparent reason, except to suggest that it is the central element in their relationship. If so, it would seem to symbolize the importance of *language* as the basis of their intersubjectivity. In other words, their relationship is inescapably mediated by and structured around language. The relationship as figured in this scene is also of course one of teacher and pupil. This is, in the first place, a very suitable and familiar situation for a substitute father, and so it under-lines the aspect of the 'double' who acts as object of identification: Charles as teacher, very precisely *in loco parentis*. But it also serves as the vehicle whereby the modalities of the pupil's relation to language, specifically, are worked out; his struggle with his Latin translation also has the wider connotation of an apprenticeship of language as such: the significance of the subject's entry into the symbolic, into language seen as in some sense alien, is dramatized by presenting it as a *foreign* language (and, moreover, one that was typical of boys' education rather than girls') rather than the 'mother tongue', thus removing the situation even further from the sphere of the mother and the imaginary. Elsewhere in Simon's novels, also, the phallic connotations of Latin are made very clear; in *L'Herbe* for instance: 'l'antique et vieux phallus ... quelque chose pour être écrit – ou décrit – en latin' (129).[40]

This 'lesson' also confirms Charles in his position of mastery over both the boy and, apparently, the functioning of this mysterious code. The question of mastery is one which Lacan raises as a 'lure', a phenomenon of the imaginary; and his 'Séminaire sur "La Lettre

Volée"' (1966) is devoted to proving that in reality no-one has mastery over the signifier. Equally, in the case of Charles one could argue that his position of mastery over Latin is undercut by his complete lack of control over the other areas of his life. But in any case it is by virtue of his initiation into language in this 'lesson' with Charles that the boy is brought into existence as subject-in-language. In fact, continuing the series of interpretations and transformations that Ricardou (1971: 124–7) has produced of the Valéry poem placed at the beginning of *La Bataille de Pharsale*, one could perhaps reinterpret: 'Le son m'enfante' as '*Leçon* m'enfante'.[41]

Several of the occurrences of this scene contain allusions to mirror-like effects, thereby recalling us to the quotient of the imaginary in the relation between Charles and the boy. But these effects actually work to disrupt the specular relation in its basic symmetry. For instance, the narrator – like Georges with De Reixach in the example from *La Route des Flandres* discussed above – cannot look his uncle in the eye, as the reader deduces from the detailed description of what the floor tiles look like (*La Bataille de Pharsale*: 220). Even more relevantly in this context, Charles's ability to see *him* is symbolized by the fact that he wears glasses (another of the 'mechanical' manifestations of vision that proliferate in Simon's texts), and when the narrator, here referred to as 'O', does glance up at Charles's face he finds that the glasses are catching the light so that he cannot see the eyes behind them: 'O. jette alors un regard rapide sur le visage maigre dont il ne peut voir les yeux cachés par un reflet sur les lunettes' (221).[42] Charles sees him but cannot himself be seen *because* of his 'seeing', i.e. his glasses; the specular identification based on looking into the double's eyes is blocked, and blocked paradoxically by a reflection as in a mirror.

This version of the scene of the Latin translation, which occurs near the end of *La Bataille de Pharsale*, does not specify *what* the glasses reflect; but in an earlier evocation of the same incident this is clearly stated: 'Il attendait, patient ou plutôt résigné, la tête légèrement incliné, les verres de ses lunettes dans cette position comme deux lunes reflétant le désordre des papiers sur son bureau éclairés par la lampe' (82).[43] That is, the glasses, representing the power of seeing, become a mirror, representing the specular relation between the narrator and Charles – *except* that what is reflected in them is not the narrator but an image of *writing*: the 'papiers'. With a truly Lacanian virtuosity, this scenario thus reveals the imaginary order of the mirror to be shot through with intervening elements of the symbolic: the subject finds himself as an object in the other's look; attempting to look back at the other, his double, he sees a mirror image not of himself but of writing, language, in his place. That is, the mirror is subverted to show the signifier *in the place of* the subject – precisely what is at issue in the entry into the symbolic.[44]

To the extent that the subject of representation and the subject-in-language can be aligned with the theoretical instances of the imaginary and the symbolic respectively, one would expect to find that the 'symbolic' subject's presentation, the modality in which it occurs in the text, was in simple terms less realistic than that of the imaginary subject. This is not in fact entirely the case, not least because, as has been shown in the preceding examples, the two orders are often shown as interacting in fairly intricate ways within the framework of a single 'scene'. That of the Latin translation, for instance, although its textual occurrences are extremely disparate and fragmentary, is nevertheless recognizable as, precisely, a *scene* of a boy getting his uncle to help him with his homework, and as such is as much a realist representation as anything else in Simon's novels.

As against this, however, there are also places in the texts where a more purely 'symbolic' subject emerges; and here it is true to say that the subject is not a realist one, and in fact disturbs the coherence of the representation. *Histoire*, for example, contains a passage which sets up a structure very similar to that of the Latin translation scene described above: a mirror reflecting letters in the place of the subject's face. But it is not a scene; the paragraph in question describes the *lettering* first and foremost, i.e. focuses specifically on the materiality of the signifier, and it is only within this matrix that first the mirror (the glass front of a bar) and then the subject appears. Moreover, the subject's appearance is extremely problematic:

COIFFURE écrit en oblique sur les volets fermant la boutique en face montant de la gauche vers la droite les hampes ou les jambages des lettres verticaux mais les barres des F et des E inclinées ... se reflétant dans la glace ... de sorte que sur les deux premières lettres de l'inscription *se superposaient en transparence* les trois bustes ... le mot SALON au-dessus de la tête *coiffée* du béret grenat la tache rouge du corsage immédiatement au-dessous de l'I et de l'F, le second F et le U *barrant le visage du personnage* accoudé au zinc, de face (*moi?*), le mot MESSIEURS peint horizontalement en caractères plus petits ...   (374, my italics)[45]

As a preliminary indication, we may note that the purely scriptural dimension of the passage is enhanced by an allusion to Rimbaud's sonnet 'Voyelles' – itself of course exploring the materiality of the signifier: 'I rouge' in Rimbaud's first line and 'corset' in the third are echoed here in 'la tache rouge du corsage immédiatement au-dessous de l'I'. The people appear only in the interstices of the letters, at one point echoing the matrix word 'coiffure' in 'coiffée'; they are anonymous, superficial and transparent, almost epiphenomenal in relation to the letters. The subject appears fleetingly and as it were *en passant*; he can hardly recognize himself, so the position of both looker and reflection is, literally, questionable – the 'moi?' in turn echoed by the last word of the novel – and, finally, his face is 'barré' by the letters: negated, or crossed out, by the signifier in a movement which recalls, one might even say parodies, the Lacanian algorithm in which the 'barre' separates signifier from signified and institutes the supremacy of the former (see 'Instance de la lettre dans l'inconscient ou la raison depuis Freud', 1966).

The idea that the subject-in-language is a position in the signifying chain, that it 'slides' under the signifier, is demonstrated with startling literalness in a passage from *La Bataille de Pharsale* (163–4) already discussed in Chapter 2 (pp. 59–60). The words 'Orion aveugle' are here materialized as letters which, breaking up the realist representation, are inscribed on the countryside seen from a passing train. They appear in sequence: 'une inexorable régularité O-R-I-O-N séparées par des intervalles mouvants de temps d'espace'; and the visual elements of representation are inscribed in the spaces between them, held in the matrix of the word: 'par exemple maintenant O talus s'abaissant rapidement R démasquant une I clôture de barbelés O prairie avec deux vaches'. The whole phrase is never present all at once – 'le mot n'étant jamais visible tout entier': it is a process rather than an entity. Most importantly, though, the subject is himself caught up in, literally *subject to*, this movement of the signifying chain: 'le mot n'étant jamais visible tout entier moi déjà plus le même ailleurs à plusieurs centaines de mètres déjà plus vieux de plusieurs secondes O-R-I-O-N'.[46] The text thus acts out with extreme clarity the primacy of the letter, the signifying chain, over the subject: in Lacan's words, 'la détermination majeure que le sujet reçoit du parcours d'un signifiant' (1966: 12).[47]

Conceptualizing the subject in Lacanian terms as 'nothing other than that which "slides in a chain of signifiers"' (Heath 1981: 79) carries the implication that this 'sliding' will have a damaging effect on claims to representational efficacy. I have already discussed this issue in general terms;[48] but the particular question of the *mobility* of the subject with reference to fictional conventions such as characterization and point of view has considerable repercussions at the level of specific texts. One important index of the extent to which the subject is constructed in language alone is the degree of mobility it has in relation to the fictional level of the novel – the extent to which the subject is just a position in language, produced by the text and moved around by the text, lacking any consistency in terms of realist representation. The degree and type of mobility varies from text to text; it is evident as early as *L'Herbe* with a discoherence in narrative point of view (analysed by Roubichou 1976), and it does not simply increase from the early novels to the later ones.

Histoire, for instance, although more radical than preceding novels in many other ways, in this particular respect remains largely within the realist format of a narrator remembering his past. The exceptions are those passages of the novel in which the 'je' – normally Charles's nephew – seems to become Charles himself: where, that is to say, the subject-in-language, as signifier, moves from one character to another and in so doing loses its consistent fictional identity. The movement whereby uncle and nephew in turn assume the position of subject is carried over into parts of *La Bataille de Pharsale*, where an unnamed first-person narrator is both doing a Latin translation, helped by his uncle (53) like the nephew in *Histoire*, and having an affair with the Dutch painter's model (48) like Charles in *Histoire*; pages 49 to 51 alternate between a description of the model and an evocation of the fair from which the nephew as schoolboy used to come home so late that his mother was worried. The paragraph on page 50 that explains the juxtaposition of the model and the fair on the grounds that both make him feel guilty *also* tacitly identifies, fuses together, nephew and uncle. There is nothing in the actual passage to suggest that the uses of 'je' in fact refer to two different characters – just as there is no reason why the same person should not do Latin homework and in later life have an affair with an artist's model; it is only the intertextual reference back to *Histoire* that establishes the difference and hence the movement of the subject, and/or conversely, the coalescence of two different characters. The configuration of characters thus changes from one novel to the next, in a kaleidoscopic succession of varying identities; *Les Géorgiques*, later, will also merge Georges and the narrator of *Histoire*.[49]

But it is later on in *La Bataille de Pharsale* that we find the clearest and most radical instance of the subject as pure positionality in discourse. This comes with the introduction of 'O' in the final section of Part II. It is immediately preceded by an evocation of death – ambiguously accidental or suicide: 'ça doit être vite fait On ne doit souffrir longtemps' (181).[50] Then, with the idea that 'je' is dead, the text breaks off and starts again, from, and with, *nothing*: 'Repartir, reprendre à zéro'.[51] O is thus first and foremost simply zero, a subject no longer endowed with any substantive attributes but solely a position, a point of intersection in a relational nexus.[52] The nexus is first of all a visual one: as already discussed in Chapter 2, O also represents the eye of the observer in relation to the object of his vision and the points marking the limits of his field of vision, resulting in a geometrical diagram with 'bissectrice', 'la ligne OT hypothénuse du triangle rectangle dont le sommet de l'angle droit se trouve aux pieds de O' (182),[53] and so on. The end of this section retains the concept of a visual figure: 'on doit se figurer l'ensemble du système comme un mobile se déformant sans cesse autour de quelques rares points fixes' (186),[54] but a more complex and fluid one, less immediately *given* in vision, and one which stresses precisely the idea of mobility. Furthermore, the very end of the section modulates from the order of the visible into that of language: '... par exemple l'intersection de la droite OO' et du trajet suivi par le pigeon dans son vol, ou encore celle des itinéraires de deux voyages, ou encore le nom de PHARSALE figurant également dans un recueil scolaire de textes latins et sur un panneau indicateur au bord d'une route de Thessalie' (186)[55] − into a *name* as point of intersection of two *texts*. This indication of O as position in a system of discourse, specifically, is developed further in Part III of the novel, where in the first few pages we find O *writing*: to his mistress, to the painter and his wife, and to his daughter Corinne. All of these relations of course define him unambiguously as the Charles of *Histoire*, but in the course of Part III O 'is' also the nephew from *Histoire* ('O traduit un texte latin ...', 220).[56] 'He' is, moreover, also the woman: the initial section 'O' already introduces 'un autre observateur (*ou observatrice*) O' (184, my italics)[57] to form the intersubjective structure of vision, the exchange of looks, discussed earlier, and later in the text we find that O has crossed over from masculine subject to feminine (and the context of the subject, perhaps, shifted from *Histoire* to echoes of Pauline Réage's *Histoire d'O*.) − in Part III, for instance:

O. voit le corps penché au-dessus d'elle ... Les bras supportés par les mains à plat sur le drap de part et d'autre des épaules d'O fléchissent, de sorte que la poitrine broussailleuse s'abaisse, les poils jaunes frôlent d'abord les pointes des seins d'O, qui se durcissent ...'   (211−13)[58]

'Position' can thus be geometric, and it can be sexual, but it is primarily discursive, in the first place because nothing links these various instances of O − the sliding of the subject in the signifying chain − except the recurrence of the graphic symbol itself, but also because the references to texts and writing mentioned above are picked up and developed further in the closing pages of the novel, which enact a *mise-en-scène* of the writing of *this* text, ending with its first sentence, and placing O as its subject of enunciation: 'O. écrit: Jaune et puis noir temps d'un battement de paupières et puis jaune de nouveau.'[59] This kind of reflexivity is of course a familiar device (from *A la Recherche du temps perdu* or Butor's *La Modification*, to cite just two examples). But what is different here is that, beyond the collapse of hero into narrator into author, we are given a subject of enunciation who is a simple zero.[60] O is in fact the ultimate signifier because it does not signify anything except as a function of its changing position in discourse.

Les Corps conducteurs, the novel written immediately after *La Bataille de Pharsale*, appears at first to have no subject discernible in the text at all. It opens with an entirely impersonal descriptive stance − a perfect illustration of Benveniste's 'histoire', in fact, except that it is in the present tense − introducing various things and people ('les jambes', 'l'infirmier', 'une jeune femme nue', etc.) from a neutral, external point of view that does not seem to be situated in any way. On the second page, however, we come across a third-person pronoun that we cannot relate to any noun already mentioned: 'Le docteur lui dit de baisser son pantalon.'[61] Because there is no nominal antecedent to attach this 'lui' to, we tend to read it as equating existentially with a first-person pronoun: 'je', that is, never substitutes for a noun in the same straightforward way that 'he' does (as in 'The doctor ... he ...'); as a shifter, in Jakobson's terminology,[62] it refers solely to the instance of enunciation. The reader is therefore more or less obliged to assume − is *placed* by the discourse in the position of assuming − that this 'lui' designates the point of view from which the description is made: in other words, the subject.

Later on, 'lui' is nominalized as 'l'homme malade', and there is ultimately no real problem in positing him as the consistent subject of the representation. He is, however, defined in the first instance by purely syntactic means, acquiring the status of subject solely by virtue of being an unattached, free-floating pronoun − an element of language which has no semantic or referential content but is a purely relational term, and as such embodies in an extreme form a fundamental characteristic of the signifying chain. The fact that it should be precisely this *absence of content* that identifies the pronoun as *subject* can be seen as significant illustration of the thesis that subjectivity is nothing other than positionality in language, as Lacan claims. There is here a foregrounding of *anaphora* which insists on the primacy not only of language but also of relationality as such.

To take this idea one stage further, one might argue that the 'pro-noun' – which is by definition a *substitute* – also crystallizes in itself the notion of subject-in-language as 'standing for' the Other excluded from language.[63] What we find here in *Les Corps conducteurs* can be interpreted as a very clear materialization at a particular point in the language system – namely the pronoun without an antecedent, i.e. a substitute for nothing – of the psychoanalytic subject as 'tenant-lieu'.

Some sections of *Les Corps conducteurs* replace the 'il' with an even less determinate 'on'. This is semantically more diffuse,[64] seeming almost to encompass the reader as well as the subject of enunciation; but it differs from 'il' most clearly in its syntactic distribution, which is far from diffuse. 'On' is solely a subject pronoun; in other cases it is indistinguishable from the other third-person pronouns (in that French, unlike English, cannot say 'it makes one ...' or 'one's', but collapses these into 'le' and 'son')[65] and can thus perhaps be seen as an extreme case of subject as pronoun, 'substituting' for an entirely undefinable substantive.

After the group of 'formalist' novels, *Les Géorgiques* initiates a return to a more representational discourse in so far as narrative and characterization become once again central concerns of the text, but it retains from *Triptyque* and *Leçon de choses* the idea of multiple narratives: here, the three stories of LSM the Napoleonic general, O/Orwell in the Spanish Civil War, and the cavalryman in the Second World War. All of these are, for the most part, simply designated as 'il'; therefore, since it is not always clear which of them is being referred to, the mobility of the subject here takes in the first place the form of multiple reference, in so far as 'il' covers three possible fictional referents.

An example of the kind of ambiguity this produces is to be found in the account of the cavalry being ambushed in Chapter 1, which is interrupted by a sentence about the process of writing *this* text, which is in turn followed by a sentence belonging to the sequence of descriptions of LSM as an old man writing his registers on the balcony overlooking the barracks. The text is as follows:

Ils comprennent alors qu'ils sont tombés dans une embuscade et qu'ils vont presque tous mourir. Aussitôt après avoir écrit cette phrase il se rend compte qu'elle est à peu près incompréhensible pour qui ne s'est pas trouvé dans une situation semblable et il relève sa main. Entre la base du pouce et celle de l'index le réseau de rides flasques puis crépelées contourne le porte-plume en courbes à peu près parallèles. (47)[66]

The first and third sentences belong unambiguously to the Second World War (as is clear from the reference to 'bombardement', 45) and the Napoleonic narratives respectively. The second sentence could belong to either (i.e. the 'il' in question could be either the twentieth-century cavalryman or LSM), not only because the break in the text could be taken to occur before or after it, but also because beyond its immediate context it fits perfectly as part of either narrative: on the one hand, if we go back in the text to the last time LSM was mentioned we find: 'Il écrit au Comité de salut public que l'on cherche à l'assassiner et que plusieurs de ses officiers qui le devançaient pour des raisons de service dans des chemins qu'il devait emprunter sont tombés dans des embuscades et ont été tués' (45)[67] – and, because of the coincidence of the two ambushes, this could quite logically continue: 'Aussitôt après avoir écrit cette phrase ...'

Equally, though, the next reference to the cavalryman continues the account of the ambush and includes this: 'Il rapporte dans un roman les circonstances et la façon dont les choses se sont déroulées ...' (52)[68] – which on the one hand reinforces the idea of the cavalryman as writer of a novel which might be *Les Géorgiques* itself; or alternatively might refer to *La Route des Flandres*, which contains a very similar ambush, and whose narrator is indeed a cavalryman: nothing (except possibly the reappearance of 'Georges' in the title *Les Géorgiques*) authorizes us to assume that the two novels have the same subject.

'Il', however, is not always the subject of enunciation: 'his' story is sometimes told by someone else. The relations between subject of enunciation and subject of statement vary for each narrative,[69] introducing a complication not found in any of Simon's other novels. The stories of LSM and O are told by someone else, an identifiably present narrator in the case of LSM, and an anonymous, absent one for O. It is only in the cavalryman's narrative that subject of enunciation and subject of statement coincide to given an autobiographical discourse, albeit in the third person. However, the narrative does not read like a straightforwardly autobiographical text; something similar to the alternation between 'il' and 'on' which we find in *Les Corps conducteurs* recurs at some points of the cavalryman's narrative – but in this case with a perfectly coherent realist explanation. Genette's distinction between point of view ('mode', in his terms) and voice (1972: 203) is pertinent here: the point of view adopted is most often, at least in Chapter 2 of the novel, a collective one with the emphasis on perception — what the cavalrymen see, hear, feel, etc. As a plural — 'Ils peuvent sentir sur leur langue et contre le palais de minuscules cristaux qui craquent sous la dent et fondent aussitôt' (79)[70] — it is virtually by definition not the narrator. Equally, the text moves easily and frequently between their point of view and description of them from the out-side, as in these two consecutive sentences: 'Ce qu'ils ont avalé, dans leurs estomacs comme un bloc de pierre froide. Ils se tiennent adossés à la paroi du wagon, recroquevillés dans leurs manteaux, silencieux et taciturnes' (80).[71]

There is also an alternation between what 'ils' perceive and, less often, what 'on' perceives: still remaining within the first two pages of Chapter 2, we can note the shift from 'ils peuvent sentir ...' to, in the next paragraph, 'on peut voir défiler lentement la campagne monotone' (79).[72] But unlike in *Les Corps conducteurs*, the coherence of these shifts is assured by the particular position of the implied subject of enunciation as *one of the group* of cavalrymen, and as therefore equally able to identify with them and to see them from the outside.

In all the above cases the mobility of the subject takes the form of a condensation on the level of the signifier — a single signifier covering two or more signifieds ('O' for Charles, his nephew and the artist's model, etc.). This is of course the standard definition of ambiguity. But the converse also occurs, and results in a phenomenon which is not reducible to ambiguity in the ordinary sense: that is, two *signifiers* for a single *signified*: in *La Route des Flandres* the signified *Georges* — the 'character' Georges — is represented in the text by the two signifiers of the first- and third-person pronouns. The narrative point of view is that of Georges throughout. Yet while this is held constant, Georges is alternately — switching every few pages — designated as 'Georges/il' and as 'je'; and these shifts are not accompanied by any other change in fictional continuity or point of view.

The result is, in the first place, the same kind of instability on the plane of representation as that created by the use of 'O', or 'il' in *Les Géorgiques*, for instance. But in this case it also seems to set up a contradiction *within* the language system itself, which at some points almost amounts to ungrammaticality. To find within a single, albeit very long, sentence — 'et ce dut être par là que *je* le vis pour la première fois ... le fixant à travers cette sorte de demi-sommeil, cette sorte de vase marron dans laquelle *j'étais* pour ainsi dire englué ... et plutôt le devinant que le voyant: c'est-à-dire ... aux trois quarts recouvert de boue − *Georges se* demandant sans exactement *se* le demander ...' 26−7, my italics)[73] − produces a slight *linguistic* shock in a way that the previously cited examples do not. By neutralizing the opposition between first and third person in this way, the sentence transgresses a structural principle of the code itself; it causes a disturbance within the signifying chain. In so far as this latter is seen as the basis of the symbolic order, it is precisely the notion of *order* that is put in question here.[74]

If the first-person sections were embedded within a third-person discourse we could perhaps arrive at a realist rationalization for the alternation by reading it as a basically authorial discourse which includes passages in direct 'speech': the character's voice, that is, contained by the author's. But *La Route des Flandres* starts and finishes with sections in the *first* person, thus effectively blocking any attempt to impose a hierarchy; *je* and *il* remain on the same level, and the contradictory positioning of the subject remains unresolved. It is also difficult to attribute any thematic significance to the shifts. At the beginning of the novel the first move into the third person seems to correlate with a loss of certainty − 'Georges se demandant' (27) − and the move back into the first person (motivated, perhaps, by the description of a mirror) with a regained confidence in the certainty of knowledge: 'Jusqu'à ce que je me rendisse compte ...' (43). But this contrast between wondering in the third person and realizing in the first is exactly reversed by the last two switches in Part I of the novel, where it is 'I' who wonders ('Et je me demandais', 88) and 'he' who realizes ('Puis il se rendit compte', 93). Throughout this first part, however, there is a sense of the first person being brought in as an attempt to *repossess* the discourse: quotation marks are used for these sections, and the 'speech' tends to start off very confidently − 'Parce que je savais parfaitement que ...' (77)[75] − and then fade away into a less sure and less personal discourse. In the second and third parts of the novel, however, even the quotation marks are not used consistently (e.g. 155), the shift sometimes occurs in the middle of a sentence and, instead of alternating sections in which either 'je' or 'Georges' appear fairly regularly, there are long passages in which neither is mentioned at all.

There is, in other words, no structural or thematic justification for the alternation between the pronouns. All that it does − but it does it all the more powerfully through lacking any such alibi − is to show

how language produces a subject whose mobility in relation to the language system, as it migrates from 'je' to 'il', in turn produces a referential clash that cannot be assimilated within the framework of realist discourse − and *La Route des Flandres* is in many other ways entirely realist. Reading the novel thus creates a curious kind of strain − to use a visual metaphor, it is like looking through a pair of badly adjusted stereoscopic lenses: instead of one three-dimensional (realist) image, we see two flat ones and we cannot make them coincide.

There is, we may conclude, considerable variety in the extent to which, and the ways in which, Simon's novels show the subject to be constructed in language as opposed to being presented as an entity which can be defined as realist, psychological, representational or imaginary. From a chronological point of view, it is roughly true to say that the realist narrator progressively disappears from the novels, at least until *Les Géorgiques* signals some kind of return to a diegetic reality which, if not immediately obvious, is nevertheless recoverable from the narrative. Before *Les Géorgiques*, however, are the two 'speakerless' novels *Triptyque* and *Leçon de choses*. These (as already discussed − see Chapter 2) differ from all Simon's other work in that they contain no realist subject, and − apparently − no subject-in-language either: nothing, in other words, that can be interpreted as the trace in language of a subject of enunciation.

The subject as pure discursive positionality is most clearly evident in *La Bataille de Pharsale* and *Les Corps conducteurs*; reduced to a mere cipher halfway through *La Bataille de Pharsale*, the subject as 'O' is simultaneously defined − more explicitly than in any of the other novels − as producer and product of the text. It is in this sense that the construction of the subject in language is relatable both to the Lacanian concept of the symbolic and to a more specifically literary problematic which concerns representation and textuality; the subject-in-language deconstructs the system of representation, and reveals the determining operations of language itself, language as 'the space, or scene, of the realization of identity ... the milieu of our trans-formation' (Heath 1972: 154).

But just as it is impossible to conceive of the symbolic and the imaginary as two completely separate orders, so the subject-in-language exists in a relation of alternation with the realist subject − language, after all, can be made to serve the ends of representation and the imaginary. The different novels strike different balances between the two: the image, the mirror and the mirage on the one hand, the letter and the autonomy of the signifier on the other, and the fluctuating movement between them.

4

WORDS AND PICTURES: THE TEXT AND ITS OTHER

One aspect of the representational dimension of Simon's novels is their construction of other representations within themselves. These play an important role in generating the text in which they are embedded, and in introducing into it a dimension of otherness, of heterogeneity. They fall into two groups: pictorial[1] and textual. The mode of incorporation into Simon's text and the use that it makes of the 'alien' representations are different for pictures and for words, mainly because of the difference in their semiological material. In the case of pictures, the material itself is alien, whereas with other texts it is a question of incorporating one discourse into another: pictures are described, texts are quoted. But this does not prevent a high level of interaction between them; in *La Bataille de Pharsale*, for instance, pictures of battles are intercut with quotations from Caesar describing other battles; or the two elements are superimposed in a quotation of a passage describing a picture (173). The strip cartoon in the same novel (the boxer on the phone to his unfaithful mistress), also combines both; firstly just in the sense that it tells a story by means of pictures, but also because it includes in the pictures the text of a dialogue, and the text is presented as another *pictorial* element:

quelques spectateurs ... tournant le dos en train de regarder sur un ring de boxe un spectacle invisible caché par un nuage blanc aux contours dentelés et à l'intérieur duquel on peut lire les mots SAVEZ-VOUS QU'IL S'EST ECHAPPE CHERI JE CRAINS QU'IL NE VOUS CHERCHE.   (66)[2]

The description of the cartoon as a whole foregrounds the spectacle and the ambivalent *look*: firstly of the figures of the spectators, as above, but later that of the woman, whose 'regard noir' (67) is directed at something which may be outside the frame of the cartoon (but 'sans la voir vraiment, regardant en réalité un spectacle intérieur') and is finally hypothesized as the *words* she has spoken, materialized into visual objects: 'peut-être la forme la couleur des mots qu'elle vient de dire': transformed, moreover, from one pictorial mode to another – from cartoon to magic lantern – 'comme s'ils lui apparaissent non pas imprimés et enfermés dans des bulles mais surgissant du néant ... à la manière de ces images des lanternes magiques' (68).[3] Thus the whole sequence describing the cartoon moves through the tension between words and pictures.

Another difference between 'other' texts and pictures is that the textual material is not necessarily a fictional representation: alongside Proust and Apuleius we find examples of journalism, poetry, letters, etc.; whereas pictures in Simon's novels – those that are actually described – are always representations. Both, however, function as anti-representational strategies. This is clearer in the case of inter-textual relations, which cut across and automatically undermine the illusion of reality, by situating the text in relation to other texts rather than to a diegetic referent. The general phenomenon of pictorial representation in literature, on the other hand, is sometimes seen as a means of reinforcing the reality effect of a text by virtue of a principle of 'complémentarité sémiologique' (Hamon 1982: 139) whereby 'le texte se présente alors comme surcodé ... et peut entrer en redondance' (ibid.);[4] the textual–fictional representation of reality is backed up with a variety of pictorial parallels which reduplicate its content – 'suivant le principe' as van Rossum-Guyon comments, 'que l'Art est plus vrai que la Vie' (1975: 90).[5] Hamon concludes: 'On pourrait donc définir le discours réaliste comme un discours *paraphrasable*. Très souvent le lisible s'articule sur le visible, et le visible inversement peut s'identifier au lisible, au racontable' (90, author's italics).[6]

Hamon gives as an example of this mechanism 'la photographie ou la carte postale dans le Nouveau Roman' (90),[7] presumably thinking of Simon in particular. Van Rossum-Guyon, on the other hand, while referring to Hamon's formulation, argues that semiological complementarity operates differently in Simon's work: far from reinforcing the reality effect (as it does in Balzac for instance), it provides a form of *reflexive commentary* on the functioning of the text: certain elements, at least, 'pourraient nous conduire à penser que la mise en spectacle n'est rien d'autre que la *figuration de la narration* en tant que celle-ci à la fois instaure et dénonce la fiction (et par là, indirectement, la réalité) ... On pourrait donc parler ici, avec Jean Ricardou, de mises en abyme partielles' (1975: 103, author's italics).[8]

It is in these terms that pictures in Simon's novels are usually discussed. There are various different ways in which pictorial elements can be seen as subverting representation. They often act as *mises en abyme*, and hence, as Dällenbach argues (1977: 174), are by definition 'denaturalizing'. The best known *mise en abyme* in Simon's novels is the portrait of the ancestor in *La Route des Flandres*, which, with its streak of what appears to be blood coming from the man's forehead, prefigures and concentrates into a single image the subsequent fate of both the ancestor himself and his descendant De Reixach; while the fact that the streak is really caused by the paint wearing away so that the reddish canvas shows through indicates also the deceptive but flawed nature of representation in general. In fact the battered quality of many of Simon's visual artefacts − flaking paint, chipped sculptures and mosaics, blurred or faded photographs and scratched pieces of film − can be interpreted as a general comment on representation as a fundamentally *imperfect* artifice.

Pictorial and/or textual representation is even more explicitly problematized in the drawing whose description constitutes a sort of prologue to *Les Géorgiques*. Despite its concern for objective accuracy, the 'froideur délibérée détaillant des anatomies stéréotypées' (12),[9] the illusion of reality is destroyed by the absence of shadows (13) − and the text stresses the formal and conventional status of the drawing by a comparison with geometry, in which 'il est *convenu* que deux droites qui se croisent *signifient* − non pas *représentent* − l'existence d'un plan' (13, my italics).[10] Moreover, the fact that *parts* of the drawing have been painted in (15) creates an uncertainty about whether it is finished or not (16); and the description contains a double contradiction: the seated man is first of all naked (11) and then wearing a blue tunic with red collar and gold epaulettes (15); and whereas we are first told that only the heads of the figures are painted in (14), a page later we read that on the seated man:

le travail de coloriage a été plus poussé. Non content de peindre le visage puissant et sanguin ... l'artiste, poursuivant plus loin, a habillé les épaules d'une tunique bleu roi ... [les] mains que le coloriste a pour ainsi dire gantées de peau humaine, légèrement rougeaude aussi.   (15)[11]

The painting thus begins to be represented as a *process*, involving changes over time, rather than a fixed and static end-product. Finally, the reference to the letter that the seated man is reading is a clear indication that the prologue refers to textual, as well as pictorial, representation. The general tone of the description is a kind of dead-pan irony that appears to be directed as much at the formal certainties of anti-representation as the naïve belief in representation; as A. C. Pugh argues in his reading of the prologue (1985), it opens up a space in which both can be put in question simultaneously.

Words and pictures: the text and its other

Related to the picture as *mise en abyme* is a more diffusely metaphorical use of the pictorial, in which diegetically real scenes are compared with paintings: the girl in the farm in *La Route des Flandres*, for instance, appears as 'quelque chose comme une de ces vieilles peintures au jus de pipe' (38), the rugby-playing English students in the showers are 'fantomatiques dans les nuages de vapeur fade, comme quelque allégorie préraphaélite de la chair vulnérable et fragile' (*Les Géorgiques*: 315), and so on. Metaphor sometimes becomes parody: the naked soldier in *La Bataille de Pharsale* is 'comme une dérisoire parodie, une dérisoire réplique de tous les Persée, les Goliath, les Léonidas, la cohorte des guerriers figés dans les bitumeuses peintures des musées' (137).[12] In any case, the effect is always to distance and derealize the image. This is perhaps why it is often used for scenes which are imagined rather than actually perceived: Louise, on the basis of what she has been told by other people, sees Marie's arrival at the house as a 'scène ... s'étant déroulée ainsi: des personnages, un groupe de personnages paisiblement assis sous le grand marronnier, comme dans un de ces tableaux impressionnistes' (*L'Herbe*: 30).[13]

A more radical subversion of representation, however, occurs when the transition from real to pictorial is not merely metaphorical but itself 'real': when a picture *generates* a new fictional sequence, or, conversely, a fictional sequence suddenly turns into a picture. Such transitions erase the diegetic boundary between different levels of representation; they correspond to Ricardou's category of the 'récit transmuté',[14] and constitute one of the most important anti-representational strategies in Simon's novels.[15] (The *intertextual* equivalent of this − if for instance a character reading a book was suddenly represented as a character in that book − does not occur.) Their importance in fact increases over the sequence of novels. But as early as *La Route des Flandres* the 'gravure galante' (a picture which itself may or may not be *diegetically* real − see p. 214) produces a sequence of narrative *actions*, recounted in a literary equivalent of the sensational style of the picture itself: 'le valet accouru au bruit du coup de feu se précipitant, habillé à la diable ...' (85).[16] But the fact that alternative possible versions are given (*perhaps* there is a maid standing behind him with her hand in front of her mouth, or *perhaps* her hand is shielding the candle flame, etc.) makes it clear that these events are not real and that the picture is acting merely as a stimulus for Georges's imagination; the diegetic borderline has not really been transgressed. In *Histoire*, similarly, the photograph in the artist's studio produces a long narrative sequence (288−307), but with the same kind of psycho-realist motivation: the narrator tries to reconstruct the events leading up to the moment at which it was taken. (And, although it has been claimed that the postcards in some sense generate the narrative,[17] they remain unambiguously pictorial and never actually assume the status of diegetic events.)

It is only with *La Bataille de Pharsale* that the diegetic boundary genuinely begins to disappear: pictures suddenly become 'reality' and vice versa. The section 'La Bataille' thus at first appears to be simply a description of a battle scene, including movement: the 'frémissements' of the leaves (101), the clouds 'continuant à glisser lentement' (102), etc.;[18] only nine pages later do we discover that it is in fact a picture, and later still that the whole section revolves around the description of four 'real' paintings.[19] In the same way, the football match played on the plain of Pharsalus, from being a narrative event ('on pouvait entendre le sifflet de l'arbitre les faibles clameurs comme des cris d'enfant', 66), reappears, ten pages later, as: 'le soleil déclinant éclairant maintenant à contre-jour les joueurs la poussière sous leurs pieds s'élevant en nuage doré, zones opaques où *la peinture – ou la mosaïque –* s'est détachée de son support par larges plaques' (76, my italics).[20] In other words, it starts off as an apparently real scene but then, half-way through the sentence, abruptly becoming a painting – *or* a mosaic: the reader is finally unable to identify it as any kind of diegetic object.

Here, unlike in the earlier texts, there is no controlling psycho-realist subject to whose imagination the sudden shift of levels could be attributed. In fact the subject at one point, in a dazzling sequence of ambiguities, appears to end up *inside* the picture: what is initially just a thematic contrast between looking at pictures of battles and being in the midst of a real battle – 'et moi non plus étranger, spectateur regardant les élégants et barbares condottieri ... mais maintenant au centre même de ce maelström: l'espace, l'air lui-même tourbillonnant' (116) – is transformed, as the separation between levels of representation collapses, into the positioning of the subject – 'moi' – in the midst of a battle in a picture: 'les tourbillons d'air épais immobilisés ... de la même matière opaque, solidifiée, étalée par le *pinceau* ... et tournoyant sans fin entre les solennelles dorures des *cadres* et *moi au centre*' (117, my italics).[21]

Les Corps conducteurs uses the device of the 'récit transmuté' even more extensively, and more systematically; the sequence of the explorers in the jungle, for instance, alternates regularly between photograph and reality, sometimes changing in mid-sentence: 'A l'approche du chef de la colonne le papillon prend de nouveau son essor, volette un moment, indécis, comme ivre, puis disparaît sur la droite hors du rectangle de la photographie' (109).[22] The novel also contains numerous paintings and drawings that play the same role; even the picture on a stamp generates a colonial adventure story in which after two pages of exciting narrative ('Comme les soldats commencent avec beaucoup de peine à surmonter la force du courant d'eau ils aperçoivent un nombre considérable de canots pleins d'Indiens armés ...', 40), the reader is suddenly confronted with: 'Le chiffre 35 suivi du mot CENTAVOS est gravé en taille-douce dans le ciel teinté sans doute par la lueur du couchant ...' (41).[23]

By this time, the representational stability of *Les Corps conducteurs* is already seriously disturbed. But this is even more true of Simon's next novel, *Triptyque*; this is not a text which *contains* pictures that generate or reflect a larger-scale fiction: it is itself produced through the interplay of three pictures. Each of these depicts a location – countryside, industrial suburb and seaside resort – and a fragmentary narrative develops out of each location; conversely, however, each narrative contains pictorial representations of the other two (as film image, postcard, cinema poster, jigsaw puzzle, etc.), so that it is impossible to define any one of them as the basic diegetic reality and the other two as pictures: the attribute of reality slips from one scene to another in a series of multiple inversions of the hierarchical relations between them. Here the referential illusion is completely demolished because the relations between the three representations form an irreducible contradiction.[24]

As is suggested by the various critical essays cited above, discussion of the pictorial in Simon's novels has seen it almost exclusively as a form of narrative reflexivity: pictures are there to act as metaphors for the text itself. While this is undoubtedly true for some of the pictures some of the time, the significance of the pictorial does also *exceed* textual self-reference. The concentration on the analogical function of pictures is challenged in a recent article by Maria Minich-Brewer (1985), which claims that 'critics of such apparently different persuasions as Jean Ricardou, Françoise van Rossum-Guyon and Jean Rousset' are all guilty of '[limiting] the rich diversity of Simon's pictorial interventions ... Since they consider painting only in its analogical relation to language, they pass over the difference between image and text, the visual and the verbal, in their determination to assign to both writing and image a structuring and compositional end' (104).[25] This welcome emphasis on the difference between the two media is, however, itself ultimately made to serve the ends of narrative reflexivity; in a slightly disappointing conclusion to an incisive argument, Minich-Brewer rejects the 'æsthetic alibi' interpretation of pictures only to replace it with the idea of pictures as a *critical* and *ironic* commentary on the rest of the narrative;[26] she does not contest the basic idea that pictures are reflexive strategies of one kind or another – straightforward or ironic.

This assumption, however, does not stand up to closer examination. In the first place, there are simply so many pictorial images in Simon's novels that it would be difficult to argue that they *all* function as forms of textual self-reference, however elastically the criteria for this are defined. At least in the 'middle period' novels, the functions and meanings of pictures are far more diverse. For instance, Simon sometimes seems quite naïvely to want to make us realize that, for instance, a bank-note or a stamp not only 'represents' a certain sum of money, but is also a *visual* representation of a certain historical or mythological reality (e.g. *Histoire*: 78): to focus the reader's attention on images that we never bother to look at properly because they are so commonplace – and also, simply, so *small*. Deguy comments on the dizzying loss of any sense of proportion implied in the detailed description of, for instance, a picture on the lid of a cigar-box: 'parce que cette chose occupe la vision comme un gouffre où la vue s'engouffre, vertigineuse distance, abîme où s'enfonce le regard versatile vers aucun fond des choses' (1962: 1010).[27] This gives an idea of the quality of *fascination* which the pictorial, like the visual in general, possesses – a fascination which exceeds and also to some extent runs counter to the self-consciously metaphorical use of pictures.

One major form in which this fascination manifests itself is the paradoxical contrast between movement and immobility. This is particularly central in *La Bataille de Pharsale*, and first of all in the stanza from *Le cimetière marin* which introduces it: 'cette flèche ailée / Qui vibre, vole, et qui ne vole pas! ... Achille immobile à grands pas!'[28] But the treatment of visual phenomena in all Simon's novels is from time to time caught up in this kind of oxymoron: reality becomes a series of freeze-frames, as movement, like that of Zeno's arrow, is broken down into separate instants. Thus a sequence from *Le Palace* contrasts the 'subterranean' continuity of the Italian's voice with the series of images it evokes: 'fixes, figées, immobiles (comme les diverses flèches lumineuses qui composaient la réclame s'allumant et s'éteignant à tour de rôle)' (66).[29] Jean-Claude Vareille, under the heading 'The energetics of immobility', sees the paradoxical relation whereby 'immobility is but the superlative expression of speed' (1985: 118) as a fundamental determinant of all Simon's writing. Pictures, however, and especially when, as in *La Bataille de Pharsale*, they depict the violent movement of battle scenes, etc., obviously pose the contradiction in a particularly acute form. Movement takes place in time and is therefore negated, frozen, by the timeless nature of pictorial representation.[30]

The two poles of the contradiction are, at different points in the texts, brought together in two opposite, but equally anti-representational, ways. As Jean Rousset demonstrates, either the dimension of time is as it were injected into the photographic 'instantané' – the photograph of the artist's studio providing the key example here: the figure which moved when the photograph was being taken is represented not by a fixed image but

la trace fuligineuse laissée par le visage au cours de ses divers changements de position restituant à l'événement son épaisseur, postulant ... la double suite des instants passés et futurs, la double série, dans le même cadrage et le même décor, des positions respectivement occupées par les divers personnages avant et après. (*Histoire*: 291)[31]

Or, conversely, real-life movement is frozen into a single image; this is the phenomenon of 'petrification' that both Rousset and Vareille comment on, whereby 'real' people (and horses) become sculptures (for instance, *La Bataille de Pharsale*: 24, 262, 268).

But despite these textual manipulations of the contradiction, the pictorial image (as opposed, here, to film)[32] is nevertheless the privileged instance of immobility and timelessness; the picture, and especially the photograph, remains that which is *fundamentally* instantaneous: 'un de ces instantanés, une de ces coupes lamelliformes pratiquées à l'intérieur de la durée', seeming to 'pour ainsi dire nier le temps' (*Histoire*: 291).[33] The photograph is the ultimate example, because it is *doubly* instantaneous; like paintings and sculpture, it represents a frozen image and one which is perceived as an immediate whole, but unlike the painting it is also *produced* instantaneously and records a particular real instant in time. Thus although pictorial images, as outlined above, undergo a range of textual transformations, they are also, at least in the novels up to *Histoire*, presented as being fixed and definite, as offering a kind of stasis and resolution that ordinary vision does not. They can do this because they stand in a different relation to time; as static records of a single instant, they possess a contrasting quality of definition and focus; they seem to be *set* in the perpetual change and flux of everything else, like islands in the sea.

It is above all the instantaneous quality of the picture that accounts for the force of attraction it exerts over the rest of the text. In this it shares some of the immediacy of the mirage as described in Chapter 1, and several of the examples of the mirage already given in fact compare the 'vision' with a picture (e.g. the 'réclame pour une marque de bière anglaise' in *La Route des Flandres*: 21).[34]

The mirage is, as I have shown in Chapter 3, relatable to the Lacanian imaginary order. If we are to account for the text's fascination with pictures, we should perhaps look at them from a similar point of view: not simply, that is, as a reflexive textual device, but as a more deeply rooted phantasy which can be traced back to the mirror stage. Evidence for this hypothesis, that the presence of pictures in the text in some way derives from the original potency of the mirror stage, can be found throughout the novels; a peculiarly noticeable feature of the texts is the frequency with which mirror images are juxtaposed with pictorial images. *Histoire*, for instance, refers to a picture 'déformé comme ces peintures qu'il faut regarder dans un miroir pour rétablir leurs vraies dimensions et découvrir ce qu'elles représentent' (93–4):[35] as though the mirror held the underlying *truth* of the image. *L'Herbe* explicitly compares them, on the basis of a common 'liquid' quality:

son visage lui apparaissant à travers la vitre des larmes ... dans la glace de la salle de bains, remontant à la surface à travers des profondeurs vertes, flou, comme liquide, dissous dans la diamantine transparence des pleurs, en émergeant peu à peu – comme l'image que le photographe met au point sur le dépoli. (163)[36]

The recurrent sequence in which photographic negatives are washed, in *Histoire*, similarly links reflections and photographs through the medium of water: one side of the tub is in shadow and so the negatives are visible in the water, while the other side reflects the sky above it. Here, however, it is the photographs which 'reflect' the subject's image – 'collées ensemble ... invisibles dans la moitié du bac que remplissait le ciel ... mais après la découpe dentelée de la crête du buisson de lierre on pouvait distinguer nos images' (411)[37] – so that the elements of mirror image, photograph and water overlap; their relations are so to speak staggered (Simon's 'chevauché'). In the same novel, the photograph taken by the Dutch artist which shows himself *in* the picture places him in the position of someone facing a mirror, both behind and in front of the camera lens.

The schema of the mirror image is echoed in a number of other such duplications of images: the *mise en abyme* on the lid of the biscuit tin in *L'Herbe*, the two portraits of the ancestor's wife in

La Route des Flandres, and the resemblance − 'de sorte que je pouvais pour ainsi dire le voir deux fois' (94) − between Charles and the portrait of the narrator's great-grandfather, which is in turn itself associated with a mirror image: 'fixant l'artiste en train de le peindre (peut-être lui-même dans une glace)' (*Histoire*: 95).[38] In the same way, the failure to recognize oneself in the mirror − as discussed in Chapter 3 − has its equivalent in several examples of failure to recognize other people in photographs. Louise mistakes her father-in-law for her husband in the photograph in the biscuit tin (*L'Herbe*: 225), the Italian can hardly recognize the man he is supposed to kill because he has only seen him in a photograph (*Le Palace*: 45, 47), and so on.

But it is the particular mode of presentation of pictures in the texts that above all suggests a close link with mirror images; the emphasis is on the picture perceived instantaneously, as an immediate and synthetic whole; as such it generates in the spectator a kind of euphoria equivalent to the infant's 'assomption jubilatoire' of his image in the mirror (Lacan 1966: 94). It is the photograph of the narrator's father in *Histoire*, for instance, that gives his mother 'cette conviction à la fois ardente et sereine qu'Il existait dans un quelque part où elle irait un jour le rejoindre un au-delà paradisiaque et vaguement oriental' (21); and the 'énorme agrandissement' is itself suffused with this almost religious adoration: 'il avait l'air de planer suspendu impondérable et souriant comme une de ces apparitions entourées d'un halo de lumière ... le voir toujours présent l'inoubliable image flottant immatérielle et auréolée de brouillard' (20).[39] It is cut off from everything around it: the imaginary appears to offer absolute, immediate presence − the image of the self as a complete entity, perceived in the moment of the mirror image, and now magically preserved in the photograph as a saintly apparition owing nothing to its context, and nothing to any process of construction. Pictures thus share the euphoric immediacy and self-contained quality of mirror images, but the fact that they are permanent objects, providing a security and stasis which the essentially fleeting mirror image does not, seems for Simon to confer on them a peculiar advantage.

The fascination of the pictorial image thus depends on its being whole, fixed and *separate* from things seen in the real world. In Simon's later texts this separation is increasingly undermined by textual procedures which both fragment images and continually cross and re-cross the borderline between pictures and reality. The process starts in *La Bataille de Pharsale* and reaches its ultimate point in *Triptyque*, where the diegetic boundary has been completely erased:

here, everything is pictorial (or cinematic) and so in a sense nothing is. Movement, both textual and diegetic, is generalized throughout the text, and this, in breaking up the 'frozen' image, dismantles the effect of fascination that pictures produce in the novels preceding *La Bataille de Pharsale*.

In these earlier texts, however, pictures serve to illuminate the connection between the Lacanian imaginary and realist literature. I have argued that the significance of pictures is rooted in the mirror stage, and hence in the imaginary ego; but it simultaneously has to do with the establishing of a psycho-realist subject who will appear as the origin of the representation, and who therefore cannot be seen as a product of the text but must be endowed with his own point of origin outside, and 'before', the text. Pictures, in fact, often perform this function, directly *representing* the idea of origin. For instance, many of them represent father figures: the photograph of Bernard's father in *Le Sacre du printemps*, that already cited of the narrator's father in *Histoire*, and the other 'portraits d'ancêtres' (28) in *Histoire*, the 'abondante galerie ou plutôt collection d'ancêtres, ou plutôt de géniteurs' (54) in *La Route des Flandres*, the posters of Marx and Stalin − father figures of the revolution − in *Le Palace*, the 'géniteurs mâles' in *Les Géorgiques*, 'ne laissant d'autre trace que l'arrogante suite des portraits ou des photographies' (170),[40] and so on.

Establishing the subject's origin in this way is essentially a question of establishing the continuity of the present with the past, and the pictorial references in the texts stress the dimension of past time that is as it were encapsulated in them. The paintings are of course often ancient objects, and so associated with the past independently of their representational content. But in Simon's novels it is actually the association between the past and *photographs* that is particularly marked; so clear, in fact, that any kind of memory can take on the quality of a photographic image − the student in *Le Palace* imagines how in later life he will remember his comrades 'immobilisés ou conservés *comme sur une photographie*, dans cette sorte de matière figée et grisâtre qu'est *le temps passé*' (33, my italics).[41] It is perhaps the documentary authenticity and exactness of the photograph, as opposed to the painting, that accounts for its stronger association with the past: it records for posterity an instant of real time. It does not, however, necessarily provide a sense of continuity: indeed Barthes suggests that the peculiar attraction of photographs lies partly in their 'contingency';[42] photography in its essence provides evidence of the past, but at the same time, evidence of the separation between past and present; as Barthes says, it simply records 'what has been'.[43]

This quality of separation and intactness is evident in the wedding photograph in *L'Herbe*:

pour ceux et celles qui, des années plus tard, regardaient la photographie, le fait de savoir que presque tous étaient morts, que ces mêmes corps aux poses nonchalantes, affectées et ridicules, étaient tous destinés ... à bientôt pourrir ... leur conféraient comme une autre virginité. (71)[44]

That is, simply by virtue of the fact that they represent the past, the pictures also represent a set of deaths; and the intervention of death means that the subject's origin cannot be seen as a transparent continuity between past and present. Rather, it becomes mysterious, distant, *troubled*: in *La Route des Flandres* we find Georges 'pensant à tous ces morts énigmatiques, figés et solennels qui dans leurs cadres dorés fixaient leurs descendants d'un regard pensif, distant' (56). Death above all signifies *absence*, and this is the only modality in which the origin can exist; the dead father in *Le Sacre du printemps* is described as 'cette absence, la présence de cette absence' (32).[45] The reference to the past, in seeking to guarantee present identity, in fact reveals only a break in continuity; presence originates only from absence.

Just as the stability of origin is undermined by death, so the efficacy of the pictorial image in general is ultimately contaminated by the tensions which result from its mode of production in, and as, a text; that is, tensions between the two-dimensional space of the picture and the linear sequentiality of writing.[46] A long passage in *Histoire* (275–81) describes a series of postcards and assigns to each of them a particular time of day – the recorded instant: 'et peut-être une heure dans la matinée', 'et environ midi',[47] and so on. The times are completely unrelated to each other (in any case they are simply the narrator's guesses): the postcards themselves do not form any kind of meaningful sequence. The text, however, does construct such a sequence, through the connections it makes between them (e.g. the repetitions of 'casque', 'coiffé', 'pantalon', and the series 'chignon' – 'achevant' – 'chevelure' – 'cheville'). The linear continuity of writing, its propensity for joining things up together, seems to be symbolized in the 'série de cartes ... au dos desquelles la même missive se poursuivait, commencée sur la première, continuée ensuite faute de place sur une seconde, et ainsi de suite' (*Histoire*: 70)[48] – disparate images traversed and linked by a single written message. Moreover, the continuity is not in fact dependent on there being a series of images: the description of even a single postcard is itself necessarily sequential.[49] The text reintroduces its own order of time,[50] and thus a different level of meaning which is partially determined by the order in which things occur. In the photograph which falls out of Marie's notebooks in *L'Herbe*, for instance, the most significant figure is her fiancé, and it is significant that he is mentioned last.

But this surplus of textual meaning comes at the cost of losing the simultaneous co-presence of all the elements of the picture – losing, in other words, the picture as totality. As Simon himself has said, 'la peinture est surface, simultanéité, l'écriture est linéarité, durée'.[51] There is thus an important difference between those pictures which are evoked by a brief reference, and those which are described in detail and at length; the latter are – inevitably – not presented as synthetic entities, but as compositions whose elements and the relations between them are specified. The photograph taken in the artist's studio falls into this latter category:

c'est-à-dire qu'en partant d'en haut et à droite (l'endroit où la vision est la plus nette) s'étend, descendant vers le bas et la gauche, un réseau de lignes d'un brun clair bordées de noir encadrant de larges losanges d'un brun foncé ornés en leur centre d'un point du même brun clair, le réseau ni les losanges ne présentent cet aspect régulier que donneraient sur une surface plane des lignes droites s'entrecroisant: au contraire chacun des losanges plus ou moins dissymétrique et étiré en divers sens.   (*Histoire*: 296)[52]

Reading this, it is difficult to visualize the picture at all. Unlike the photograph of the narrator's father, we have no sense here of a total image or of the impact that it can make. Description of this factual and detailed kind is inevitably deconstructive: the image literally disintegrates as soon as the text gets to grips with it (an effect which is itself represented in the many images of torn and fragmented pictures, in *Le Palace*, for instance).

In other words, the most important obstacle to the efficacy of the picture is simply the fact that it is presented via language; it is actually invisible, and does not exist except in the form of a written description, like the landscape *inscribed* in the window ('le paysage qui *s'inscrit* dans la fenêtre'), as the opening of *Le Palace* puts it. This is the contradiction that, as A. C. Pugh defines it, founds literary representation: 'The image, to be "visible", must deny its linguistic status, and to be readable, it must put its visibility in doubt' (1985: 66). It is only by holding the image at a distance that the text can fleetingly take advantage of its imaginary force, the force of an immediate, indissoluble whole. As soon as it moves in to produce a description, it inevitably *textualizes* the image – which thus re-enters the order of writing (and hence of the symbolic), as a system of relations between elements.

The 'otherness' of pictures in relation to the text is thus relative and variable. This is also true, although with the differences outlined at the beginning of this chapter, of the text's other 'other': the issue of *quotation* and intertextual reference. One important version of this is of course Simon's quotation of himself. The intertextual dimension of the corpus is, as I have already noted, extremely marked; an extensive network of allusions, overlaps and permutations of textual material is gradually built up and modified with each successive text, so that the experience of reading Simon involves a mixture of recognition and displacement.[53] The dual figure of the old woman, for instance, initially Marie and Sabine in *L'Herbe*, diverges and reconverges across subsequent novels, producing the grandmother and her friends in *Histoire* and *Les Géorgiques*, the ancient crone in *La Route des Flandres* and (as the idiot's mother) *Les Géorgiques*, the old lady in the hotel in *Les Corps conducteurs*, the old peasant woman in *Triptyque*, and Batti in *Les Géorgiques*. As a result, the corpus appears as a system of relations between elements: a system whose elements move around, and a system within which the writer as *bricoleur* can move around, reassembling elements into new patterns. The Proustian image of the work as a kind of mobile architecture, as 'une église où des fidèles sauraient peu à peu apprendre des vérités et découvrir des harmonies, le grand plan d'ensemble' (*A la Recherche du temps perdu*: III, 1040)[54] comes to mind here, but with the difference that for Proust what is at stake is an ontological relationship to time and truth, whereas in Simon's case the emphasis is on the text as a structure of relations, above all between words: the most striking feature of his reworkings of material already used is that these are not simply a repetition of the same experience (of war, childhood, etc.), but of the same *words*: experience and words seem indissociable, and memory is always already a 'form of words'. As just one example of this, we may consider the following passage from *Les Géorgiques* in relation to the much earlier *L'Herbe*:

on battait les tapis ... d'où s'échappait comme un subtil et faible parfum de choses fanées (les bouquets de roses pâlies, les guirlandes décolorées mêlées aux fades volutes décoratives) tandis que les pendeloques du lustre soudain dérangées, agitées par les courants d'air, s'entrechoquaient dans une cascade de tintements légers, cristallins, semblables à ces musiques aigrelettes au son desquelles se meuvent, tournent sur eux-mêmes et s'inclinent des automates costumés en marquis et en bergères comme ceux que l'on pouvait voir, gracieux et mélancoliques, sous la forme de porcelaines de Saxe ...(173)[55]

Underlying the description of what the carpet smells like is a reference to *L'Herbe*: the 'subtil et faible parfum de choses fanées (les bouquets de roses pâlies)' unmistakably echoes the 'odeur de bouquets flétris ... l'exhalaison discrète ... des jours fanés' (*L'Herbe*: 20)[56] of Marie's room. The passage moves from the carpet to the chandelier; and even this entirely 'natural' metonymic transition turns out to be motivated by a link with *L'Herbe*: the description of Marie's room on page 20 is immediately preceded by a reference to time and the sun, both of which recur together in the dining-room clock in *L'Herbe* which is decorated with a 'soleil doré' (67), but also with 'guirlandes' (67) as in line 2 of the above passage from *Les Géorgiques*. It is, surely, the 'pendule du salon'[57] which reappears here transformed into 'les pendeloques du lustre': the phonetic link between the words is confirmed by the sounds the objects made – the clock's 'tintement aigrelet' (*L'Herbe*: 68) echoed in the chandelier's 'tintements ... semblables à ces musiques aigrelettes' – and by the 'marquis ... gracieux et mélancoliques' who are equally reminiscent of the figures evoked by the funereal futility of the decorations on the clock: 'comme si ... il avait su, lui, le gracieux siècle, et ses gracieuses marquises dévergondées, et ses marquis aux perruques poudrées, cyniques, libertins, encyclopédiques et désespérés, qu'on allait bientôt leur couper le cou' (*L'Herbe*: 68).[58] (And the reference here to the Revolution is, of course, far more central to *Les Géorgiques* than it is to *L'Herbe*.) Finally, 'porcelaines de Saxe' refers us once again to *L'Herbe* and descriptions of Sabine in her youth.

The functioning of this kind of intertextuality is largely implicit; the text does not draw attention to it. In contrast, references to *other* writers' texts are usually very noticeable, and the way in which they are used is equally clear. At the beginning of this chapter I have argued that the phenomenon of intertextuality is *per se* anti-representational; the intrusion of other discourses into the text inevitably breaks up the homogeneity which the 'reality effect' requires. *La Bataille de Pharsale*, with its multiplicity of fragments of other texts, is a particularly good example of the disorientating effect that this has on the representational dimension of the novel. But the particular use that Simon makes of other texts reinforces the effect considerably. The way they are juxtaposed with Simon's own writing produces an ironic commentary on the futility of their claims to representational adequacy. This is perhaps most obviously true of the critical re-writing of the selected sections of Orwell's *Homage to Catalonia* that appear in *Les Géorgiques*, where the problems of writing, particularly in its attempt to represent reality, are systematically posed, and O's account of what happened in Barcelona during the Spanish Civil War is constantly criticized for its distortions and omissions[59] – on the question of Soviet participation, for instance:

Mais il n'en parla pas non plus. Soit qu'il s'interdît aussi de lever la tête vers les fenêtres éclairées tard dans la nuit. Soit qu'il eût décidé de n'en rien dire, du moins à ce stade de son récit. Non qu'il ignorât alors la présence de ces sortes de gens. Il savait qu'ils existaient quelque part, c'est-à-dire comme on sait (pas connaît) quelque chose apprise à travers des articles de journaux ou dans des livres, sans se faire une idée exacte de leur réalité.   (337)[60]

Similar treatment, however, is given to John Reid's *Ten Days that Shook the World* in *Histoire*; an extract recounting Lenin addressing a meeting (139–40) is incongruously inserted between an episode showing Lambert and the narrator as children quarrelling, and another in which the narrator, again as a child, struggles with his Latin translation – failing, that is, to make words mean anything. Thus the drama and seriousness of the Reid passage are corroded by the context which frames it; later in the novel, also, a brief fragment of Reid is juxtaposed with, and opposed to, a disguised quotation from Marx followed by an explicitly ironic comment from the narrator: '*l'immense ovation qui se prolongea pendant plusieurs minutes* Quand elle se répète pour la deuxième fois plus rien qu'une farce Et la combienième maintenant' (381, author's italics).[61]

The main target of Simon's irony is political or historical narrative, but it is not limited to this. The textbook *Leçon de choses* appears in a similar mode in, precisely, *Leçon de choses*; and the fragments of Proust which recur throughout *La Bataille de Pharsale* are at one point the object of a savagely derisive mutilation: 'tous laids souvenir voluptueu kil emporté de chézelle lui permetté de sefer unidé dé zatitudezardante zoupâmé kel pouvé tavoir avek d'otr' (178).[62] The conventionality of written signs is parodied by caricaturing phonetic spelling, and their capacity to signify is thereby negated: in this version, the signified of Proust's language becomes almost inaccessible behind the impenetrably bizarre appearance of the signifier.

Simon's use of intertextuality can be seen as part of a wider attitude to writing. It is not surprising that his references to other writers should be handled in such a way as to discredit literary and historiographic representation if writing is defined essentially by its inadequacy as a means of representation. The *theme* of writing is also very prominent. It is manifested in the character of Pierre, the writer, and his relationship with Georges, who has nothing but contempt for his father's work ('Je n'ai surtout pas envie d'aligner encore des mots

107

et des mots et encore des mots. Est-ce qu'à la fin tu n'en as pas assez toi aussi?', *La Route des Flandres*: 36);[63] in the newspaper reporting of the Spanish Civil War and the cynicism with which it is treated in *Le Palace*, and in the unsuccessful attempts of the three protagonists of *Les Géorgiques* to impose some kind of intelligible form on their experiences by writing them down. The message, although conveyed with varying degrees of irony, is in each case the same: writing is unable to express the true nature of experience.

The converse theme of illiteracy serves as a further attack on writing, and an equally ironic one: it is the illiterate who believe more strongly than anyone else in its efficacy. Thus the academic Pierre's faith in the written word is derided by his son but echoed, and even outdone, by his father, 'le vieux paysan illettré ... pénétré, imbu d'une superstitieuse confiance dans ces mots ... ce que renferment les livres' (*L'Herbe*: 231).[64] The *illiterate* is an important figure in the texts; illiteracy constitutes a form of passive resistance to the dominance of writing, while being simultaneously a kind of noble despair, as expressed by the illiterate guard in *Le Palace* 'saisissant ... la feuille de papier qu'il tient à deux mains, la serrant comme si ç'avait été non une simple feuille de papier mais un ennemi, un adversaire qu'il s'agissait de maintenir et de maîtriser ... devant le visage d'aigle empreint dans cet instant d'un indicible et ombrageux désespoir' (191).[65]

In the literate culture to which Simon and his readers by definition belong, the written text is normally taken for tranted; what his texts do – as for instance in the parodically phonetic transcription of Proust quoted earlier – is to block our normal automatic perception of writing as transparent medium or instrument, and present it as something strange. This of course is exactly the formalist technique of defamiliarization,[66] and it takes several different forms. Illiteracy, for instance, while it provides an ironic critique of writing, is also significant for the process of defamiliarization in simply marking a moment of opacity within the prevailing ideology of writing as transparency, as an automatic and entirely abstract process. The written text is, usually, received by characters in the novels as something alien and rebarbative; descriptions of reading stress its difficulty, by breaking it down into a sequence of small physical actions, presenting it as though in slow motion – Batti, for instance, struggling with the peremptory letters she receives from LSM,

avec chaque fois la même perplexité, la même appréhension, avant de monter dans sa chambre, tâtonner dans un tiroir à la recherche de l'étui sur le fermoir duquel s'escrimaient maladroitement les ongles cassés, jusqu'à ce qu'elle parvienne à l'ouvrir, saisissant sur le rembourrage de velours râpé une de ces paires de lunettes à monture de fer, à l'arceau garni d'un lambeau de baptiste jaunie entortillé de fil noir, en dépliant les branches, les passant avec soin derrière les oreilles, refermant l'étui, se décidant enfin (se résignant) à faire sauter le cachet de cire, s'approchant de la fenêtre, ses lèvres remuant silencieusement tandis qu'entre les paupières flasques ses prunelles glissaient lentement de gauche à droite, revenaient vivement sur la gauche pour repartir une nouvelle fois en sens inverse, les paupières s'abaissant chaque fois un peu plus, les sourcils froncés, les lèvres continuant à mouler les mots les uns après les autres. (463)[67]

Writing, too, is seen as a question of *physical* effort; the illiterate guard trying to read the laissez-passer in *Le Palace* reminds the student of the Italian, 'appuyant de toutes ses forces sur le crayon, traçant non pas sur mais dans la page de carnet de profonds sillons, comme si le papier, le fragile, dangereux et impalpable support de signes, d'abstractions, devait être affronté et maîtrisé au prix d'un violent effort physique' (191).[68]

Defamiliarizing writing means, essentially, presenting it as a physical activity carried out on a *material* substance; and the substance most often mentioned is stone. Not only are there several passages referring to the ambiguous possibility of permanence conferred on writing by stone (analogous, perhaps, to the 'petrification' of visual images described earlier in this chapter), but it is embodied in the very name of the principal writer figure, Pierre; while another important writer, LSM, is himself represented by a marble bust. Writing, in Simon's novels, is above all *inscription*: the crude awkwardness that results from the struggle against the resistance of stone − 'la pointe appuyée avec force pour entamer le marbre déraillant parfois de sorte que la plupart des lettres ont cet aspect à la fois gauche et saccadé' (*Histoire*: 409)[69] − is emblematic of writing in general. Similarly, it is his waning physical strength that prevents the old general in *Les Géorgiques* from writing clearly − 'les lettres tantôt trop grandes, tantôt presque escamotées, griffonnées, comme si la force lui manquait' (373).

The result is a text which is almost unreadable: 'les lignes se distendant, divergeant, les corrections, les ratures, les surcharges se multipliant' (ibid.).[70] Illegibility, as in this example and many others, is the other major figure of *opacity*: to the illiterate subject corresponds the *illegible* text. The text becomes a mere thing: signs which cannot be deciphered cease to be signs and have to be seen as unfamiliar and incomprehensible objects. Examples and images of various kinds of illegibility are scattered widely throughout the novels: ink which has faded, broken-off words on torn posters ('UNION POUR LE PROG', *Histoire*: 234), inscriptions which cannot be read because they have worn away ('les incompréhensibles vestiges d'un langage incohérent', *Histoire*: 410),[71] and so on. What they all have in common is that in thus presenting texts as opaque and imperfect objects, they serve as indices of the materiality of writing: if the text were a purely abstract system of signs it would not be subject to the kind of damage and deterioration that is emphasized here.

This in fact takes two main forms, relating to the two general themes of discontinuity and of time passing. The illegible text is either broken into *fragments*, or *worn away* by the passage of time. In the above example from *Les Géorgiques* it is the writer himself, close to death, who is worn out; and the ink of the writing in his registers has also gradually become powdery in the course of time, so that the writing seems to be crumbling away (76). This idea is frequently linked with death; the inscription on the wife's gravestone, for instance, is so worn that it has to be *felt* rather than read – a striking instance of the materiality of the text:

sur la pierre grenue et rongée l'inscription, l'épitaphe, le visiteur se penchant pour lire (ou plutôt devinant en creux légers dans la pierre ...) les mots ... lisant au fur et à mesure que son doigt suivait les lettres alignées MARIE ANNE ... puis grattant la pierre de l'ongle, effritant les écailles jaunes des lichens, disant HASSEL ..., la fin du nom tout à fait effacée, la pierre à cet endroit éclatée, les caractères redevenant lisibles un peu plus loin. (163)[72]

And on another grave, this time in *Le Palace*, 'les lettres dorées des plaintives inscriptions courant parmi les fleurs de perles mauves' (105) also become increasingly dilapidated, imitating the decay of the corpse they are commemorating, and 'ne proposant plus à la fin au visiteur qu'un énigmatique squelette de langage où adhère encore par endroits la chair raccornie de lambeaux de voyelles et de lambeaux de diphtongues' (ibid.).[73]

Here in fact the text is both worn away *and* fragmented into 'shreds'; *Le Palace* in particular is full of discontinuous, dislocated writing – the message on the banner, for instance, is not only interrupted but back to front (30). Quotations, of course, are always fragments; and so intertextuality itself can be seen as a form of fragmentation. The quotation is a piece of language broken off from another text; and both in its 'otherness' and in its fragmentary status it draws attention to its materiality as text. This is emphasized even more when it is obviously incomplete, and unidentifiable; a few words suddenly intruding enigmatically into the text: 'ou du moins sentiment de ta mort' on page 67 of *La Bataille de Pharsale* for instance, is not even recognisable *as* a quotation until it is given in full, and with full bibliographical apparatus, much nearer the end of the book: 'et Lucain, Phars., VII, 470–473: "Puissent les dieux te donner non pas la mort, qui est le châtiment réservé à tous, mais, après ton destin fatal, le sentiment de ta mort …' (235).[74]

As a fragment of other writing inserted into a new context, the quotation not only sets up semantic and textual tensions, but also creates an awareness of its *spatial* relations with its context. By invoking the two-dimensional space of the page, the textual fragment brings our perception of writing closer to the *pictorial*; and this provides yet another way of defamiliarizing it. Thus, quotations in the form of titles, headlines, road-signs, etc., are presented with precise attention to the shapes of their letters and the visual lay-out of the words.[75] *Le Palace* is full of this kind of typographical interest; and as a result its text becomes visually very spaced out and discontinuous, constantly broken up by phrases in capital letters. The disjunction is made more acute by the switch of languages from French to Spanish, and, in one case, English as well:

… et de nouveau en noir sur le fond vert:
SUPERIOR VUELTA ABAJO SEGARS MANUFACTURED IN HAVANA
INDUSTRIA STREET No 520
la mention certifiée par une signature calligraphiée …   (165)[76]

There are also long descriptions of the ornately decorated guarantee on the lid of a cigar-box (164–5), and the messages on a series of political posters (178–9), both reproducing the actual format of the lettering.

Quotations, however, are not the only instance in which the pictorial aspects of writing are foregrounded. Writing sometimes actually seems to merge with drawing: the smudged hand-written name 'Xailoum' on the list of LSM's horses is also a picture of a flowing mane (*Les Géorgiques*: 71). And in *La Bataille de Pharsale* there is of course the pictorial joke of the little hand drawn in the text (15) pointing ambiguously to heaven and/or the public lavatory. Graffiti, also, are often a combination of words and drawing, and the letters themselves are always described as opaque two-dimensional shapes. The pictorial character of letters is most striking when they belong to a different alphabet: the Greek letters scratched on the wall of the farm in *La Bataille de Pharsale* are an extreme example of *alien* writing described purely as a structure of spatial relations:

Il y avait aussi les initiales BΠT répétées trois fois en différentes grandeurs ΔMP et aussi les lettres Δ et Π inscrites dans l'angle formé par la partie supérieure d'un immense Σ dont l'angle inférieur contenait en tout petits chiffres la date 1966.   (37)[77]

This in fact also exemplifies a final strategy for the defamiliarization of writing, namely the extensive quotation and thematization of foreign languages. The examples of 'typographical' quotation given above bring into play Spanish, English and Greek; elsewhere in Simon's novels there are sometimes quite lengthy passages in Italian (*Les Géorgiques*: 48) and Latin (the various translation passages in *Histoire* and *La Bataille de Pharsale*). I have already discussed the significance of foreign languages and of translation in relation to Lacan's symbolic order, and will return to this in the next chapter; but there is also an evident and simple sense in which the foreign words in the text signify the 'otherness' of *all* writing.[78] This is precisely the effect that the various different defamiliarization techniques all work to produce; whether writing is presented as foreign, as pictorial, as a physical process or an object vulnerable to physical damage, it is always shown in its materiality; and therefore, since this runs counter to our normal perception of it, in its strange opacity and 'otherness'. Both these emphases can be found also in the concept of the symbolic order, since this is grounded in the materiality of the signifier and defines language as fundamentally alien; indeed Lacan sometimes refers to the symbolic as the Other. But the otherness of writing in Simon's texts in fact exceeds the Lacanian definition of the symbolic: it is *also* − in so far as words are juxtaposed with pictures − a function of its implication in the pictorial, and hence the imaginary. That is, writing is defamiliarized being seen (like an image) rather than read (like a text).

Pictures and words, imaginary and symbolic, transparency and opacity, sameness and difference themselves, thus form a complex of parallels and oppositions that are difficult to disentangle. Taking Simon's text as base-line, we can see how it constructs pictures as essentially different from itself as text. But pictures as instances of the imaginary signify, for the *subject*, homogeneity (wholeness, etc.) rather than difference; they are in a sense closer to him. Whereas writing is, in the same sense, fundamentally other because it belongs to the symbolic. Within this global otherness, however, the text also introduces differences between itself and other texts; and these differences are concretely materialized in its actual fabric. But, from the point of view of this matrix text, the other texts can never be *as* other as pictures, because they are the same semiological material.

Words and pictures: the text and its other

But, again, one of the ways in which it emphasizes the otherness and materiality of writing is by using and describing it in a specifically pictorial fashion; and this tends to minimize the initial opposition between pictures and text. Text, subject, picture and 'other' text form a series of sliding, kaleidoscopic patterns in relation to each other, and the position of the *other* — to the text, to the subject — seems to be occupied by words and pictures in turn.

5

THE UNSEEN AND THE UNSAID

The relationship between the visual and the textual exists in the first place between elements *in* the texts: as a series of parallels and inter-connections on the one hand, differences and tensions on the other. I have examined some of these in previous chapters. But the basic relation can also be traced through its negative version − that is, through the significance of what is *not* seen and what is *not* said or written. There are, in other words, two different kinds of censorship at work in the novels; and these activities also play a part in the overall textual economy of vision and language, representation and generative textuality. This chapter will therefore look at the varying modes of existence of the unseen and the unsaid in Simon's novels and the parallels between them, at their relation to desire and their relevance to the question of realism. Both kinds of censorship tend to work against representational coherence, as will be seen, but they do so in rather ambiguous ways; and both are themselves to some degree reappropriated by, drawn back into, the sphere of fascination and desire that they are in the first place resisting.

I argued in Chapter 2 that it is precisely the incompleteness of vision that poses it as an object of desire, and that within this dialectic of the visible and the invisible the object is both elusive and in a sense inexhaustible. Correlatively, desire is a never-ending process, as is vision. But that which is specifically presented in the text as *unseen* − as hidden − constitutes a particular variation on the basic structure of desiring vision.

In *Histoire*, which differs from Simon's other novels in its greater concentration on the figure of the mother, the idea of incomplete visibility is especially strong, with the emphasis on what is not seen; the mother's sexuality, since it cannot be acknowledged, is presented as invisible and enclosed: she is referred to, several times, as a garden hidden behind a high wall, implying both that she represses her own sexuality towards men in general and also that she is a repressed object of desire for her son − she is simultaneously the impenetrable wall and the inviolable flower:

114

elle pareille − avec son corps caché sous les rigides baleines des corsets, les rigides et bruissantes jupes, son visage sereine enduit de décentes crèmes et de décents voiles de poudre − à l'un de ces hauts murs nus bordant une rue, impénétrables, hautains, secrets, dont seuls dépassent les sommets des touffes de lauriers ou de camellias aux inviolables fleurs immobiles dans les sombres et rigides verdures et derrière lesquels on entend (on croit entendre) comme des bruits de jets d'eau, des chants d'oiseaux   (23)[1]

− although even here the ambiguity of 'murs *nus*' coming after references to her clothes suggests that the invisibility is not complete.

The principal figure of the unseen, however, is the *curtain*. It is above all the curtain that conceals, wholly or partially, the desirable woman and/or the sexual activity of a couple; even the old king of the Picasso engraving in *Les Corps conducteurs* watches 'à travers la fente d'un rideau le couple d'amants enlacés' (131)[2] − and there are many other examples of this scene. Moreover, this pervasive image is *also* used as a metaphor for linguistic meaning, and thus serves to link the textual and the visual axes − as, for instance, when Simon starts his paper 'La fiction mot à mot' (1972) with a quotation from Lacan's early paper 'Propos sur la causalité psychique' (1946) which takes 'rideau' as an example of the polysemic nature of the word.[3] But the curtain in fact turns out to be illustrating not only polysemy but the elusive and covert nature of meaning in its basic principle − Lacan concludes his paragraph: 'Rideau! C'est une image enfin du sens en tant que sens, qui pour se découvrir doit se dévoiler' (1966: 166−7),[4] and Simon quotes this too (1972: 73). The domain of censorship is clear: *all* meaning has to be 'unveiled' and uncovered.

As far as its visual implications are concerned the curtain differs from the image of the wall quoted above in so far as, while the wall in a sense *is* the woman, the curtain is at least initially a separate entity. It is more mobile, more manipulable, one could almost say more *flirtatious* than the wall. Nevertheless, it still serves in the first instance to arrest the penetrating power of male vision, by hiding the woman who stands behind it. There are three main occurrences of this situation: in *La Route des Flandres*, the farmer in whose barn the soldiers are quartered locks his supposedly adulterous wife in her bedroom, and she looks out of the window from behind the curtain; secondly, in *Le Palace*, the student sees a naked woman in the room across the courtyard from his; and thirdly, the subject of *La Bataille de Pharsale* watches, from the pavement café opposite, the window of the room in which he thinks his mistress is making love to somebody else.

In each case, what matters to the man who is looking is less the woman herself than the composite image of the woman-behind-the-curtain: it is the visual structure of the *mise-en-scène* that is dominant. Georges, for instance, just misses seeing the woman; what captures his gaze and what the text therefore concentrates on and describes in some detail is the curtain itself:

Georges regarda aussi ... mais sans doute pas assez vite car à l'une des fenêtres du premier étage de la maison il n'eut que le temps de voir le rideau qui retombait, un de ces rideaux de filet bon marché comme on en vend dans les foires et dont le motif représentait un paon à la longue queue retombante encadré dans un losange dont les côtés obliques dessinaient comme des marches selon les mailles du filet, la queue du paon se balançant une ou deux fois, puis s'immobilisant.   (*La Route des Flandres*: 61–2)[5]

The image evokes the existence of something hidden, and in so doing implies a contrast between appearance and reality. Other *nouveaux romanciers* such as Robbe-Grillet also frequently exploit the deceptive nature of appearances, but they do so in a rather more playful fashion. Moreover, the opposition of appearance and reality is equally characteristic of the more traditionally realist novel; and we can in fact find at least one instance where it takes this same form of the woman behind the curtain: Stendhal's hero Julien in the garden of the hôtel de la Mole, looking furtively up at Mathilde's bedroom window. In a similar vein, Balzac's recurrent use of the theatre[6] as a textual device for contrasting the illusion of the *mise-en-scène* with the backstage reality (the two sides again separated by a curtain) constitutes part of a whole system of metaphors involving appearance versus reality, surface versus depth, and so on.

Images like these encapsulate in an almost exemplary form an obscure but close connection between the *hidden* and the *real*: in the realist novel, things are not what they seem. Moreover, this assumption directly serves the reality effect, by virtue of what is essentially a false syllogism – if the real is hidden then the hidden must be real. The realist text, in other words, performs a kind of logical sleight of hand: having established that appearances are deceptive, it 'follows' that reality is by definition hidden – and *therefore*, conversely, anything that is hidden will tend to give a stronger impression of reality than anything which is overtly visible. This is the point of Plato's story about Zeuxis and Parrhasios, which Lacan quotes in his 'Qu'est-ce qu'un tableau?': Parrhasios paints on a wall a veil so life-like that Zeuxis asks him what is behind it. Lacan comments that this 'rend clair qu'à vouloir tromper un homme, ce qu'on lui présente c'est la peinture d'un voile, c'est-à-dire de quelque chose au-delà de quoi il demande de voir' (1973: 102)[7] – and Plato's veil corresponds exactly to the curtain. The concealment of the real also contributes to the didacticism of the realist novel, implying two complementary lessons: it is foolish to trust to first impressions, and perseverance is rewarded. The reader of these novels has to *work* for the truth, struggling through the whole novel before it is revealed to him.[8]

The equation of the real with the hidden has implications for the status of the visible – which, in the terms of this definition, would appear to lose its realist credibility. If the value of the real is protected by maintaining its invisibility for as long as possible, then conversely the visible will be devalued, and reduced to the level of mere appearance. Whereas I have been arguing the opposite – that it is the investment of desire in the visible that founds and supports the realist aspect of Simon's novels. In fact, however, two conflicting notions of the real are involved here. In the context of Simon's novels, representation of the 'real' means representation of what the subject perceives as real, making no claims at all as to the *objective* accuracy of his perception. The real here has to be understood as a perceptual and psychological rather than an epistemological concept – as a vision experienced as real by the subject – and its 'truth' is therefore purely phenomenological: not truth versus appearance, but the truth *of* an appearance, in the sense of something presented by the text as being 'really' perceived by a psycho-realist subject. The opposition is no longer, as it was in Balzac's novels, between subjective illusion and objective truth, but between subjective psychological realism and non-representational discourse.

This distinction is also relevant to the larger question of knowledge versus desire. In classical realism, vision and the manipulation of invisibility serve above all as instruments of knowledge. This emphasis is very clear even in Proust, for instance: what Swann feels when he too is looking for a woman hidden behind a curtain is 'le désir de connaître la vérité ... Il savait que la réalité des circonstances, qu'il eût donné sa vie pour restituer exactement, était lisible derrière cette fenêtre striée de lumière' (*A la Recherche*, I: 274).[9] In contrast, the subjective or phenomenological status of the visible in Simon's novels in effect excludes it from the realm of positive knowledge: rather than a means of supplying true information about the world, the visible in general becomes, as I have tried to show, an object of desire.

And, in so far as the visible is concealed, whatever is concealing it *also* becomes impregnated with desire. The net curtain in *La Route des Flandres*, as quoted above, captures Georges's gaze; and in a later version of the same episode, it is clear that the curtain itself has become invested with the 'life' that it initially seemed to obliterate: 'le paon palpitant tout entier avec le rideau son cou galbé s'infléchissant en forme d'S ... le rideau continuant à osciller après qu'elle l'eût laissé retomber palpitant comme une chose vivante comme la vie qui se cachait derrière' (*La Route des Flandres*: 270).[10] From being a barrier to vision, an obstacle between the subject and the object of his desire, the curtain seems to end up as a substitute object – even, at one point, a naked stomach: 'le rideau de tulle ... respirant faiblement comme un ventre' (*La Bataille de Pharsale*: 102)[11] – absorbing into itself the desire of the gaze.[12] It thus becomes erotic in its own right – tantalizing the gaze in a kind of strip-tease, continually promising and deferring the pleasure of vision. The most explicit account of this process is given in a version of the curtain which – perhaps in compensation for the explicitness – operates a displacement in relation to the basic image of the real desirable woman, but simultaneously emphasizes its purely visual quality: here the curtain is concealing a cinema screen –

le rideau bariolé de réclames retrouvé chaque fois avec la même impatience et la même sécurisante satisfaction, car s'il s'interposait, faisait *obstacle, retardait le plaisir*, il était en même temps *le garant, la promesse* que, derrière *son aveugle opacité*, se tenaient quelque part, prêtes d'un instant à l'autre à scintiller dans le grésillement de l'appareil de projection, les *visions attendues* de chevauchées, de baisers et de combats.

(*Les Géorgiques*: 206, my italics)[13]

One might note here also that the imaginary, escapist qualities often associated with film images are a further indication of the extent to which Simon has shifted the terrain of vision, from the classic realist concern with perception and knowledge, to issues of phantasy and desire.

The build-up of tension is further increased when the curtain is repeated in several different versions, producing more layers of concealment – the scene in *La Bataille de Pharsale* contrives an accumulation of reflections which serve to hide the curtain which in turn hides the woman:

le reflet dans le vantail de la fenêtre à demi fermé toujours rempli aux deux tiers par l'angle de l'immeuble et à un tiers par du ciel, les larges mailles du rideau de filet derrière la vitre plus visibles dans la partie gris sombre que dans la bande remplie par le bleu clair, la forme boursouflée du nuage se faufilant d'un vantail à l'autre pour ainsi dire en se contorsionnant sur la surface inégale de verre, glissant et disparaissant, l'image reflétée de la façade d'angle, balcons, fenêtres, sinueuse aussi, comme ces reflets dans l'eau,

(10–11)[14]

but it is noticeable that all these screens are only partial: the window half closed, the clouds reflected in only part of it, the clouds themselves in sinuous movement, and the curtain made of 'larges mailles'. Rather than a total blocking of vision, there is a plurality of veils, one on top of the other, and all with gaps in them, so that there is always a chance of getting the gaps aligned and being able to see through the curtain to the woman.

The role that the curtain plays in generating sexual excitement is made particularly clear in those few occasions in the texts where the man is *in* the room, actually making love to the woman, and the curtain nevertheless still figures as part of the scene. There are two rather equivocal instances of this in *La Bataille de Pharsale*, one which does not actually mention the presence of a woman (85) and one which repeats the initial scene of the novel but from inside the room and from the woman's point of view: 'Le rideau tiré ne laisse passer qu'une lumière atténuée. O voit le corps penché au-dessus d'elle' (211).[15] The clearest example, though, comes from *La Route des Flandres*: towards the end of the novel, Georges is in bed with Corinne and suddenly remembers the curtain with the peacock (270) – so that the presence of the curtain is here motivated solely by its efficacy as a phantasy.

More specifically, it becomes a kind of *fetish*. Fetishism is another modality of desiring vision, but one which paradoxically has more to do with *not* seeing than with seeing; or, more precisely, it is based on a mechanism of 'disavowal' designed to ensure that these two positions can co-exist.[16] Erotic less in what it reveals than in what it conceals, the function of the fetish, according to Freud, is to cover up and substitute for the lack of a penis on the woman's – originally the mother's – body. The *completely* naked female body is actually, in Simon's terms, 'terrifying' and a 'trap' (*Histoire*: 295), because its not having a penis evokes the threat of castration. What is both puzzling and frightening about the naked body of the artist's model is its matter-of-fact obviousness, its lack of *mystery* on one level creating a further mystery: 'sa paisible et banale nudité tellement dépourvue de mystère qu'il en émanait cette espèce de mystère au second degré caché au-delà du visible, du palpable, cette terrifiant énigme, insoluble, vertigineuse' (*Histoire*: 306).[17] The phrase 'nudité tellement dépourvue de mystère' can be read as a sort of transformation or condensation: lacking the mystery needed to disguise that other and far more important lack – of a penis. This is provided by the fetish; and the curtain, as fetish, is necessary in order to preserve the desirability of the female body which when completely visible is too threatening to stimulate desire.

119

This fetishistic structuring of desire is complicated and intensified by *movement*. The importance of the contrast between, and paradoxical equation of, movement and stillness throughout Simon's writing has been discussed in the previous chapter; but in the case of the curtain it acquires a more specific meaning. The passage from *La Route des Flandres* cited earlier shows the curtain 'palpitant' like a living creature; in the one from *La Bataille de Pharsale* the reflections of the clouds are described as 'se faufilant ... se contorsionnant ... glissant et disparaissant', but the curtain in this case is not moving, and the passage goes on to underline the contrast: 'Mais immobile. Les mailles du rideau immobile aussi' (11). The opposition between the still and the moving curtain in fact continues to punctuate the whole text of *La Bataille de Pharsale* – 'Peut-être le rideau derrière le vantail de droite avait-il légèrement bougé ou le vent?' (20), 'le rideau de filet absolument immobile aussi' (47), etc.[18] In *La Route des Flandres*, similarly, the curtain is first seen falling back into place but is subsequently still (271); and in *Le Palace*, the naked woman is drawing the curtain across her body.

It is the moving curtain in particular that becomes erotic. It intensifies the fascination of the object by transforming it into something evanescent, both more accessible and more elusive; and, by offering the possibility of a brief glimpse of the woman's body, it *concentrates* the gaze. Movement is, once again, an essential feature of the strip-tease – but with the difference that the stripper's sequence of movements is ritualized and teleological, whereas the random, accidental movements of the curtain alternately reveal and cover up again – a combination of strip-tease and fan-dance. In the episode of the boy's visit to the opera in *Les Géorgiques*, the curtain is in fact twice juxtaposed with the similar movement of the fluttering fans in the audience (27 and 31). In its oscillation between hiding and revealing, the moving curtain allows precisely the contradictory co-existence of seeing and not seeing that constitutes the disavowal that underlies fetishism; an oscillation that occurs most explicitly in the episode in *Histoire* where the narrator asks Hélène to shave her pubic hair. Here it is specifically the woman's genitals that are alternately concealed and revealed, and the emphasis on seeing is clear: 'la main dessus le cachant puis le dévoilant puis le recouvrant courant vite jusqu'au lit Fais voir dis-je oh fais voir' (135).[19]

But the moving curtain has a further significance as well. It can operate as a sign of the woman as subject: if she, rather than the wind, is moving the curtain, it means that she is looking out and presumably looking back at the man, transforming him into the object of *her* look.

(The window itself is in fact ambiguous in just the same way: it serves to frame the image, to present the woman *as* image, offered to vision, as though in a picture or on a stage; while on the other hand the fact that she is at the window at all is because *she* is *looking out*.) The subject in *La Bataille de Pharsale* therefore has two reasons for staring at the curtain and hoping that it will move: if it does it may reveal the figure of the woman, but will in any case be a sign that she is 'observant le premier observateur ... à travers les mailles du rideau de filet' (184)[20] – a sign, in other words, of her interest in him. Here the curtain participates in an exchange of looks, and in this kind of reversibility of the look whereby subject and object continually exchange positions.[21] The curtain assumes a particular role within this configuration: in hiding the desirable object of the look, the curtain is by the same token hiding that other object of desire which is the other's look. But, in this second case too, the curtain does not simply hide the object: it is what makes it possible to *imagine* its existence. Rather than seeing a woman who is not looking at him, the curtain enables him not to see a woman who might be looking at him – and the curtain's movement is the trace of that possible other look, of, as Lacan says, 'un regard par moi imaginé au champ de l'Autre' (1973: 79).[22] The curtain, then, can also be seen as symbolizing the impossibility of locating the other's look, as a figure of its 'unapprehensibility'.[23]

What the curtain offers is a particular kind of eroticism deriving from a production – almost in the theatrical sense, since the curtain is of course also associated with the stage – of the female body as incomplete and ephemeral: only part of it is visible, and only for a moment. Barthes points to something very similar when he asks 'L'endroit le plus érotique d'un corps n'est-il pas *là où le vêtement baille*?' (1973: 19, author's italics), and moreover goes on to define it as a specifically *textual* pleasure: 'Dans la perversion (qui est le régime du plaisir textuel) ... c'est l'intermittence, comme l'a bien dit la psychanalyse, qui est érotique' (ibid.) – and concludes, in terms which define exactly the particular pleasure of Simon's texts: 'c'est ce scintillement même qui séduit, ou encore: la mise en scène d'une apparition–disparition' (ibid.).[24] The scene in *Le Palace* where the student watches the American's window emphasizes both the momentariness – 'la voyant alors, juste une fraction de seconde' (173) – and the incompleteness of the vision: just a *section* of 'le corps nu [qui] ... n'était pas entièrement visible, étroitement encastré entre les deux verticales et même en partie masqué par le côté gauche du rectangle de la fenêtre qui partageait exactement en deux la cuisse droite' (ibid.)[25] — and there is an echo, perhaps, of the underlying castration anxiety which the fetish is designed to assuage in the almost sadistic[26] reduction of the body to 'un de ces baroques échafaudages d'objets disparates superposés ... qui semblent tenir sans pesanteur sur le doigt de l'équilibriste' (174).[27]

But it is the moment of disappearance which most crucially *marks* the vision, and which the student struggles to recreate in his memory: 'Mais comment était-ce, comment était-ce? Rien qu'un instant, l'espace d'une fraction de seconde à peine. Puis elle tira le rideau, se supprimant, se gommant, s'effaçant elle-même' (174–5). The movement captured here, of a sudden vivid apparition which almost immediately fades into nothingness — 'entrevue, elle aussi sortie du néant et retournée à jamais l'instant après au néant' (175)[28] — is typical of the mirage as it is found in Simon's texts.

It is thus an essentially instantaneous, fleeting moment that the text attempts to capture. But Simon speaks also of a countervailing persistence, of 'l'apparition disparue restant là sans doute par l'effet d'une persistence rétinienne, devant à sa brièveté même ... cette prolongation d'existence, de sorte qu'il lui semblait toujours continuer à la voir' (175);[29] and it is in fact this after-effect of the image that in this case is inscribed in the text. The representation of the instant is to some extent negated as the text builds up a specifically verbal momentum, actually destroying the fleeting quality of the apparition as it works on it, producing four pages of detailed description, breaking the 'instant' down into a 'suite d'images simples' (175)[30] and, most strikingly of all, devoting a whole page to an almost word for word repetition of an earlier account of the same event — thereby referring to itself rather than to the ostensible object of the representation. The text fixes the image in a kind of slow motion replay, and so amplifies it and *makes it last*. Rather than having as its essential aim the accurate reproduction of the incident, therefore, the text may be seen as maximizing the pleasure of the vision in a *non-representational* way, by distorting it, drawing it out, creating a parallel textual pleasure of deferral and repetition. In this way the difference between desire for the visible *per se* and desire which materializes in *writing* the visible becomes clear: Simon's texts reach towards an object which is simultaneously constructed by their own activity. I have referred in Chapter 1 to the textual 'modalization' of the visible, its reconstitution as object of desire inscribed in a text; the passage from *Le Palace* cited above provides further illustration of this.

In one case the image of the curtain hiding the woman who stands behind it is reversed, as the curtain becomes the draped material − 'le vieux rideau drapé contre le mur en guise de fond' (*Histoire*: 296)[31] − *in front of* which the artist's nude model poses. One whole section of *Histoire* (288–307) is devoted to describing a photograph taken in the studio, showing the Dutch artist Van Velden, the model, and the narrator's uncle Charles. The central focus of the description is the naked female body and Charles's reaction to it; and although the model is the exact opposite of the woman behind the curtain − and is the most clearly *exhibitionist* version of the woman as seen object − the same kind of fetishization of the curtain nevertheless still operates. That is, Charles cannot actually look at the model herself, and instead stares fixedly at the material behind her − which is consequently described in obsessive detail (296–7). In fact the underlying significance of the fetish comes across even more strongly here, since the curtain is no longer actually preventing him from seeing the naked female body: he is rather *choosing* to avert his eyes, to look at − i.e. to fetishize − 'the last impression before the uncanny and traumatic one', as Freud puts it (vol. 21: 155).

The disturbance which this sight is presumed (by the narrator, who begins to merge indistinguishably with Charles at this point) to cause in his psyche is in fact so extreme that it is translated into an odd kind of turbulence in the text itself: a more or less realist *visual* version of fetishism and censorship − i.e. Charles looking at the curtain − leads immediately to a reference to the inadequacy of language and 'l'innommable' in its unreliable relation to the 'nommé'. At this point the visual coherence of the representation itself is suddenly disrupted; having alluded to the linguistic dimension and then explicitly abandoned it: 'non pas disant mais sentant' (279),[32] the text erupts in an extraordinary explosion, and confusion, of language which apparently makes no sense at all within the framework of the realist scene. Anthony Pugh defines this paragraph as 'le premier exemple dans le texte simonien d'une écriture radicalement non-représentative, non-narrative, et surtout non-visuelle' (1975: 388).[33] It is particularly odd in that it consists of a single paragraph, after which the text goes back to its previous and more normal mode, with the narrator wondering what Charles felt, and so on; and there seems to be no very cogent reason as to why the sight of the nude model should occasion such an acute and obscure kind of disruption.

If, however, the reader goes back a few pages to the description of Charles's entry into the studio, a tentative explanation begins to be possible. He is described as being 'comme un adolescent attardé, gauche et pour ainsi dire virginal' (294),[34] although, we are told, it is at least thirty-five years since his birth and fifteen since he lost his virginity; and the juxtaposition of these two biographical facts leads to a comparison of his mother with 'une autre femme', but involving 'la même partie de son corps, quoique utilisée, si l'on peut se permettre cette expression, en sens inverse' (294).[35] Is it, in other words, perhaps the *mother's* body, the mother's sexual organs, that are responsible for the kind of representational black-out that the text undergoes on page 297? Pugh, in his treatment of the paragraph in question, finds in it an echo of an earlier evocation of the mother's hair (33). In fact, however, there is a more complex and revealing correlation between, not this paragraph, but the description two pages earlier of Charles's *first* glimpse of the model, and the *first* description in the novel of the mother glimpsed on her death bed with the priest administering the last rites (18–19). The similarities between these two passages are so striking that it is worth looking at them in detail. Charles's first sight of the model is described as follows:

ou encore *distinguant dans l'entrebaillement des tentures* qui fermaient l'entreé ...
(étendue avec cette tranquille indifférence ou plutôt évidence d'objet, ou plutôt d'entité, au milieu de ce décor de meubles de cuisine, de guitares sans cordes et de vieux *tapis fanés* suspendus en guise de cloisons de sorte qu'ils cuisinaient, dormaient et s'accouplaient à l'abri de *guirlandes de fleurs* et de *feuillages* jaunis se balançant sur des fonds *rougeâtres*, comme un éphémère et poussiéreux campement de *pourpre* et de *lauriers fanés*)
... un *fragment* (entre les deux parallèles ou *l'angle aigu de l'ouverture*), une *section*: du *blanc et du noir*: une hanche, la barre d'ombre entre les cuisses, le creux d'un flanc respirant: quelque chose d'insolite: cette matité, cet éclat, cette tiédeur devinée, cette inoffensive et terrifiante *immobilité* de piège).
(295, my italics, author's ellipses)[36]

When we read this passage in conjunction with the scene of the mother on her death bed, a whole series of lexical echoes becomes apparent. Thus in the scene with the mother there is an equivalent of the 'tentures' in the priest's robes; and it is behind these that 'un instant j'avais pu voir ou plutôt entrevoir le visage de maman' (19)[37] – which is very close to 'distinguant dans l'entrebaillement des tentures' quoted above (and both reproduce the schema of vision partially obstructed by a kind of curtain). The description of the robes as 'l'immobile ruée des vagues violettes les taches de sang les feuilles' (19)[38] is similarly echoed almost point for point in the later passage: 'immobile'/'immobilité', 'violettes'/'pourpre', 'taches de sang'/ 'rougeâtres', 'feuilles'/'feuillages' (and also 'lauriers'). The priest is 'piétinant sur le tapis les guirlandes de roses' (18),[39] and this recurs as the 'vieux tapis fanés' and the 'guirlandes de fleurs' which are also, perhaps, an echo of the mother's 'oreillers festonnés' (19);[40] the word 'fané' appears once in the first passage ('lilas fané', 19), and twice in the second. Both also show a juxtaposition of black and white – the mother's hand 'affleurant la petite boule *noire* et immédiatement au-dessous se détachant sur la *blancheur* des oreillers'[41] and the model's body reduced to 'du blanc et du noir'. Similarly, 'aigu' and 'section' in the passage reprinted above can be seen as derived from the emphasis on the mother's face as being 'comme une lame de couteau vue de face le nez aussi comme une lame de couteau' (19).[42]

The most important correlation, though, is that which establishes the form, and indeed the conditions of possibility, of both visions: as with the woman behind the curtain in *Le Palace*, in both cases only part of the woman's body is visible, inserted in a geometrically defined frame which limits what can be seen and cuts off all the rest: thus 'entrevoir le visage de maman ... dans un *triangle limité* par le bras incliné le fronton du pied du lit en bois marqueté le montant à droit' (19, my italics)[43] corresponds to 'un fragment (entre les deux parallèles ou *l'angle aigu de l'ouverture*), une *section*'. Both women's bodies are fetishized by being seen as incomplete 'sections'. It is, moreover, partly because this is the basis of both visions that they are brought into such a close relation in the text, despite being separated by two hundred and seventy-five pages. But the connection is above all determined by the subject's – indifferently the narrator's or Charles's – unconscious desire for the mother. The second scene with the model ultimately reads as a slightly more 'acceptable' re-invention of what cannot be expressed in the first scene with the mother: a displacement on to the model, the sexually available woman par excellence, of the idea of the mother's sexuality, the inaccessibility of which is further reinforced by the imminence of her death. The process of displacement can be read in the material lexical traces of the first scene which remain in the second. Conversely, the repressed desire for the mother is reactivated by the association with the nude model, and the disarray which this causes in turn generates – in a further displacement from the initial sight of the model to the version of it given two pages later – the sudden explosion of non-representational textuality.

More fundamentally, however, the very structure of fetishistic desire, and fetishistic vision, is rooted in a peculiarly ambiguous relation to the real. Fetishism is based on disavowal: and this involves, precisely, the simultaneous acceptance and denial of what is 'really' there – or not there. The psychic 'compromise', as Freud calls it, which results from the conflict between perceived reality and 'the force of the counter-wish' (154), is re-enacted in the similarly ambivalent 'compromise' of a literary discourse which oscillates continuously between the construction of visual objects of desire and the subversion of all forms of representation. In this discourse, therefore, invisibility is not just a guarantee of reality, and the curtain is both far more and far less than a guarantee of invisibility.

The examples discussed so far have already indicated that the curtain is part of a fetishistic staging of desire. As well as generating desire, however, in some cases the curtain actually produces the *visible* itself. In addition to its theatrical connotations, it also participates in a more cinematic regime of desire, sometimes becoming the equivalent of the cinema screen. In his article on Simon, Deguy points out that with the invention of cinema and then television, 'screen' has become an ambiguous term: it is both that which hides the object and that on which the image of the object is presented – with the second meaning becoming dominant: 'l'écran n'est plus ce qui masque, mais le temple où se représente, irréalisé, le réel comme image' (1962: 1016).[44] This ambiguity mirrors the larger ambiguity of seen/unseen in Simon's texts: thus the curtain in *Le Palace*, lit from behind, is also the semi-transparent surface on which the woman's body *becomes visible*, 'par l'effet de la lumière qui avait dessiné en ombres chinoises sinueuses et mouvantes le sinueux contour du bras levé, du sein, de la hanche et de la cuisse ondulant, s'étirant, se distendant sur l'étoffe brusquement tirée' (144) – and again later: 'les ombres chinoises vert–noir projetées sur le rideau' (175).[45]

Much earlier in *Le Palace*, though, we find a different and more extreme version of the curtain producing the visible: a figurative curtain and an imaginary vision. (Here, in other words, the realist logic of the curtain hiding the visible and thus making it real is exactly reversed: the curtain *produces* a visible which is *not* real.) The narrator has returned to the site of the hotel occupied during the Civil War, which has now been demolished. The curtain, an eminently 'moving' one, is formed by birds, echoing the connection set up by the 'palpitant' bird on the curtain in *La Route des Flandres*. In this case, however, it is not a lace peacock but the flock of pigeons in the square: 'ils s'envolaient brusquement ... un palpitant et neigeux rideau parcouru de remous, de courants multiples' (23) – and behind it there appears, as a hallucinatory mirage, the old building of the hotel: 'comme un rideau mouvant par delà lequel, à travers la glace du bar, il lui semblait le voir, intact, dressant son architecture rocailleuse, boursouflée' (23–4). Then, as the curtain falls away, the mirage disappears with it and the present-day scene returns – 'le frémissant voile de pigeons ondulant, fléchissant, retombant, s'affaissant enfin, la muraille froide et nue de la banque réapparaissant de nouveau, géométrique, carrée ...' (24) – but now including, as a final effect of the curtain, a new apparition: 'géométrique, carrée, et se détachant là-dessus, le visage peint en train de lui sourire, et lui se demandant depuis combien de temps elle était assise là'. That is, a mysterious woman, 'sa jeune et lourde chair comme un mystérieux bouillonnement, un secret' (24),[46] appears out of nowhere as though by magic, as though the association between the curtain and the desirable woman were so powerful that the one irresistibly produces the other.

But a further, and crucial, function of the curtain is to be found in a variation which is the reverse of this: instead of magically bringing into being something behind it, the curtain serves to conceal *nothing*. That is, what it hides is revealed as nothing, as an absence; the final occurrence[47] of the curtain with the peacock, near the end of *La Route des Flandres*, dismisses as empty illusion the idea that there was ever anything at all behind it:

sans plus de consistance que ce rideau sur lequel nous croyions voir le paon brodé remuer palpiter respirer imaginant rêvant à ce qu'il y avait derrière n'ayant même pas vu sans doute le visage coupé en deux la main qui l'avait laissé retomber épiant passionnément le faible mouvement d'un courant d'air;
(274–5)[48]

and a few pages earlier, even a detailed and more optimistic description of the curtain leads immediately to the idea of *death* as, precisely, the knowledge that there is after all no mystery and nothing hidden, the 'décevant secret qu'est la certitude de l'absence de tout secret et de tout mystère' (270).[49] In this formulation – the secret is that there is no secret – the curtain does indeed serve to *negate* the visible, not by concealing it but by showing that there is nothing to be seen; this is in a sense the truth behind the fetish, which comes into being as a strategy for concealing, not 'something', but an absence – whose momentary revelation is thus an index of the *failure* of the fetish. In these moments of dysphoria the curtain works *against* desire, by undoing the whole configuration of seen and unseen.

Beyond this, however, since the configuration of woman and curtain acts as a privileged instance of the real in fiction, it also undermines the *representational* axis of the text. Most of the time, the simple fact of the curtain's presence is seen as a kind of guarantee that it is hiding something 'real' – to this extent, Simon's novels, albeit somewhat perversely, endorse the hidden/real equation of classic realist discourse. It is thus along these lines that Dällenbach interprets 'le pouvoir de fascination que détient dans *La route* le fameux "rideau de paon"' – i.e. as a sign of the revelation of reality: 'métaphore emblématique d'un livre hanté par le dévoilement et intéressé par tout ce qui fait signe, il invite précisément à voir derrière et à scruter, pour la mettre au jour, la part d'invisible que le visible réserve' (1982: 306).[50] The curtain, in other words, usually creates and maintains an illusion of reality. But when it turns out that what the curtain is hiding is not the plenitude of the real but, precisely, the secret that there is nothing there after all, then – although in all Simon's novels these moments of disclosure are very rare – all the other realist instances of the curtain are retrospectively contaminated by the suspicion that they too are illusory, and the equation of real and hidden is no longer viable. Whereas in most realist fiction the reader's willingness to persevere with the narrative unravelling of illusion is rewarded with the final delivery of the truth, the reader of *La Route des Flandres*, for instance, works his way through almost the whole novel before discovering that there is no truth and no reality. Appearances in Simon's novels are not set up in order to be contrasted with, and dissipated by, a substantive objective reality – rather, they are the plenitude that contrasts with the nothingness revealed at the end of *La Route des Flandres*, but also in the last words of *L'Herbe*: 'puis quelques gouttes encore, puis, un long moment après, une autre – puis plus rien'.[51] In fact several of the novels end with a similar dissolving of appearance into nothingness: *Les Corps conducteurs* terminated by an eclipse of vision, and *Triptyque* and *Leçon de choses*, both of which end with a light being switched off and visibility giving way to darkness.

This nothingness is the secret that the curtain is ultimately hiding; but the fact is that it *does* hide it most of the time. Although the moments of 'la certitude de l'absence' (*La Route des Flandres*: 270) often occur at the end of the novels, they are never definitively established: the phantasy of plenitude, of the visible and the represented, always returns. And the image of the woman behind the curtain gets caught up in these large-scale opposing but inconclusive movements by which a fictional referent is alternately posited and dissolved.

Similar issues concerning the status of representation are raised by the verbal equivalent of invisibility: the unsaid. There are in fact three different categories of 'unsaid'. The first can be equated simply with the unknown − with questions which are posed in the texts and then left unanswered. An obvious example here is the motive behind De Reixach's death (was it suicide, and if so why?), which is dwelt upon at length in *La Route des Flandres* but never resolved. An equally insistent questioning surrounds the death of the general in *Le Palace* with its 'étalage de variations sur la même lancinante interrogation: ¿QUIEN ASESINO A SANTIAGO?' (35);[52] and this novel also explores, although in less declamatory fashion, the even more ominous disappearance of the American (pp. 207, 210). It is in *Les Géorgiques*, however, that the accumulation of unanswered questions, of gaps in the knowledge of the narrative, is greatest. They occur both in relation to O's experiences in Barcelona and to LSM, in his relationship with his brother, Batti's actions after his death, and so on. The account of LSM's life is crucially determined by the fact that the subject who is narrating it does not *know* what happened and has to build up a tentative interpretation on the basis of inadequate information; and this, clearly, has a certain effect on the illusion of reality constructed and/or deconstructed by the text.[53]

In his discussion of this aspect of *La Route des Flandres*, Lucien Dällenbach comes to the conclusion that there is 'Chez Simon, nulle volonté d'en finir avec le sens mais reconnaissance implicite, au contraire, qu'on n'en a jamais fini avec lui, dans la mesure où le régime sémantique simonien est, fondamentalement, celui de l'énigme' (1982: 305).[54] In fact, though, this kind of positing of an enigma − an unknown − is not the same thing as a view of meaning as infinite process. A 'régime sémantique de l'énigme' is a hermeneutic code: it creates in the reader a desire to solve the enigma, to find the answer. When this proves impossible (and this is not always the case: there are secrets which *are* revealed in Simon's novels), the expectations that have been set up are certainly frustrated, and to that extent the text breaks the rules of realism − but only realist fiction of a rather naïve kind; there are plenty of novels which leave the reader with similar mysteries unresolved and which nevertheless remain entirely within the limits of a representational use of language − a use, in other words, which presupposes that words refer in a determinate and specifiable fashion to entities in the real world. The mystery surrounding Julien's motives for shooting Madame de Rênal, for instance, or the fact that we never know whether George Burton in *L'Emploi du temps* was the victim of an accident or an attempted murder, does not, despite the centrality of these incidents, turn the novels in question into pure 'adventures of writing'.

It could even be argued that whenever it proclaims the existence of a particular unknown the text at least situates itself within the domain of fictional *knowledge*, and consequently within a problematic that remains essentially realist. 'Wanting to know' is, after all, the principal source of motivation for the reader of realist fiction, which for that reason carefully cultivates and exploits it. The point here is that even if the knowledge is not supplied, the *operations* of meaning are not totally changed by its absence; meaning is still taken to be basically unproblematic, a full and finite relation between signifier and signified. Knowledge may be withheld, but it is still assumed that language is a perfectly adequate instrument with which to search for it. This is so even in the extreme case of Iglésia's language which is reduced to a few grunts and mumblings, but nevertheless allows Georges and Blum to '[reconstituer] ... l'histoire entière' (*La Route des Flandres*: 137).[55] A reference to vision occurs here too: the knowledge is symbolized by a *picture* which is gradually *restored* by their conversations: the role of language, in other words, is to get at a truth that pre-exists it, that is waiting to be revealed, 'comme la surface d'un tableau obscurci par les vernis et la crasse et qu'un restaurateur révélerait par plaques – essayant, expérimentant ça et là sur de petits morceaux différentes formules de nettoyants' (137).[56] A whole series of connections between text and visual representation and true knowledge are condensed in this image: truth – the 'whole story' – is a painting, and language is the cleaning agent which restores it.

The second type of *unsaid* is not missing knowledge but repressed knowledge. In this case, the link between language and representation is looser and more ambiguous; the lacunæ imposed by censorship work against representation not only by the incompleteness they create but even more so because their gaps themselves become *generative* of textual activity, while still remaining within a global concept of positive and definable meaning. Here it is a question of censorship in the psychoanalytic sense, and of the absences in the text that are the traces of its activity.[57] One example of this has already been discussed: the paragraph in *Histoire* (297) with its sudden disruption of the established discourse and its association, as I have argued, with the mother's body. But censorship becomes a major *theme* in several of the novels, and acquires a range of political and psychological connotations: all of which, however, have in common the fact that when censorship is explicitly thematized in this way it is always located in other texts, not in the discourse of the principal subject.

One of the earliest examples is Marie's collection of notebooks in *L'Herbe*; these provide a counterpoint to the main narrative, and are characterized as much by what is left out of them as by what is actually recorded in them. Thus Louise knows even before she looks at them that 'elle n'allait y trouver ni journal, ni mémoires, ni lettres jaunies, ni quoi que ce soit de ce genre' (120);[58] and this stress on what is not there, on the unsaid or unwritten, is interpreted as a refusal to place any importance on personal experience – an idea so indecent that it is not even made conscious: 'des sortes d'idées (tenir un journal, écrire l'histoire de sa propre vie) qui n'étaient même pas capables d'effleurer l'esprit de celle qui les avaient tenues' (ibid.).[59] It is true that in one sense Marie's life puts in question the whole idea of repression; the main point of presenting us with a life of total self-sacrifice and total asexuality is to demonstrate that it is *not* lived as difficult, painful or unnatural. But the question of personal history is posed on a slightly different level here: what *is* repressed is the desire to 'écrire l'histoire de sa propre vie', because in the context of the novel as a whole 'personal history' is a contradiction in terms. History is precisely what makes Marie's life insignificant or invisible, and conversely from the point of view of the individual life it is history that is insignificant and invisible.

The invisibility of history is the main subject of my next chapter; but it is also relevant here in so far as one of its manifestations is the theme of political censorship, which is prominent in *Le Palace*, with the question of Santiago's assassination, the newspapers' claims that it was the fifth column, the American's cynicism about this and his subsequent disappearance. In *Les Géorgiques* too, the republicans in the Spanish Civil War are shown as censoring information about the participation of the Russians and various other political issues. O writes his account of the war, and this is also presented as a censored version of the facts: Simon's text becomes almost monotonous in its cataloguing of things that O leaves out – for instance, 'il ne parla pas des cortèges, ni des insidieuses et meurtrières manchettes des journaux [both of course prominent in *Le Palace*] ni des rivalités entre les différentes casernes aux différents parrainages' (331), 'passant sans les voir (en tout cas il n'en parla pas – ou peut-être faisaient-ils partie ... de ces choses qu'il avait décidé une fois pour toutes de ne plus voir' (336), 'Mais il n'en parla pas non plus' (337),[60] etc. Here censorship and the refusal of knowledge are also posed as a question of vision: the things he has decided not to *see* thus forming a negative version of the transformation in *Les Géorgiques* of the visible into an object of knowledge rather than desire (see Introduction). But this 'unsaid' and 'unseen' is not the completely calculated and knowing construct of the political leaders themselves: O's position lies somewhere in between the conscious political censorship that implies control and power, and the unconscious censorship that leaves its subject vulnerable to his own naïveté. O's simple trust in words, his hope that language itself will sort out his experiences for him − 'il pense aussi peut-être que ... les obligations de la construction syntaxique feront ressortir des rapports de cause à effet' (311) − results only in a proliferation of lacunæ: 'Il y aura cependant des trous dans son récit, des points obscurs, des incohérences même' (ibid.).[61] O does not fully possess his 'adventure', and therefore becomes its victim or, more exactly, the victim of his own narrative:

son aventure (ou plutôt l'aventure qu'il (O.) essayait maintenant de raconter) ressemblait à un de ces romans dont le narrateur qui menait l'enquête serait non pas l'assassin, comme dans certaines versions sophistiquées, mais le mort lui-même.   (340)[62]

− and his 'death' leads in turn to the 'drowning' of the reader: 'noyant le lecteur dans une profusion de détails oiseux dont l'accumulation lui sert à dissimuler *le maillon caché de la chaîne, l'information manquante*' (ibid., my italics).[63] The operations are carried out by the victim, that is, by the unconscious subject caught up in, rather than controlling, his discourse; the concept of censorship veers from the level of political manipulation to that of psychic repression.[64]

In *Les Géorgiques* the theme of censorship is also important with reference to LSM's story. In the first place, the very existence of his papers was kept secret by his descendant, the 'vieille dame', because she disapproved so strongly of his having voted for the death of the king that she suppressed the evidence of this that was to be found in the papers, by hiding them in the secret cupboard under the stairs. This too counts as political censorship, of an amateur kind; and in fact the old lady proves to be a more skilful censor than the Spanish communists, because she manages to conceal not only the unacceptable knowledge, but also the fact that it has actually been censored − whereas the Spanish newspapers are 'tellement censurées que certaines de leurs pages ... étaient à peu près entièrement blanches' (305).[65] More important than the secret of the regicide, however, is that of LSM's brother, the renegade monarchist. This is revealed only at the end of Chapter III; and the terms of the revelation stress the point that the brother was a secret, an *unsaid*: '"Tu veux dire:

pourquoi est-ce qu'on n'en a jamais parlé? Eh bien voilà: précisément!''' (256).[66] In other words, what is significant about the
brother is 'precisely' that he is censored, that he is excluded from
language, and *by* language; he is the figure

> dont il ne devait rester plus tard aucune trace, pas un médaillon, *pas une lettre,*
> *pas un papier témoignant qu'il avait été* (sauf ces deux simples mots: mon
> frère, quand il s'agit de partager ses biens, et cette affiche, ces trois *colonnes*
> *imprimées qui n'attestaient de son existence que par le jugement qui la lui*
> *enlevait*), lui dont il était même défendu maintenant de *prononcer le nom.*
>
> (420, my italics)[67]

But there is also a peculiar facial sign associated with censorship:
the 'rictus'. LSM's impassive face is 'intraitablement fermé sur son
secret, avec ce mince rictus qui tiraillait peut-être encore les lèvres'
(404); and O gives his idealized account of events in Spain, 'écrivant
... pour ainsi dire la bouche en coin, tiraillée de côté par un rictus
à la fois railleur et nerveux' (332).[68] The 'rictus' remains as a kind
of paralinguistic trace of the unsaid, and as a discreet link between
the two almost diametrically opposed characters of O and LSM –
linking them in the one activity they have in common, that of
censorship.

Apart from this explicit thematizing of censorship, always with
reference to someone else's text, there are some brief allusions made *en*
passant to similar mechanisms in the subject's own discourse: the
'lapsus' whereby he reads 'COUPS' for 'COURS' in the newspaper
headline, for instance (*La Bataille de Pharsale*: 65). Or there are
instances that are not even commented on but are simply very clear
traces of censorship: again in *La Bataille de Pharsale* (and just after a
mention of the curtain), a sudden break in the text is followed by a
reference to something unspecified remembered on a right-hand page:
'Disant que la jalousie est comme ... comme ... Me rappelant l'endroit: environ dans le premier tiers en haut d'une page de droite'
(20);[69] and the phrase 'page de droite' is repeated at intervals throughout the novel in conjunction with 'jalousie' and with allusions to
Proust;[70] but it remains a blank page, as though he cannot quite
remember it: 'jalousie où donc page de droite en haut' (90).[71] The
quotation itself is still censored. In *Histoire*, similarly, the newspaper
headlines about the suicide of a woman who is probably the narrator's
wife are never explained, but break violently into the flow of the text,
and are themselves broken off, unfinished: 'SE JETTE DU QUATRI-
EME ETA' (251), 'MET FIN A SES JOURS EN SE JETANT D'UN'
(389);[72] the only complete version is upside down (366).

In these examples the activity of censorship is made very evident. The cryptic fragments left in the text, markedly unconnected to what precedes and follows them, act as a sign of something missing, and their repetition underlines the compulsive nature of the phenomenon. Elsewhere, however, the breaks and gaps are not so blatant, and yet it is still possible to trace a movement of dissimulation in the language. Critical work on Simon's texts has produced numerous examples of this kind of occultation or dispersal of meaning, which may be more or less systematic. Lotringer, for instance, shows how the 'scène occultée de la *noyade nocturne*'[73] in *Triptyque* (i.e. there are clear indications that the little girl has drowned, but the incident is never actually represented) is alluded to throughout the novel in various forms of 'noyer' − including the pun on 'drown'/'walnut tree' − which are planted, like clues, all over the text; and he contrasts this with other less carefully orchestrated trails of displaced or 'sliding' signification.[74]

From a different theoretical point of view, Ricardou's work on the detailed micro-structures of Simon's texts results in a number of what one might call micro-insights concerning the displacement of signifiers. One example concerns the letter 'O' in *La Bataille de Pharsale* − its appearances but also its disappearance from, for instance, the quotation from Proust that is first cited on page 22 of the novel: 'édicules Rambuteau s'appelaient des pistières Sans doute en son enfance n'avait-il pas entendu l'o et cela lui était resté'.[75] Ricardou interprets this as follows: 'La citation de Proust où tel personnage nomme pistières les édicules Rambuteau permet notamment d'entendre que la lettre O (mise en evidence par effacement indu puisque chez Poe la "lettre" volée est dissimulée par ostentation réfléchie) est porteuse d'une "piste".'[76] The disappearing 'O', he argues, links 'Orion' with 'noir' and 'Verona' with 'envers' (1971: 150). It is however possible to follow the 'piste' in a different direction as well: 'O' leads to Orion, and Orion leads, mythically and etymologically, to *urine*.[77] The quotation from Proust is thus doubly determined in relation to Orion: 'pissotières'/'urine', the subtraction of 'o' giving 'pistières' which signals its status as a 'piste' of meaning (which may be compared with Lacan's comment on, precisely, interpreting Poe's 'Lettre volée': 'Dépistons donc sa foulée là où elle nous dépiste', 1966: 31),[78] while 'piste' is at the same time phonetically suggestive of the source of the quotation: Proust, also censored from Simon's text. Moreover, this second and fragmentary occurrence of the quotation comes just after a mention of that other mark of censorship, the cryptic 'page de droite' (*La Bataille de Pharsale*: 38).

Sometimes the 'piste' seems to lead to a word which does not appear at all, but which in spite of or because of its absence structures a whole section of the text; here the effects of censorship are clearly discernible as a *force* in the construction of meanings — as a kind of magnetic field which orientates the passage in question around a central determining absence. An example is the following passage from *Histoire*:

veuf mot boiteux tronqué restant pour ainsi dire en suspens coupé contre nature comme l'anglais half moitié sectionné cut off coupé de quelque chose qui manque soudain dans la bouche les lèvres prononçant VF continuant à faire fff comme un bruit d'air froissé déchiré par le passage rapide étincelant et meurtrier d'une lame. (91–2)[79]

The description is of Charles, whose wife killed herself because of his adultery; and the image is clearly one of castration: his wife's suicide has in effect castrated him. But this point is made solely by a play on the material qualities of the signifier 'veuf' and its associations with other similar sounding words in English: 'half', 'cut off'. There are references to 'something missing': the phallus, but also perhaps a missing *word* ('quelque chose qui manque soudain *dans la bouche*') whose absence means that the whole passage is 'restant pour ainsi dire en suspens'. And the word is — surely — *'knife'*: underlying the other English words ending in *f* and also the reference to 'une lame'. But if these are so to speak generated by the repressed signifier 'knife', where does 'knife' itself come from? It is partly determined by the conjunction of the phonetically similar 'veuf' and the idea of castration; but the text also reminds us several times that Charles is 'naïf', and particularly where women are concerned: 'Ce pauvre Charles: avec les femmes il était d'une naïveté ...' (76).[80] 'Knife' thus condenses into one bilingual signifier the proposition that naïvety, i.e. inability to cope with women, leads to widowhood and castration; and is itself repressed, but recoverable from the effects — the displacement along the chain of signifiers — that its repression has on the organization of the overt discourse of the text.

Language itself can thus be seen as a kind of curtain, as Simon's quotation of Lacan's curtain as metaphor for the operations of meaning — 'qui pour se découvrir doit se dévoiler' — suggests. Language does not simply communicate, but serves equally to conceal 'something' — in the case outlined above, a certain content of repressed meaning. And like the visual image of the curtain, language too is eroticized to the extent that it hides imperfectly, *deferring* the revelation of what lies behind it. The word 'libidineux', for instance, evokes in the subject of *La Bataille de Pharsale* 'ce même trouble, ce même émoi un peu honteux, la conscience d'un interdit transgressé' (139), because it simultaneously points to and disguises a fuller, less abstract semantic content ('lit, bite, nœud'), which in turn colours the actual phonic material of the signifier: 'le mot libidineux avec sa consonance un peu rose, un peu molle, plissée pour ainsi dire par la répétition des mêmes syllabes et de sons évocateurs (lit, bite, nœud)' (139);[81] the word itself, 'plissée' like the folds of the curtain, has absorbed the sensual quality of its semi-concealed associations.

The play of language, refusing an immediately given meaning, is the verbal equivalent of the movements of the curtain. It is thus not surprising that foreign words, with their obscurity of meaning, should be particularly strongly invested with sexual energy. Spanish, for instance, possesses a particular kind of eroticism, thought of as being inherent in the language itself: even the extremely banal letters from the mother's girl-friend in *Histoire* are 'parfumées de la lourde sensualité qui semble émaner de cette langue des noms des mots eux-mêmes' (35).[82] The association of Spanish with the mother no doubt accounts for some of the desire invested in it, but even where there is no such link foreign languages are still fetishized because of their partial impenetrability; the obscene Latin words that the boy in *Histoire* pursues through the pages of the dictionary are a 'secret capital' (117) whose power to excite him seems to derive less from their being obscene than from their being foreign, and therefore mysterious: 'L'excitation, l'espèce de fièvre, les mots latins, crus, violents que leur aspect dépaysant, exotique pour ainsi dire, leur sens incertain, chargeaient d'un pouvoir ambigu, multiple' (ibid.).[83]

The configuration of opacity and transparency, visible and invisible, offered by the imperfectly understood Latin phrases is, moreover, *reduplicated* in the subject-matter of the two fragments that the boy is shown to be reading (pp. 119 and 124). They are given verbatim in the text, as though to emphasize that it is their actual texture and opacity that is desired; initially, they form an area of concealment, or resistance to interpretation. But in a second phase this is then overcome, and their meaning is revealed, albeit incompletely and unclearly; and *what* it reveals – what it means – is, in the first case, the phallus initially hidden under 'le pan de mon vêtement' and then 'unveiled'; and in the second, a woman 'toute nue sous sa chevelure':

læta proximat rosa serta renudata crinibusque dissolutis accourant couronnée de roses joyeuse toute nue sous sa chevelure dénouée crinière toison que je

136

pouvais sentir dans ma main crins à la fois soyeux et rêches m'échappant
ondulant ondoyant.   (124)[84]

Here the erotic focus is not the naked body as such but the hair which,
in the significantly expanded translation of 'crinibusque dissolutis',
becomes the moving curtain semi-covering her nakedness, like a fetish.
Thus the movement of the text, *both* in its signifier and its signified,
hovers between revelation and concealment. The two features of
language which emerge most strongly and most indissolubly here are
its erotic power and its teasing resistance to interpretation; and the signified — the woman's hair, both beautiful and elusive ('m'échappant')
— coincides with, and comes to act almost as a metaphor for, the
action of the signifier.

The curtain partially hides the woman, and in so doing becomes
a fetish; and, to the extent that it allows meaning to be partially
hidden, language is similarly fetishized, becoming an object of desire
in its own right. The parallel between language and curtain, however,
does not stop there. I have already argued that on one level the
function of the curtain is to cover up the fact that there is *nothing*
behind it: and language can do this too. At this point the notion of
a hidden meaning, meaning as a concealed but definite presence, gives
way to the idea that what lies behind the surface activity of language
is simply an absence of meaning. There are, in other words, certain
points in the texts at which the very idea that language is meaningful
is seen to be an illusion. One important example of this occurs towards
the end of *La Route des Flandres* when Georges finally realizes that
his search for the truth about Corinne and De Reixach — also a search
for his own identity — is doomed to failure; the extract already cited
in this context (p. 127) in fact begins as follows:

qu'avais-je cherché en elle espéré poursuivi jusque sur son corps dans son
corps des mots des sons aussi fou que lui avec ses illusoires feuilles de papier
noircies de pattes de mouche des paroles que prononçaient nos lèvres pour
nous abuser nous-mêmes vivre une vie de sons sans plus de réalité sans plus
de consistance que ce rideau sur lequel nous croyions voir le paon brodé
remuer ...   (274–5)[85]

All he has found are words, which are not 'real', and whose meaningless emptiness is the basis for comparing them with, precisely,
the curtain. From being a major *example* of the relation between
language and referent, the schema of curtain and woman now
assumes the status of a reflexive *image* of that relation: the curtain
is language and the woman's body is, by implication, the referent
'pursued' behind language.[86] What is especially striking here is that

the moment at which the equation becomes most explicit is the negative one: that is, language is figured as curtain just at the moment at which the curtain is shown to have nothing behind it − at which the referent of language dramatically disappears. It also brings about a final identification between Georges and his father, whom he had previously despised, seeing him as endlessly producing meaningless words as a kind of smokescreen to conceal the futility of his life − now he realizes that he is himself 'aussi fou que lui', and that this is perhaps a general condition: we all live with the illusion that language is possessed of 'réalité' and 'consistance'. Whereas 'really' the *relation* in which meaning should consist, the relation between signifier and signified, is not there because the signified has no independent existence; language is reduced to the single dimension of the signifier, as the equation 'des mots des sons' implies.

Another curtain of meaningless sound appears in *Triptyque*, in the noise of the crickets − behind which there is not a meaningful and qualitatively distinct reality, but merely a further curtain of sound: 'l'un d'eux, puis un autre, s'interrompt brusquement, laissant place alors (*comme un rideau ouvrant sur un autre rideau*) à la même stridulation' (207, my italics). Beneath one layer of signifiers there is just another layer, so that the sounds themselves are as it were neutralized into silence, cancelling each other out as the 'chant strident ... tisse comme une seconde nappe de silence' (206).[87] There is no accumulation of depth and no consistency; the layers never build up into anything; language is just a series of surfaces that shift across one another. Thus although this idea of an infinite regression is close to the characterization of Simon's texts given by Dällenbach and cited earlier here − 'reconnaissance implicite ... qu'on n'en a jamais fini avec [le sens]' − there is in fact a crucial difference. Dällenbach's 'régime sémantique de l'énigme' implies a depth of meaning (he also talks about *La Route des Flandres*'s 'obsession du sens et de la profondeur', 305)[88] which is the exact opposite of the conception of language implied by the curtain with nothing behind it − that is, language defined as pure *surface*. In these terms, it has no room for mystery, no depth within which an enigma could be contained. In fact it cannot contain anything − in *La Bataille de Pharsale*, words are merely empty bubbles, 'venant crever à la surface comme des bulles vides comme des bulles et rien d'autre ...' − and language can function only as long as one does not try to penetrate it in depth: 'Clair pour qui ne cherche pas à l'approfondir' (91).[89] Depth, weight and fullness are all excluded here; and this effects a far more radical subversion of traditional realism than the one outlined by Dällenbach:

it presents language as incapable of carrying any dimension of reference to a reality outside it. The enigmatic, secretive aspects of the novels, despite their lacunæ and their undoubted difference from conventional realism, ultimately present less of a threat to the status of representation than do the passages quoted here, in which a kind of aporia is reached.

Referring to two of these passages – from *La Route des Flandres* and *La Bataille de Pharsale* – Stephen Heath comments: 'that attempt to *see behind*, to arrest the movement of signification, blinds itself to the reality without depth of the movement of language as system' (1972: 160, author's italics), and goes on to extend this to the whole of Simon's work: 'Simon defines the reality or, better, the realism of his work exactly in the presentation of a text and not in an "elsewhere" or a "behind"' (160). To generalize in this way makes Simon's texts seem more homogeneous than they really are; but the stress on lack of depth seems to me more relevant than Dällenbach's formulation. Heath does not, however, discuss the question of the *efficacy* of the illusion: the main point of what Georges says in the passage quoted above, for instance, is that we normally fool ourselves into living as though words did have a substantive meaning. The ambiguous logic of the curtain metaphor is that even though there really is nothing behind it, the fact that the curtain *conceals* the absence means that it creates an illusion of depth and presence – which is sometimes exposed and destroyed, but at other times actually 'works', in the sense that the surface produces an effect of depth. As Jean-Louis Baudry puts it in a critique of realist conceptions of the text, it is

comme si, en apparaissant autre qu'elle n'est, il y avait dans toute surface une sorte de pli, un miroitement d'ombre qui laisse croire à un jeu de la profondeur, alors qu'il n'est que le symptôme d'un repliement de la surface sur elle-même ... On assiste donc à un renversement du modèle imaginaire de la connaissance. Alors que pour toute la pensée métaphysique la surface cache la profondeur, la profondeur ne sera plus qu'un effet d'illusion de la surface qui interdit de la considérer pour elle-même.   (1968: 135)[90]

In a similar way, it is the property of the curtain – of language as surface – to make its own 'folds' appear as something at once more substantial and more mysterious.

This conception of language is thematized at various places in all the novels. But it is only in *Les Corps conducteurs*, *Triptyque* and *Leçon de choses* that it is consistently put into practice. In *Les Corps conducteurs*, for instance, even that most potent producer of illusion, the net curtain with the peacock, is taken up again to reappear devoid of all the fascination which surrounds it in *La Route des Flandres*, functioning in this transformed context solely as a *textual* element and, specifically, as an intertextual link with other points in the corpus of Simon's novels:

A l'intérieur de la vitrine, contre la glace, leurs pans retombant derrière les photographies, deux rideaux de dentelle brodés de guirlandes de feuilles entourant un oiseau s'écartent en deux courbes symétriques. Soit saleté, soit qu'ils aient été teintes, ou encore jaunies par le soleil, ils sont d'une couleur pisseuse. Suivant le quadrillage des mailles du filet, les dessins ont des contours en escaliers. Bien qu'il soit fragmenté et télescopé par les plis, on peut reconnaître dans l'oiseau un paon à la longue queue tombante. (26)[91]

The text here is recycling a number of key images from Simon's past work – the curtain itself, but also photographs, the 'guirlandes de feuilles' from *Histoire*, and an allusion to the various attributes of Orion in 'soleil' and 'pisseuse' – and inserting them into a different kind of textual system which defuses them as representational images. Notably, the curtain is no longer hiding anything because it is *behind* the display of photographs. Or rather, what it is hiding is only parts of *itself*, 'fragmenté et télescopé par les plis': and here we find exactly Baudry's 'sorte de pli, un miroitement d'ombre qui laisse croire à un jeu de la profondeur' – except that now the mechanism is demystified, as it is made clear that the whole play of concealment takes place on the surface, and is nothing more than language doubling back on itself. The fact that the peacock is 'fragmenté' can also be read as an indication that it has lost the impact peculiar to the image and the imaginary, whose wholeness and immediacy is here deconstructed by the work of the text.

Within the whole corpus of novels, one can therefore distinguish two different positions occupied by language in relation, not merely to representation in a positive sense, but more specifically here to the status of the unsaid. Language either covers up – and thereby simultaneously betrays the presence of – a hidden meaning, that is, a potentially definable semantic content which is unknown or has been censored; or, alternatively, it is the screen which simultaneously conceals and reveals a fundamental absence of meaning. In this second case, what is not said is no longer something specific: it is the all-pervading 'secret qu'est la certitude de l'absence de tout secret'. Thus we find repeated on a smaller scale, within the area of the unsaid, a version of the same fluctuation in relation to representation as is discernible in the co-existence of visual and textual elements in Simon's work. The figuration of the unseen participates in the same kind of fluctuation, running parallel to and in a sense dramatizing the movement between 'knowing' and not knowing, saying and not saying – the ambiguities of disavowal – and the concomitant paradoxical production of something visible out of the invisible, of desire out of what is initially set up as an obstacle to desire. At the same time, the lacunæ caused by the unseen can generate a disturbance in the language of the text which itself disrupts the representation at certain points. In other words, what is most striking in the functioning of the unsaid and the unseen is the number of different versions of both which occur, the range of different ways in which they act on the representational dimension of the novels, and the intricacy and flexibility with which they echo and cut across each other.

6

THE INVISIBILITY OF HISTORY

Simon's writing is centrally concerned with history,[1] and presents a view of it that is totally pessimistic. In the novels a wide range of historical events is represented, from the Spanish Civil War and the Second World War to the French Revolution, the battles of ancient Greece and Rome, and colonialism in Latin America; underlying this variety, however, they have in common the fact that they are always violent, and always end − in so far as they can be said to have any definable outcome at all − in renewed oppression. This, however, is shown as almost accidental: the overriding impression given by the depiction of 'history' in all the novels is one of incomprehensible confusion.

To describe the relationship between real historical events and texts like this presupposes that the texts in question are representational, and this is only partially true; realist depiction of 'historical' scenes − scenes of war, for instance − occurs in the same intermittent and fragile fashion as do other elements of representation in Simon's novels. As an additional complication, moreover, the reader is also confronted with fairly frequent abstract statements about history in general: statements that on one level, therefore, seem to require us to engage with Simon's quasi-theoretical views on history. But, equally, the overall functioning of the texts is obviously not that of theory or historiography; in fact, the various possible and problematic relations between history and writing are explicitly questioned in them (as will be discussed at the end of this chapter). There are thus two issues involved. In the first place, this is one of the thematic areas in which the reader is aware of a substantive view being expressed by the author; but its expression, however vehement it becomes at times, is fragmentary and, in places, contradictory: it is a question of piecing together its component elements and elucidating the assumptions behind it. Secondly, it needs to be relocated within the double parameters of fiction and textuality that operate throughout Simon's writing, and which here have the effect of transforming the *concept* of history into a rhetorical *figure*.

Because there is no common measure between the events of history and the scale of personal experience – the narrator of *Histoire*, for instance, cannot see any connection between the Spanish Civil War as a historical entity and his own participation in it – the historical process appears random and chaotic, lacking any kind of logic. Simon sometimes seems to believe that this is all it really is; sometimes, on the other hand, he talks as though there is an *order* to history, but one which is beyond the reach of our understanding. The first position – that there is nothing over and above the manifest chaos of events – predominates in *Histoire*; whereas *La Route des Flandres*, *Le Palace* and especially *Les Géorgiques* contain more evidence of the second, i.e. of a mysterious force ('l'impitoyable, arrogante et mystérieuse Histoire', *Le Palace*: 18)[2] destroying everything in its path ('cette olympienne et froide progression, ce lent glacier en marche depuis le commencement des temps, broyant, écrasant tout', *La Route des Flandres*: 279),[3] and operating with 'facetious perversity' (*Les Géorgiques*: 340) – with a blind, and usually cruel,[4] irony: 'et, comme toujours, agissant (l'Histoire) avec sa terrifiante démesure, son incrédible et pesant humour' (ibid.).[5] (The rhetorical status of history, as a kind of abstract personification, is evident here.)

But any such order or logic is by definition inaccessible to us; the strange periods of inertia in the midst of war, for instance, are determined by 'Des lois peut-être (un ordre ou plutôt une ordonnance impossible à détecter mais d'une nature aussi imprescriptible, aussi mathématique que celles qui président aux spirales des coquillages ...)' (*Les Géorgiques*: 131).[6] We can never know whether the order exists or not: but then it would not make much difference if we did, since it is in any case both all-powerful and entirely impersonal – hence the ironic uncertainty with which the irony of History is itself treated: 'Et il était en train de s'y employer quand l'Histoire (ou le destin – ou quoi d'autre?: l'interne logique de la matière? ses implacables mécanismes?) en décida autrement' (*Les Géorgiques*: 352)[7] and the reduction of the two alternative hypotheses about it to the succinctly indifferent formula: 'l'Histoire, la futilité, la fatalité' (400).[8]

It follows that man does not make history: he *undergoes* it: or, as Pierre says in *L'Herbe*, 'endurer l'Histoire (pas s'y résigner: l'endurer), c'est la faire' (36)[9] – passive endurance is the only valid attitude. Any kind of humanist or rationalist conception of history is mere delusion; and Simon is sarcastic about man's arrogant belief that he can intervene in the historical process – or indeed the comforting belief that history is intelligible, because rational and hence susceptible of moral justification, or that progress is possible. Perhaps the strongest statement of his position comes in the last words of *La Route des Flandres*, which refute, bitterly and relentlessly, all of these various illusions: 'le monde arrêté figé s'effritant se dépiautant s'écroulant peu à peu par morceaux comme une bâtisse abandonnée, inutilisable, livrée à l'incohérent, nonchalant, impersonnel et destructeur travail du temps'.[10]

Faced with such a nihilistic attitude, critics, especially those on the left, have reacted uneasily. As Deguy says, 'On comprend que la position politique de Claude Simon, position *paralysée* plus répandue qu'on ne pourrait croire, a des chances d'être inconfortable' (1962: 1028, author's italics).[11] There is a tendency to minimize his cynicism or to explain it away; thus Jacques Leenhardt, for instance, argues (1975, especially 127–9) that Simon's views are directly determined by his experiences in Spain; the traumatic 'auto-assassination' of the left is at the root of Simon's conception of history as 'non-transcendance', which is thus nothing more than the automatic result of a very particular historical conjuncture. While there is little doubt that the events of 1936 were traumatic for Simon, to take this as a total explanation is a kind of short-circuiting of the intratextual configurations of his work – of, that is, the incidence of *other* discursive or thematic factors on the 'theme' of history. For instance, there is an obvious logical connection between history and memory: views of history, as official versions of collective memory, suffer from all the problems which Simon associates with individual memory – its unreliability, its 'foisonnant et rigoureux désordre' (*Histoire*: 296)[12] and so on – but in a more acute form because they are no longer located within what is at least nominally a single consciousness. Hence the double contrast in *Le Palace*: between the present and the past of personal memory, but also between personal memory and the official 'historical' explanations of the past.

An equally determining, if less obvious, link can also be traced between his conception of history on the one hand and, on the other, the pervasive primacy of the visual in his work. The historical process as such cannot literally be *seen*, and Simon's choice of epigraph for *L'Herbe* makes precisely this point: 'Personne ne fait l'Histoire, on ne la voit pas, pas plus qu'on ne voit l'herbe pousser.'[13] He also stresses throughout his novels how the individual – the narrator in *Histoire*, for instance, participating in the Spanish Civil War – can

144

perceive only small fragments of history, and cannot relate them to any coherent whole. This emphasis is to some extent reinforced by the generic constraints of realist fiction, with its inbuilt privileging of individual experience, but Simon takes it to extreme lengths: for him, anything which is not accessible to the senses is hardly accessible at all.

As such it becomes in a way simply unreal for the subject; at the same time, however, it can also be theorized as corresponding to the Lacanian order of, precisely, the *real* as that which the subject always 'misses': 'du réel comme rencontre − la rencontre en tant qu'elle peut être manquée, qu'essentiellement elle est la rencontre manquée' (1973: 54).[14] That is, in this definition the real is what remains inaccessible, resists meaning, and exists in opposition to both the symbolic and the imaginary (and is obviously quite different, therefore, from the 'real' of realist fiction, which in Lacanian terms equates with the imaginary).

History is meaningless *because it is invisible.* It is the opposite of the image, and of the *presence* of the visible to consciousness; it is absence, death (the dominant image in *Le Palace* is that of a hidden corpse, rotting away out of sight); but more than anything else it is the negativity that escapes consciousness, evacuates meaning and constantly seeps away from us: hence, in the same novel, the metaphor of the body that should have given birth to the revolution but is instead 'se vidant dans une infime, incessante et vaine hémorragie ... une invisible fissure au centre même de son corps' (230) − or again, the mysterious 'mince et sournois chuintement de fuite, cette espèce d'invisible et permanente hémorragie' (151).[15] The fight against Franco, and by extension political struggle in general, is defined as hæmorrhage, as loss: the 'fuite' of history from vision and hence consciousness.

Thus, also, the student's failure to make sense of history is equated with the idea that there is something that he has missed *seeing*:

Sans doute y avait-il quelque chose qu'il n'avait pas su voir, qui lui avait échappé, et peut-être alors pourrait-il s'introduire, se loger, resquiller lui aussi une place dans cette dérivée tangentielle, comestible et optimiste de la métaphysique baptisée carpe ou Histoire,   (134)[16]

and the comparison he goes on to make, between the humanist conception of history and a first-class train compartment from whose windows the comfortably installed passengers can *look out* at the world ('regardant par la fenêtre avec une expression de charitable dégoût', 135), reinforces the underlying assumption here which, as the sarcastic tone ('Il devait bien y avoir un truc')[17] implies, is that history, at least for him, *not* visible.

It is, moreover, invisible in a very different sense from the invisibility constructed by the figure of the woman behind the curtain – and its variations – discussed in the previous chapter. There the emphasis was on the construction, precisely, and the manipulation of a partial, conditional and very ambiguous concealment; and much attention was given to the means of concealment – the curtain itself. Here, in contrast, there is nothing very obvious behind which history could be said to be hiding; indeed the images in question are less those of concealment (apart from the corpse in *Le Palace*) than of a more fundamental loss and absence. The invisibility of history, in other words, is absolute and unconditional; there can be no *play* involved in it, and it is not implicated in the fetishistic manœuvering of desire that the curtain is. The connection between desire and vision in the form of concealment – revelation is simply broken; the unconditional invisibility of history allows for no investment of desire but is either unpleasurable or simply meaningless.

That history should be so totally invisible is hardly surprising when one remembers that in Simon's writing the central figure of 'Achille immobile à grands pas' serves to define all perceptual reality as essentially discontinuous: if even simple physical movement escapes perception, there is surely no chance at all that the large-scale events and the causal connections between them that constitute 'History' will be perceptible. Characteristically, we find 'les choses se passant, comme dans ces mouvements de terrains lentement et sournoisement minés, par de brusques à-coups' (*L'Herbe*: 68); Pierre and Sabine have aged 'par une suite de soudaines mutations' (69).[18] And it is because of this impossibility of representing continuous change, that when History is brought, or rather *forced* into vision, it can only be a parody of itself: History as spectacle has the jerky unreality and the inherent ridiculousness of a speeded-up film:[19] 'l'Histoire ... tournant à la parodie, au bouffon: un de ces films projetés à l'accéléré, avec ses foules, ses personnages ataxiques, aux gestes incohérents, inachevés – ou achevés trop tôt' (*Les Géorgiques*: 385).[20]

What is at issue here is the relation between history and the individual consciousness;[21] this is of course an extremely complex area, and one that has been the subject of much debate. For the purposes of the present discussion, however, the general theoretical arguments are relevant only in so far as they help to clarify the much narrower question of exactly what Simon thinks history is, and is not: while it appears in the texts simply as 'l'Histoire', the object of his attacks is actually (and inevitably) a certain *kind* of theorization of history.

His position is in fact usually interpreted as a rejection of Marxism. It undoubtedly is that: in the representation of the Spanish Civil War in both *Le Palace* and *Les Géorgiques*, but also the Latin American writers' conference in *Les Corps conducteurs*, and the character of Lambert in *Histoire*. Moreover, in the context of twentieth-century political debate Marxism can certainly be seen as his most important and relevant target. But it is important to note that at the same time, alongside Marxism–Leninism, he is *also* attacking a significantly different conception of history: namely, the belief in progress, the social perfectibility of mankind and 'la déesse Raison la Vertu' (*La Route des Flandres*: 312)[22] that stems from eighteenth-century rationalism. References to the Enlightenment are particularly prominent in *La Route des Flandres*,[23] and their main focus is the question of history. Their presentation is rather confused; Simon does not, for instance, make any clear distinction between Rousseau, who is the figure he mentions most often, and the *philosophes*; and so he tends to give the impression that in attacking notions of universal reason and of history as progress, he is holding Rousseau responsible for them. Pierre's last conversation with Georges before the latter leaves for the front, for instance, is essentially a summary of some of Rousseau's ideas, presented as above all a rational explanation of historical events, of war and trade as successive phases but functional equivalents, and both of them as 'la conséquence de l'ancestrale terreur de la faim et la mort' (35).[24] There are also one or two equally dismissive allusions to the modern liberalism which traces its descendance from the values of the Enlightenment, but in the process degenerates from philosophy into journalism – from Rousseau to 'l'honorable Manchester Guar ...' (*Le Palace*: 17).

In fact when Simon criticizes the actual ideological content of humanist conceptions of history, the object of the attack is almost always liberal rationalism rather than Marxism. What he rejects, in other words, is the belief in civilization and the harmonious progress of mankind towards reason and virtue, the belief that violence is not – as he thinks it is – permanent and ineradicable. In contrast, his opposition to Marxism seems to centre less on its theoretical tenets and more on its practical consequences, as these had been shown in Spain, for instance; thus even when he describes the actual Marxist texts the emphasis is on the contrast between 'leur profusion d'interminables et patientes démonstrations, leur aspect de manuels à l'usage des écoles du soir' (*Les Géorgiques*: 319)[25] and the violence that their ideas generate when put into practice.

Nevertheless, Marxism and Enlightenment thought have in common the simple fact that both are *theoretical systems*: and this for Simon is the most important thing about them. The parallels which structure *Les Géorgiques*, for instance, place both theories in the same historical relation to a revolution: as Rousseau is to France in 1789, so Marx and Lenin are to Spain in 1936. They are treated as more or less equivalent in that both are first and foremost set *against* personal experience. Any differences between them are subsumed in this overriding opposition between abstract theory (of any kind) versus the sense impressions of the individual. Moreover, the dominant sense is always sight: it is a question of what has been *seen* as against what has been *read*. This contrast comes across with equal force in the case of both Marxism and the Enlightenment; on the one hand O in *Les Géorgiques* finds that his first-hand experience of events conflicts with what he has learnt from reading Marx ('l'autre Bible dont ... son adolescence avait été nourrie', 283),[26] and in order to go on believing Marx he has to *stop seeing* ('ces choses qu'il avait décidé une fois pour toutes de ne plus voir', 336)[27] – and in exactly the same way, the eighteenth-century ancestor's disillusionment with Rousseau – 'une morale larmoyante et suisse dont il n'aurait jamais pu avoir connaissance si sa fortune, son rang, ne lui en avait donné les moyens, c'est-à-dire le loisir et le pouvoir de *lire*' (*La Route des Flandres*: 194, my italics) – is the result of what he has himself seen in battle, 'de sorte qu'à présent il ne lui restait plus qu'à *regarder ou plutôt éviter de regarder* ... se débander de tous côtés cette racaille ...' (ibid., my italics).[28] Under the pressure of what he has seen, the Enlightenment theories – 'ce que (... l'idyllique et larmoyant règne de la Raison et de la Vertu) les lectures lui avaient fait entrevoir' (202) – are emptied of meaning, becoming merely 'quelque chose en quoi il avait cru et à quoi maintenant il ne *voyait* même plus de sens' (ibid., my italics)[29] – and the idiom in this context takes on an almost literal force: you cannot *see* any meaning in explanations of history.

The underlying assumption here is that we can only make sense of that which we have personally experienced. Intelligibility as the end-product of a process of abstract reasoning is, for Simon, impossible; he does not of course assume that what he perceives is necessarily objectively real – this is made clear by the constant searching and questioning of the evidence of his senses and his memory – or, conversely, that what is not perceptible cannot exist objectively: it is, however, definitively out of reach; even if there is a 'mysterious' invisible historical order (and he is never sure whether there is or not), it does not exist for the subject in any meaningful sense. Perceptual reality, in other words, is flawed: but it is all that we have got. The subject's relation to reality is exclusively defined in terms of perception; indeed Simon sometimes writes as though 'invisible' *equals* 'unreal': what cannot be seen is 'privée de réalité, comme la fumée quand on fume dans le noir, qu'on ne peut pas la voir, et qu'alors quelque chose de brûlant seulement ... échappe ensuite par la bouche, le nez, sans véritable existence' (*Histoire*: 390).[30]

There is therefore a sense in which Simon's attacks on the false transparency of 'theorized' history conceal a *demand* that history be immediately present to consciousness, because the only alternative is a history constructed solely as hæmorrhage and lack. There is no possibility, in this view which manages in a strange way to be both uncomfortably cynical and uncomfortably naïve, of taking account of any structures which underpin or go beyond individual consciousness. An intelligible conception of history must either derive directly from perception, or remain a fallacious abstraction.[31]

This is the basis for his rejection of Marxist, Rousseauesque and rationalist theories of history; and, despite his own tendency to treat them as equivalent, there are in fact significant differences as regards the force of his critique, firstly between Rousseau and the *philosophes*, and secondly between both of these and Marxism. The reliance of the *philosophes* on general explanatory models of different aspects of reality in effect pre-empts the whole issue of the position of the individual consciousness; perception itself is seen as a purely mechanical process of transcription of images of objects onto the brain; and, more abstractly, the relation between thought, action and circumstances is also entirely mechanical. Thus the *problem* of the relation between general abstract truths and personal experience is never posed, because it is simply assumed that there is no disjunction between the two. (It is, of course, this exclusion of the individual self from the operations of reason that forms the basis of the criticisms of Enlightenment rationalism made by English writers such as Burke and Coleridge.)[32]

As a result of their foreclosure of the problem, it could be argued that – even if only by omission – history is assumed by the *philosophes* to be directly *present* to consciousness; it is this tendency to conceive of reality as nothing more than immediate *surface*, as a kind of transparent, graspable – in psychoanalytic terms, imaginary – rationality, that Adorno and Horkheimer, for instance, criticize in Enlightenment thought.[33] As such, it is only a short step to a conception of the objects of theoretical knowledge, including history, as being at least metaphorically 'visible' – and the visual metaphor is in fact deeply embedded in the *philosophes*' own discourse, to the extent of giving the movement its very name: the terms 'Enlightenment' and 'Lumières', and the frequent use of 'lumières' and 'raison' as interchangeable, surely presuppose the possibility of *seeing* the truth.

Rousseau himself commonly substitutes 'lumières' for 'raison', and his writing is equally full of visual metaphors for the act of understanding. But he differs from the *philosophes* in that he does recognize a disjunction between individual experience and generalizable truths,[34] and in that throughout his work he places much greater emphasis on the individual. As an alternative to the functioning of universal reason, he puts forward, in the *Confessions* for instance, the notion of an immediate and intuitive apprehension of the truths of nature. This, of course, corresponds to Simon's ideal of a directly, as it were *perfectly* perceptible reality; but the almost mystical formulation of it that Rousseau gives makes it impossible for him to believe in it.

In their very different ways, therefore, both Rousseau and the *philosophes* can be said to hold positions which contain, however implicitly or negatively, the assumption that objects of theoretical knowledge are perceptible, in the sense of being immediately present to consciousness. More explicitly, they both lack any explanation of why the converse might be the case – any way, that is, of accounting for the individual's *inability* to see history happening around him, for instance. So it is perhaps not unreasonable to argue that their metaphor of visibility is an *operational* metaphor, in that it underpins a particular model of the process of understanding. To this extent, they embody something close to Simon's own dream of a visible history, a 'scintillante et exaltante vision' – a history, in other words, which could become an object of desire. In rejecting this position he is thus refusing a view which he wishes were true, but knows is not: and this seems to make his rejection of it all the more vehemently sarcastic: 'Nous y voilà: l'Histoire ... Comme l'Immaculée Conception: scintillante et exaltante vision traditionnellement réservée aux cœurs simples et aux esprits forts, bonne conscience du dénonciateur et du philosophe' (*La Route des Flandres*: 187)[35] – and all the more cogent: the *philosophes* and Rousseau (alluded to above in 'cœur simple' and 'dénonciateur')[36] have no real answer to his critique of them.

Marx's theory of history, on the other hand, nowhere assumes that its functioning is present to consciousness; in fact the Marxist theory of ideology provides an explanation of precisely the disjunction between the two – and it is on this point that its relation to Simon's position differs most sharply from that of Rousseau and the *philosophes*: the historical process *cannot* be immediately accessible to the ideologically bound world-views of its participants; but it can, in principle, be made intelligible as the result of a process of theoretical work.[37] In this case, then, Simon is rejecting a position which is far more fundamentally alien to his own than are the ideas of the Enlightenment. (And the heterogeneity of the two opposing views involved here in turn gives Marxism a rather greater purchase on Simon's: his belief that history is an entirely impersonal and arbitrary force, for instance, can be situated and accounted for quite unproblematically within Marxist theory as a typical form of petit-bourgeois alienation.)[38]

Simon's attitude to history is so basic to his view of the world in general that it directly or indirectly affects many different areas of his writing. It is, for instance, in the light of the general predominance of spatial (and hence visual) over temporal structure that one can best understand the importance his novels attach to *geography*: an importance, in other words, that is determined contrastively, on the basis of an implicit comparison with history. Unlike history, geographical realities can figure as objects of desire: an obvious example is LSM's passionate attachment to his estate, for instance. Geography is in fact especially evident in *Les Géorgiques*, whose very title refers us etymologically to the *land*; geo-graphy, as 'land-writing', offers a kind of matrix for the production and interpretation of the text, in the sense that what is written is a series of relationships to the land: agricultural, in the case of LSM's letters to Batti about the management of his estate; strategic, in the accounts of the movements of Napoleon's armies and the Second World War cavalry; political, perhaps, in O's travels through Spain. Historical battles appear in LSM's writing above all in terms of strategies based on topography, on the lie of the land. Moreover, the 'visibility' of geography is reinforced by its close connections with another major sub-category of the visible: pictorial representation, albeit in this case of a very schematic kind; the representation of the earth is introduced in the mention of the map and the globe included in the description of the drawing which opens *Les Géorgiques*, and these initiate a series of references to maps of various kinds – notably the plan of his estate which LSM carries everywhere with him as his only tangible link with his own land, and symbol of its status as 'lost object' of desire. History is written, but geography is drawn.

Wars are normally thought of as part of history, and, viewed in this way, each war is different because it happened at a different time. But wars also tend to happen in the same places, as Simon points out in *L'Herbe*, where he refers to 'des lieux de tous temps réservés à cet usage ... ces plaines, ces deux ou trois fleuves dont l'Europe avait pris l'habitude de se servir comme de champs clos, d'égouts naturels (34)[39] – and *La Bataille de Pharsale* similarly exploits the coincidence in, and the confusion generated by, the fact that the plain of Pharsalus was the site not only of the Roman battle but also that of Kynos Képhalai in which the Greeks lost their independence (218). Thus the principal result of this focusing on places, this rearticulation of history onto geography, is to reduce history to mere repetition and to preclude any perception of change:

Mais c'étaient les mêmes chemins, les mêmes mares gelées, les mêmes forêts silencieuses qu'avaient traversé et retraversé les hordes successives de pillards, d'incendiaires et d'assassins, depuis celles venues du fond de l'Asie, et ensuite d'hommes aux barbes rouges habillés de fer ... et plus tard des armées aux pieds simplement enveloppés de chiffons, et après d'autres encore, et toujours les mêmes vallées ... simplement parce que c'était le meilleur passage qui menait de l'Est à l'Ouest. (*Les Géorgiques*: 136)[40]

Seen in this perspective, human agency, too, is reduced to a blind undifferentiated force; the fact that the people involved were 'autres' (or at least 'successives' which hovers somewhere in between identity and difference) is overshadowed by the emphasis on the *same* roads, the *same* valleys, and so on. Geography, in other words, serves to reinforce Simon's attack on the humanist conception of history.

In *Les Géorgiques*, people are seen primarily in terms of their relationship to the land: sometimes rooted in it, like Batti who never moves away from the chateau, but more often wandering or fleeing, caught up in the perpetual 'errance' across the face of the earth that figures more or less prominently in all Simon's novels.[41] At once aimless and forced, 'errance' represents a kind of basic human condition; it is thus fittingly exemplified in the first place by the gipsies, 'venus tout droit du fond de l'Asie, des âges, sortis tels quels des entrailles du monde' (*Les Géorgiques*: 308) and subject to 'les lois immémoriales de l'errance' (213).[42] But the nomadic existence of soldiers is also constantly emphasized, both here and in *La Route des Flandres*; as is, in the latter novel, that of refugees from war: 'ces civils qui s'obstinaient de façon incompréhensible à errer traînant une valise crevée ou poussant devant eux de ces voiturettes d'enfant chargées de vagues bagages' (17).[43]

Religion, too, contributes to 'l'errance', generating 'ces multitudes terribles et migratrices tourbillonnant sans fin à la surface de la terre errant de l'Orient à l'Occident à travers le temps et l'espace se traînant de lieux saints en lieux saints' (*Histoire*: 245)[44] − and this example makes particularly clear the extent to which 'errance', in its endless processes of displacement, is a form of desire for the land, here valorized as sacred but at the same time always lacking, always decentred: no one holy place is sufficient to arrest the movement of desire. It is as though the most primitive function that human communities perform is to materialize the spatial dimensions of the earth by the trajectories that they are continually inscribing on it.

Civilized individuals, however, are equally part of the phenomenon; returning to *Les Géorgiques*, we find both O and LSM's brother forced into flight, in both cases for political (i.e. 'historical') reasons. The effect of flight, however, is to turn them into animals (O is 'chassé comme une bête', 361, and the brother appears to Batti as 'la bête traquée', 413),[45] to return them to the most primitive state of humanity − comparable, perhaps, to the 'errance à trois dimensions, comme forcés à voler sans but' of the insects in *L'Herbe*: 'comme si quelque tourment les forçait ainsi à errer sur place' (22).[46] While LSM himself is not actually fleeing, he nevertheless spends his life being posted from one end of Europe to the other; he becomes in fact so closely identified with ceaseless travelling that the narrator imagines his ghost still pursuing 'cette interminable errance ... d'un coin à l'autre de cette Europe qu'il avait défiée, parcourue et reparcourue en tout sens dans un va-et-vient sans cesse recommencé qui le ramenait sans cesse aux mêmes lieux' (243−4).[47]

Movement which never achieves anything and has no definitive goal, 'errance' undercuts the rationalist conception of history as progress. Occasionally, in fact, the text makes a specific causal connection between 'errance' and the *ir*rational − i.e. invisible, ungraspable − nature of historical reality: at the end of *Le Palace* the image of history concretized as the invisible, unnameable, monstrous corpse is *what makes* the soldiers wander aimlessly round the city, and what makes them regress to the natural, a-historical state of animals − in this case, vultures:

peut-être tournaient-ils en rond dans la ville à la recherche de l'introuvable ennemi, de cette chose qui n'avait pas de nom, pas de visage, pas d'apparence, condamnés à errer sans fin comme ce juif de la légende qui ne pouvait trouver le repos, semblables à ces bancs d'oiseaux inquiets, plaintifs et sauvages qu'on voit voleter interminablement en gémissant au-dessus de quelque chose d'invisible, quelque charogne, quelque bête agonisante, quelque monstre.

(224−5)[48]

This kind of privileging of a spatial, rather than a temporal apprehension of reality is a further manifestation of Simon's implicit demand for *presence*, and as such can perhaps be seen as a precondition for a particular textual strategy observable in some of the novels. This institutes a *figurative* spatialization of history itself — almost as though, in transferring it onto a spatial plane, it were attempting to evade the conceptual impasse of history as failed presence, attempting to produce a figure of history which would be in a sense visible. But, as will be seen, the strategy is full of contradictions.

In *L'Herbe*, for instance, Marie's experiences during the war are used by Pierre as an illustration of the 'reality' of history as opposed to the 'official' rationalist view of it; and the contrast is expressed in an essentially spatial metaphor. Marie, who according to this view should be *outside* the defined, containable area of History — like the other non-combatants, 'placés, pensait-on, de droite et de fait, hors de ce qu'on nous avait appris ... à considérer comme le cheptel vif de l'Histoire' (34) — in reality gets caught up in it; and this teaches us that

l'Histoire n'est pas, comme voudraient le faire croire les manuels scolaires, une série discontinue de dates, de traités et de batailles spectaculaires et cliquetantes (assimilable ... aux autres genres de fléaux aux manifestations sporadiques se produisant à heures, lieux et dates bien définis ...) mais au contraire sans limite, et non seulement dans le temps (ne s'arrêtant, ne ralentissant, ne s'interrompant jamais, permanente, à la facon des séances de cinéma ...) mais aussi dans ses effets. (35)[49]

The main point here is that history is *limitless*, not only in time but also in space; and the question of its visibility is also posed, in a slightly contradictory way: while 'spectacular' battles are rejected as part of the rationalist illusion, the later comparison with cinema does suggest that history is perhaps, after all, a never-ending series of images.

A much larger contradiction, however, arises between the formulation given here and the figurative presentation of history in some of the later novels. Thus the comparison with cinema is replaced in *Le Palace* by the stress on the *invisible* historical factors mentioned earlier in this chapter. But the most important difference is that the metaphor of *demarcation*, seen as misleading in *L'Herbe*, is actually taken over and used by the text itself. Far from being an undifferentiated, all-pervasive force, history takes the form of, precisely, a delimited *space*; it is seen as operating within limits, introducing a conceptual division of reality into historical and non-historical areas.

In the ironically titled *Histoire*, for instance, a photograph of a battle-field in a history textbook seems (in its concentration on the *land*, once again) to mark out a boundary between history and the amorphous wastes of non-history:

> comme si celle-ci (l'Histoire) s'arrêtait, là, comme si la longue suite des chapitres ... la longue suite des images qui les illustraient ... n'avaient été écrites, sculptées, peintes, gravées, qu'en vue de cette seule fin, ce seul aboutissement, cette apothéose: les étendues grisâtres, mornes, informes, sans traces humaines. (*Histoire*: 116)[50]

But it is in *Les Géorgiques* that the demarcation is most obvious; certain people, places, or situations are repeatedly presented as outside history, or even as having been ejected from it. A typical example occurs in the scene where the twentieth-century cavalrymen, working in the intense cold, light a fire in the snow, and are described as 'pro-jetés, comme hors de l'Histoire, ou livrés à quelque chose qui se situait au-delà de toute mesure ... l'état (temps, espace, froid) où devait être le monde à l'époque des cavernes, des mammouths, des bisons' (119).[51] Thus it is now prehistory − or, more generally, non-history − that is limitless, 'beyond all measure', and surrounds a *limited* area of history.

The clearest instance of this image of history as a localized space is in fact a place: Spain. In order to reach Spain, O has to reverse the direction of history and 'remonte à toute vitesse *l'espace* de plusieurs siècles' (319, my italics); Spain is 'oublié par l'histoire' (320), its inhabitants are 'populations restées elles-mêmes à l'état sauvage, primitif' (344);[52] pushed out to the edge of the continent, its *geo-graphical* position on the map ensures that rather than participating in a historical process itself defined here in images of movement in *space* ('glissé', 'expulsé', etc.), it is merely history's dustbin, 'repoussé par la géographie, comme un récipient ... où par l'effet de la pesanteur avait glissé, était venu s'amasser, s'accumuler ce que les autres pays avaient péniblement et peu à peu expulsé au cours des siècles' (320).[53]

If history is a certain area carved out of reality, and if it can be shown that certain elements are situated outside it, and described as eternal, immemorial, unchanging, etc., one might expect other elements to be contained within it. In fact, however, it is much more difficult to find anything unambiguously included in it; while there are numerous prominent references to phenomena located 'hors de l'Histoire', the converse metaphor hardly occurs. Also, even apparently historical realities tend to disintegrate into a kind of empty irony. For instance, the name of the ancestor in *Les Géorgiques*, Lacombe St Michel, and his descendants, has an eminently historical significance since it is 'le nom qui avait fait basculer le scrutin fatal' (171)[54] – the name of the regicide, of the man who voted for the death of Louis XVI. It can further be seen as a vehicle of history in that it links past generations to the present through the male line: the old lady imagines 'les trois orgasmes, les trois éjaculations de semence mâle à travers lesquelles le nom s'était conservé jusqu'à elle' (195).[55] The name would thus appear to guarantee the continuity of lineage and so of at least one aspect of history.

But its historical presence is in fact extremely fragile – on two different levels. Textually, it generates an *absence*: in so far as it is a historical signifier – the name of the regicide – it is subject to a kind of taboo, and never actually given in the text except as initials and in oblique allusions. (And, similarly, the way in which LSM's brother is 'written out' of history is by scrupulously obliterating any occurrence of his name, 420). Secondly, the thematic development of the name demonstrates how, as a vehicle of history, it does not itself survive. The names of dukes and princes which used to be borne by regiments are replaced by simple numbers after the Revolution (371), and this reorganization creates 'a new geography': the victory once again of geography over history. The extinction of the lineage of horses, which functions throughout *Les Géorgiques* as an ironic parallel to the family line, is symbolized by the crossing out of their names (67). More insidiously, in some cases the name does not disappear but is devalued, as its historical credentials are abused by unworthy descendants (148). This perversion of the name jeopardizes the historical validity it is meant to maintain; names cannot in fact unambiguously guarantee the domain of history.

This is particularly evident where the name migrates, as it were, from history to geography: from a noble lineage to a *place*. As a girl, the old lady 'portait encore le nom auquel personne maintenant ne répondait' (144); now it has become 'plus rien donc, par la suite, à partir du jour où elle avait été mariée: un bruit, un simple assemblage de lettres qui sur la carte ou le panneau d'un carrefour n'indiquait maintenant plus que l'emplacement d'un hameau et du château en ruines vendu depuis longtemps' (144).[56] People's names degenerate into place names and are thus lost to the domain of history.

There is however a further stage to this degeneration, reached when 'le nom fameux, le blason, ne figuraient plus, dérisoires, qu'abusivement utilisés sur les étiquettes d'une marque d'apéritif bon marché vendu dans les épiceries' (151).[57] The glorious ancestral family name, in other words, ends up as the brand name of a commercial product, at the service of the act of exchange which is, as will be shown later in this chapter, fundamentally antagonistic to history.

The adventures of the ancestral name, its elliptical function in the text and its displacement from family history to topography and thence to commerce, would thus seem to indicate that history, as an area of figurative space, has at best a highly ambiguous content. Nothing is solidly established as lying within its boundaries. On the one hand, this can be interpreted as confirming the earlier view of history in *L'Herbe*: that is, we are wrong to assume that history can be contained within the fixed boundaries of rationalist categories. The figurative presentation of history as a limited space is basically no different from this, and is therefore equally illusory; and the fact that the space turns out to be empty is a consequence and a sign of its illusory nature.

Its emptiness is also, however, directly relevant to the basic theme of history's invisibility. The strategy of 'spatialization' works to *exclude*, but does not include anything. Thus a textual device which appears on one level to translate history into a visual figure – to 'materialize', as Simon himself would say, a definite area which could be 'seen' as historical reality – ends up paradoxically with nothing in it: history is an empty space. Or, to use an alternative image, it is like an area of shadow lying on the text: only as things emerge from it do they become visible.

Indeed, phenomena that are specifically presented as outside history tend to acquire particularly strong visual associations, as though the a-historical and the visible belong together almost by definition. This is all the more striking in that it produces some unexpected conjunctions, in phenomena that do not appear to fall into either category – that have no obvious visual dimension and that are normally considered to be part of the historical process. One such is the act of *exchange*. Unlike Marx, for whom changing forms of economic exchange are one of the touchstones of historical development, and unlike Rousseau whose noble savage is innocent of any commercial activity, Simon rather surprisingly locates exchange outside history and regards it as simply a constant of human nature, a universal function which has existed unchanged since the beginning of time (thus he imagines the commercial travellers on the plain of Pharsalus deposited there as the result of a natural disaster 'dans des temps très anciens', *La Bataille de Pharsale*: 152),[58] and asserts itself in all circumstances: even life in the prisoner-of-war camps is dominated by the bartering of useless objects (*La Route des Flandres*: 171). The activity of exchange is an end in itself; more than that, it is a basic and *instinctive* form of human behaviour − as basic an instinct, in fact, as sex and violence: he refers to 'actes élémentaires et brutaux comme le meurtre, le troc ou le coït' (*Les Géorgiques*: 173).[59] Through being linked in this way with nature, acquiring all the characteristics of a biological function, commercial exchange automatically becomes a-historical. (It in fact comes very close to the natural, cyclical transmutations of matter, also described as 'exchanges' that figure so prominently in *L'Herbe*: for instance, 'le compliqué et subtil mécanisme d'échanges et de métamorphoses par quoi l'air invisible lui-même se mue par une série de transformations', 212.)[60]

A less explicit example, but one which nevertheless shows how the equation of exchange with non-history structures quite large sections of the text, can be seen in the episode in *Les Géorgiques* of the boy's visit to the cinema (205−12), including an interpolated passage in italics referring to the narrator's later experiences as a prisoner of war. Here the text alternates the theme of exchange with that of people left outside history; it starts with a description of advertisements, representing commercial exchange, 'un quotidien mercantile' (206),[61] and then moves to the audience, which consists largely of the gipsies, described as representatives of humanity in its original, unchanging state; this is then interrupted by the memory of the prisoners hoarding cigarette butts 'parce que deux cigarettes se *négocient* là contre une gamelle de soupe' (209, my italics); they, like the fugitives, are 'semblables maintenant à des bêtes affamées' (209) because for them it is 'comme si l'été, le temps, l'Histoire, pourrissaient eux-mêmes, se décomposaient' (209). Removed from History, they are engaged in *exchanging* their possessions: 'marchandant à mi-voix ... de dérisoires trésors'.[62] Thus the to-and-fro movement of the text weaves together the notion of exchange with whatever lies beyond the limits of history.

Moreover, this same episode also offers evidence of the association between exchange and the *visual* − in a typically imaginary mode: exchange is first presented in the form of cinema advertisements, i.e. visual images on the screen (208). So there is a clear textual connection between exchange, as a form of *non*-history, and visual spectacle: to the invisibility of history (the real) corresponds the visibility of non-history (the imaginary).

The most fully developed form of this connection occurs in *Histoire*. The account of the narrator's visit to the bank contains several descriptions of bank-notes (p. 78, 81, 84, 93–4, 99) – that is, of the currency of commercial exchange – and in each case the notes are treated as, first and foremost, pictorial images. They 'represent' in two distinct ways at once: a certain financial value, but also a certain visual reality. Here exchange is once again conceived of as a process of transmutation (the bank works to 'transmuter, c'est-à-dire leur faire subir cette opération qui consiste à convertir de la matière brute, rugueuse, en quelque chose de ... commode à stocker et à acheter', 80), and this time the final stage of the metamorphosis is a bank-note, that is, a visual image: 'l'opération suivante consistant à transmuter une seconde fois tout ça en papier filigrane *décoré de divinités financières ou mercantiles*' (ibid., my italics).[63] Money is the abstract symbol which comes to replace the real objects whose value it 'represents'; a derealizing process, 'a sort of sublimation' (81), which one can perhaps see as running parallel to that transformation of the real into its image, the 'representability' of the real, which is the principal theme of Deguy's article on *Le Palace*. The long description of the poster on the wall of the bank (93–4), which depicts coins and bank-notes which themselves depict Richelieu and other historical figures, adds a second layer of pictorial representation – it is a picture of a picture – and thus insists further on the link between exchange and the image, while at the same time using the similarity of the images to reiterate the unchanging, a-historical nature of exchange:

comme si le même modèle au masque pensif, impitoyable et désabusé posant pour le même peintre avait revêtu chez un costumier de théâtre leurs défroques successives, réincarnations, *réapparitions sporadiques d'un unique personnage répété à travers les siècles* dans la même attitude tranquille, perfide et lasse devant d'allégoriques fonds de glaives, de trophées, de galions, d'épis et de balances.   (94, my italics)[64]

Here, in other words, the essential characteristic of exchange – its a-historicity – is presented as inseparable from its manifestation as image; and via the example of financial exchange, non-history is implicitly associated with visibility.

An equivalent connection is made, but more indirectly and on a more theoretical level, through the figure of the *mother*. I have already (Chapter 3) commented on the association in Simon's texts between the mother and the visual image, and its relevance to the concept of the imaginary order. Equally, however, references to the mother's womb form the starting point for a thematization of *time* that is essentially non-historical: a desire to return to the womb, perceptible in many of Simon's male characters, which is also a desire to escape from the passage of time. Thus in *Le Sacre du printemps*, Bernard's reaction against 'la lente, l'inexorable notion du temps' (222) is to imagine the cord of the telephone on which he is speaking to Edith as

une sorte de cordon ombilical menant symboliquement à une femme, au sein tiède et noir dont est issue toute vie et après quoi soupire la chair nostalgique et gémissante hantée par le désir, et plus que le désir le besoin, et plus que le besoin la nécessité d'y retourner, d'y mourir à nouveau.   (222)[65]

The evocation of the womb is 'nostalgique', and is furthermore associated with death, as though the state before birth were also a kind of non-life. The same configuration of timelessness, death and the womb is apparent in Montès's thoughts as he sits beside Rose's dead body: 'Comme si, assis là dans *le temps aboli* à côté de Rose *morte* ... il se trouvait ramené à un état en quelque sorte *fœtal*, lovée dans la douloureuse et torturante (dit-on) quiétude d'une vie *intra-utérine*' (*Le Vent*: 186, my italics).[66]

In the much later novel *Les Géorgiques*, we find a peculiar insistence on the distinction between patrilineal kinship and the beginnings of an alternative maternal kinship system: the difference between the 'frère de sang' and the 'frère de lait'. LSM, in other words, is a kind of brother to Batti because both were breast-fed by her mother – she is 'non pas du même sang mais du même lait que lui' (367), and thus 'pour ainsi dire comme un autre frère. C'est-à-dire plus qu'une sœur: non du même sang mais du même lait qu'eux, avec laquelle ils n'avaient fait qu'un' (405);[67] and this is given some recognition by the family who have her taught to read and write with the two boys 'comme une redevance, un dû, un paiement en retour du lait qu'ils avaient sucé' (406).[68] But the main difference, of course, between the alliances based on 'blood' and on 'milk', is that the latter creates only siblings; it is limited to a single generation. In this way too, then, the maternal goes together with 'le temps aboli' and is the opposite of historical time.

The clearest instance, however, of this antagonism between history and the maternal time of the womb occurs with the 'abortion' of the socialist revolution in *Le Palace*. Here the exemplarily historical event of the Civil War is several times portrayed as a fœtus unnaturally torn from the mother's womb; history, seen as the result of man's attempt to take control of events, is revealed to be 'un fœtus à trop grosse tête langé dans du papier imprimé, rien qu'un petit macrocéphale décédé avant terme parce que les docteurs n'étaient pas du même avis et jeté aux égouts dans un linceul de mots' (16).[69]

Non-history, then, has maternal connotations, and is visible and/or pictorial. Constructing history in opposition to this therefore by the same token opposes it, as an instance of the real, to the imaginary. However, the Lacanian real is defined not only by its contrast with the imaginary, but also with the symbolic order; and in Simon's texts this takes the form of a prominent and conflictual juxtaposition of history and *writing*. Thus the above quotation, with its evocation of the fœtus wrapped in newspaper, is in fact opposing the womb to history in the context of writing. But this is not because the two go together in any straightforward way: the effect of their juxtaposition is to highlight the problems inherent in each of them. The attempts of LSM and O in *Les Géorgiques* to write historical accounts, for instance, provide a fictional context in which the whole issue of the problematic relation between historical events and our perception of them is once again raised, but now formulated within the general framework of language. O is ridiculed, for instance, for his naïve belief that the syntactic structures of language mirror and reveal causal structures in historical events (311). Writing history appears as an enterprise whose motivations and end products both have little to do with the accurate representation of events; and the illusion that they do is, further, shown to consist of two parallel and complicit illusions about writing on the one hand and history on the other. That is, the humanist intellectual's optimistic faith in a rational history goes hand in hand with an almost arrogant confidence in the unproblematic nature of writing. This is the case with O, and with 'l'enthousiaste armée des correspondants étrangers de la presse libérale' (16)[70] in *Le Palace*; but above all with Pierre, whose letter to Georges laments the destruction of Enlightenment texts in the bombing of the library at Leipzig in these terms:

l'Histoire dira plus tard ce que l'humanité a perdu l'autre jour en quelques minutes, l'héritage de plusieurs siècles, dans le bombardement de ce qui était la plus précieuse bibliothèque du monde, tout cela est d'une infinie tristesse, ton vieux père.   (*La Route des Flandres*: 223)[71]

As an etymologist – someone who writes about the history of words – Pierre embodies the reciprocal implication of writing and history in a particularly close form. Georges, on the other hand, dismisses both the value of writing and the rationality of history: writing and what is written about are lacking in reality *because* any reality they might have is conferred on them by a human mind which itself does not really exist: 'griffonnages sans autre existence réelle que celle attribuée à eux par un esprit lui non plus sans existence réelle pour représenter des choses imaginées par lui et peut-être aussi dépourvues d'existence' (*La Route des Flandres*: 245).[72]

From a very different angle, the defamiliarization of writing discussed in Chapter 4 also has the effect of bringing it into alignment with history. The presentation of writing as opaque and illegible, as non-signifying, in effect removes it from the domain of the symbolic; therefore, far from providing a means of rescuing history from meaninglessness, writing rejoins history in the same inaccessible area of the real.

The novels (particularly *Histoire*) also contain many derisive references to history textbooks – the 'manuel d'Histoire' which is the most simplistic, reductive and self-confident version of the equation of history and writing. As such, it has a distinctive style that can easily be parodied; thus we find in the opening pages of *Les Géorgiques* long passages of baldly factual discourse written in the 'historic present':

Le 16 ventôse de l'an III il entre au Comité de salut public. De Milan il règle le cérémonial de la visite de l'empereur dans le royaume d'Italie. En pleine Terreur il est élu secrétaire de la Convention et sauve une royaliste qu'il épousera en seconde noces. (22)[73]

On closer inspection, however, these passages turn out to contain equally dead-pan references to 'facts' about LSM that belong to a rather different order of experience: 'Il voit des points noirs', 'C'est un colosse',[74] for instance. But even without these discrepancies, the parody and its object are obvious: the very flatness of the style foregrounds and thus serves to cast doubt on the assumption that neutral, factual discourse is possible. What it caricatures is an ideal of objective historical discourse – ironically, very close to the kind of writing that Benveniste calls, precisely, *histoire*[75] – thereby implying that the ideal is unattainable.

This in turn can be seen as one particular and extreme form of the question of representational writing in general. It remains to determine more explicitly the place of history within this problematic. In the course of this book I have tried to show how Simon's writing is held in the tension of two contrary movements: a basically representational discourse which attempts to translate sense impressions, especially visual ones, into language, and secondly, working against this, an orientation towards the autonomous generative impulses within language itself.

The text outlines a figurative area, designated as historical, which is then revealed to be empty; and this – the invisibility of history – has an effect on both discourses. The distinction made earlier in this chapter between two kinds of invisibility, one relative and the other absolute, is materialized by the two textual structures of the *curtain* hiding the desirable woman and the *empty space* of history. The curtain has been shown to be an image also of linguistic censorship, hence of a kind of textual repression, creating on the representational level of the discourse gaps which allow a freer kind of associative word-play to break through – that is, they act as *generative* lacunæ. To put it another way, the curtain is obviously hiding something behind it. The empty space, in contrast, seems to be a patent and radical absence – a manifestation not of repression but perhaps of something closer to Lacan's 'forclusion', as Leclaire describes it: 'un trou originel qui ne serait jamais susceptible de retrouver sa substance puisqu'elle n'aurait jamais été autre que substance de trou'.[76] As such, it plays no part in the generative mechanisms of autonomous textuality.

But the figure of the empty space is also relevant to the position of history in the representational discourse of Simon's novels. In so far as it designates the absence, rather than concealment, of history one might be tempted to interpret it as a realist statement: 'saying', in effect, that there is no such thing as history. But this is contradicted, elsewhere in the texts, by other more obviously substantive statements that history is *something* – is a mysterious but powerful force at work overriding men's actions, and so on. History is, in other words, 'represented', but *only* in this very abstract sense: there is a particular kind of rhetoric, involving abstract personification and generalized proclamations about 'l'Histoire', which remains very separate from the rest of the discourse – in which, in so far as realist discourse is, for Simon, founded on a notion of the visible, and in so far as history is invisible, it is excluded from the more concretely representational mode of his writing.

There are, in other words, three related but apparently conflicting factors: history is presented figuratively as an empty space; history is said to exist, in abstract and generalized terms; and history is not *shown* in action because it is invisible. Attempting to put these together, one can conclude that, firstly, the 'empty space' is not to be taken literally (it is after all a metaphor) – history does exist for Simon. However, it cannot be shown existing: and if we now relate the empty space to this third point, it becomes possible to see it as signifying, metaphorically, something rather different, and rather more congruent with its own status as an instance of figurative language: that is, it points specifically to the problems attaching to the *textual representation* of history. In other words, it is not that history is not there, in reality; it is rather that − like the taboo historical name of LSM − it cannot be represented. That is, the empty space is a figure of the unrepresentable: history forms an empty space, *in the text*. And the figure itself reads, finally, as a reflexive manifestation of the invisibility of history.

It is in this sense that Simon's figuration of history can be compared with the Lacanian notion of 'une certaine limite, qui s'appelle le réel' (1973: 49):[77] the real as, in Alan Sheridan's definition, 'that before which the imaginary faltered, that over which the symbolic stumbles, that which is refractory, resistant ... the ineliminable residue of all articulation, the foreclosed element, that which may be approached, but never grasped' (1977b: 280).

Thus despite its central and enduring importance as a theme in Simon's novels, history occupies a rather anomalous position in relation to the text. It is in fact the only major thematic element that does not engage with questions of language in a positive and productive way; its significance, ultimately, is that it marks out the limits of representation by creating a kind of no-go area − an area of *impasse* in the texts.

7

FICTION WORD BY WORD

The general approach I have adopted in writing about Simon's novels
has above all emphasized their functioning as *texts*, looking at the
texture of the writing, the actual signifying (lexical, rhetorical, even
syntactic) material. Working in this way, as it were from a position
of permanent close-up, leads to a concentration on *detail* which I
would argue is the most productive way of reading his novels: because
the risks involved – principally, the risk of failing to see the wood
for the trees, of presenting the novels as nothing more than a succession of tiny verbal fragments – seem to me to be outweighed by the
different kind of *access* to the text that is opened up when one begins
to 'remonter les veinules du sens',[1] as Barthes has described it (1970:
19), and to bring into focus the small-scale but pervasive and insistent
manœuvres that are involved in writing the visible.

Simon himself, constructing his novels 'par le cheminement même
de l'écriture' (1972: 74),[2] has of course always been less interested in
the wood than in the trees: one of his best-known theoretical papers,
'La fiction mot à mot', would seem by its very title to offer at least
some kind of authorial sanction for concentration on textual detail.
However, this approach is not entirely neutral as regards the status
of representation: breaking the text down, taking each fragment as
it comes, also means working against the illusion of reality, which
operates on the level of much larger stretches of writing: which can
only 'take off' if it has a much longer textual runway. It need not
occupy the whole of the text, and it can be contested and to some
extent fragmented itself, but the point is that where it does function,
it does so *as a whole* – the imaginary, as Lacan makes clear, is all
to do with wholeness.

   At the same time, therefore – despite the inevitably anti-representational effect of concentrating on fragments of text – I have tried
to emphasize how a countervailing illusionist discourse in Simon's
work also exerts a strong, recurrent and very characteristic pressure.

165

I have further argued that the theoretical position he adopts in 'La fiction mot à mot', in its bias towards, precisely, the anti-representational 'word by word', fails to recognize this. The title itself, in part, stresses the activity of words relating to other words, and this is reinforced by the intertextual allusion to the boy's incompetent 'mot à mot' Latin translation in *Histoire*: a caricatural example of a text in which the subject-matter has become completely irrelevant, and the (Latin) word's referent is completely eclipsed by its problematic relation to another (French) word.

But the essay's title as a whole is significantly more ambiguous: given the explicit argument contained in the paper, the retention of 'fiction', where one might rather have expected a less representationally loaded term such as 'writing' or 'text', seems oddly out of place: 'la fiction mot à mot', if one takes its implications seriously, reads less as a conjunction of object and technique, end and means, and more as a contradiction in terms. As such, it compresses into one short phrase the tension set up throughout Simon's writing between the holistic illusion of 'fiction' and the deconstructing, dis-integrated literality of the 'mot à mot'.

Simon's misrecognition of visual representation in his novels is indicative of a wider sense in which his own conscious ideas about writing seem somehow cut off from the active workings of the text. He is himself of course very aware of the disjunction between 'le Claude Simon travaillant' and 'celui de la vie quotidienne'; and in the interview from which this remark is taken he also quotes Raoul Dufy to the effect that 'il faut savoir abandonner le tableau que l'on voudrait faire au profit de celui qui *se* fait' (Interview with L. Janvier, 1972).[3] And the texts themselves suggest, even more strongly than these comments, that his writing always *escapes* him; as though the productive force of the language is to a large extent the result of unconscious motivations. This is no doubt true of all writers, to varying degrees; and in Simon's case the generative impulses, the scope and richness of his textual obsessions, seem particularly close to the unconscious. His novels are therefore in some ways the opposite of the usual stereotype of the *nouveau roman*. They are certainly not the schematic, rationalistic, over-intellectualized productions popularly associated with Robbe-Grillet or Butor, for instance. This is of course an extremely simplistic and reductive view of these two writers; but it would still be true to say that they are 'intellectual' in a way that Simon is not.

As well as this separation between literary theory and textual practice, it seems to me that within the novels themselves there is an evident disjunction between the quality of the ideas that are expressed in the form of large-scale consciously elaborated themes, and the power of something which is not just 'style', but a stratum at which issues of desire, fascination, loss and fear inform, in obscure and entangled ways, the whole substance of the text. Even the representational, 'defamiliarizing' precision of many of his descriptions derives from the peculiar intensity of a *desiring* vision. It is on this level, I would argue, that the real subtlety and the real inventiveness of his writing is to be found, whereas discussion of the overt themes and ideas (nature, death, war, history, etc.) fairly quickly reaches a point of exhaustion. Thus in the case of history, for example, I have suggested in Chapter 6 that Simon's rather over-simplified *conception* of historical action holds less interest for the reader of his novels than the textual activity of the *figure* of history, which comes to signify the unrepresentable in general.

Another specific problem concerning the status of consciously expressed attitudes in Simon's texts is: how do women read them? The representation of female characters throughout the novels is (with the sole exceptions of Louise in *L'Herbe* and perhaps Batti in *Les Géorgiques*) uniformly negative and stereotyped: old women are either terrifying (*Histoire*), ridiculous (Sabine), or a-sexually saintly (Marie), while young women are exclusively sexual, visual objects. It is clear that Simon's 'ideas' about women are unambiguously reactionary; and many female readers find the novels offensive for that reason. I myself do not, with the exception of the depiction of Sabine in *L'Herbe*, for reasons that I think are connected with the disjunction of levels mentioned above. It seems to me that the representation of the female characters is so transparently determined by a configuration of half-acknowledged fears and desires that the question of attaching any kind of objectivity to them simply does not arise: they are an extreme case of the visible as object of phantasy, and hence of fictional representation as phantasy. In a sense, what is being represented is not a woman but, as I have shown, the construction of male sexuality – not a realist character but the projection of the subject's phantasies. The exception is of course *L'Herbe*, in which there is no male subject; here, therefore, the reader has no way of *placing* the image of Sabine (or indeed Marie and Louise) in relation to a male psyche. But the other images of women are placed, and hence relativized, in exactly that way. It is also relevant that Simon's protagonists are in no sense triumphant sexual heroes – the dominant feelings are failure, fear, desperation and above all loss.

The representation of women – or, more accurately, of phantasies about women – is in fact a good example of the differential but interrelated functioning of distinct levels of the text. The fear which is directly perceptible in many of the narrator's comments about women is also central to the fetishistic play of concealment discussed in Chapter 5, in which the woman's 'terrifying' naked body becomes desirable in so far as it is only partially and momentarily visible; and the structure of fetishism itself is further involved, through the ambiguity of disavowal, in a more abstract questioning of the status of the real in representation. Finally, fetishism consists above all in a *manipulation* of vision, in order to construct the object as desirable, and this closely resembles the *textual* manipulation of the object of vision that I have characterized as 'modalization'; writing the visible, in other words, echoes the mechanisms of fetishistic vision.

This brings us back to the basic issue: what exactly is the relation between the textual and the visual? The preceding six chapters have examined different aspects of this question, and we are perhaps now in a position to draw these together and reach some general conclusions. In its initial formulation, the relation appears as a simple polarity of the text versus the visual: writing, that is, inevitably pulls against the image – pulls it to pieces, in fact, and dissolves it into words. But posed on this level the relation remains entirely abstract, because the visual in this context has no real existence; it exists only in so far as it is signified in the discourse of the text. To grasp the relation more concretely, therefore, we have to look at the opposition between two *discourses*, one of which has the visible as its fictional referent, while the other remains within the field of generative textuality and has no referent of any kind. For convenience I shall refer to them as 'visual discourse' and 'generative discourse' respectively. The fact that they are basically different is immediately evident on reading the novels, in the sense that the presence or absence of a fictional referent is always observable; and I have tried to explore in some detail the ways in which Simon's text alternates between them.

That is, there is a continuous double movement in which the mirage of 'fiction' is produced by the visual discourse and then countered by the generative discourse, which in turn gives way as another visual representation emerges. All these terms – fiction, mirage, image, representation, the visible – refer to different but often interchangeable versions of the imaginary; from which moreover they derive their peculiar force. Fiction, in other words, always *returns*: the imaginary constantly re-forms after each disruption,

> comme la surface de l'eau se referme sur un caillou, le paysage reflété un moment brisé, fracassé, dissocié en une multitude incohérente d'éclats, de débris enchevêtrés de ciel et d'arbres (c'est-à-dire non plus le ciel, les arbres, mais des flaques brouillées de bleu, de vert, de noir), se reformant, le bleu, le vert, le noir se regroupant, se coagulant pour ainsi dire, s'ordonnant, ondulant encore un peu comme de dangereux serpents, puis s'immobilisant, et plus rien alors que la surface vernie, perfide, sereine et mystérieuse où s'ordonne la paisible opulence des branches, du ciel, des nuages paisibles et lents, plus rien maintenant que cette surface laquée et impénétrable.

(*La Route des Flandres*: 232)[4]

This long and richly developed description is actually, in context, a simile for the process of repressing traumatic memories of war-time, and as such it explicitly brings into play the notion of the unconscious. The alternate opening and closing mechanism which Lacan ascribes to the unconscious is also echoed here in the description of the pebble breaking open, but then being swallowed up by, the water. Although the emphasis is on the moment of closure, i.e. the restoration of the imaginary in the form of the mirror-like surface and the unified image reflected in it, the passage also refers to the opposite aspect whereby the mirror is shattered by the stone which sinks to the bottom – preventing, in Malcolm Bowie's phrase, the 'false fixities of the Imaginary' (1979: 131) from becoming permanently established. In fact it leads on to a comparison with, and clear criticism of, the kind of *writing* that precisely does not disrupt the imaginary, but covers over gaps and disruptions: 'phrases ... infiniment rassurantes, aussi lisses, aussi polies, aussi glacées et aussi peu solides que la surface miroitante de l'eau' (*La Route des Flandres*: 232).[5] Thus the description as a whole can be read as a simile for both phases of the alternating movement, and, by extension, for the permanent and irresolvable tension set up in Simon's texts between the two discourses.

In fact, however, the relations between the visual and the generative discourses are rather more complex than this model, taken on its own, allows for. Looking more closely at the texts reveals that while the discourses remain distinct, they are not always opposed: or at least, the opposition between them is a dialectical rather than a static one. In other words, the text does see-saw between the two poles of the discourses, as outlined above, without ever stabilizing, but at the same time there is also a sense in which the opposition *itself* is not stabilized either. On the evidence of the texts, one cannot simply say that one discourse promotes and modalizes the visible while the other negates it. Thus the supposedly pure textual productivity of generative word-play sometimes actually generates 'visions' (Chapter 2); while conversely we have seen how apparently straightforward visual description often has the effect of disintegrating pictorial images and making them invisible (Chapter 4). It is not only, in other words, a question of fluctuation, but also of the interpenetration of the two modes of writing, and in some places the reversibility of the terms of the opposition.

The passage from *La Route des Flandres* that I have just quoted provides further illustration of these ambiguities. In the first place, its appearance in the text is over-determined: it is generated by a link between visually similar signifieds − from the remembered horses' watering-place to the imagined pool − but also, simultaneously, by a purely verbal transition: 'l'abreuvoir où il fallait *casser la glace*' (232)[6] leads in, via a pun on 'glace' (ice/mirror), to the stone 'break-ing' ('brisé, fracassé') the 'mirror' of the water. Similarly, the description itself, with its precise notation of light, movement and colour, is a typical example of visual discourse − and yet it is explicitly introduced as a simile, an instance of figurative language. And, while the simile is itself presented in an entirely representational discourse, it describes (initially) the destruction of a representation; and in so doing brings into play a tension relevant, on a larger scale, to the whole enterprise of writing the visible: the 'débris' of a shattered *visual* representation consists of meaningless fragments of colours − 'c'est-à-dire non plus le ciel, les arbres, mais des flaques brouillées de bleu, de vert, de noir' − which are themselves still necessarily represented in language as visible objects; i.e. an attack on visual representation can only be *narrated* in a representational discourse.

As for the *cause* of this kind of instability in the actual terms of the opposition, we may seek an explanation firstly in the psycho-analytical model of the interdependence of symbolic and imaginary, discussed in Chapter 3 (pp. 76−8): neither 'order' is pure and autonomous − they exist solely by virtue of their reciprocal impli-cation in one another, and the Other, in Lacan's terms, intervenes in the specular relation right from the start. This is an explanation on the level of general theory, and principally concerns the *subject*.

Another reason, however, can be found on a more concrete and specific level. Each of the two discourses could in principle exist quite independently of the other: a text consisting entirely of visual discourse, or entirely of generative discourse, is perfectly possible. But in the case of Simon's texts, they co-exist; and once their relation is seen not as a conceptual polarity but as the material juxtaposition of particular sequences of each within a particular text, the *object*'s position (object of representation, of vision and of desire) becomes ambiguous: and this ambiguity arises because, although for the most part the two discourses have opposite or at least different functions, there is a crucial area in which they overlap.

That is: visual discourse modalizes the visible in order to produce it as a phantasized object of desire (see Chapter 2); this usually involves a certain derealization of the object, and various other textual effects which approximately reproduce the subject's control over the phantasy, and which are in themselves, I have argued, a kind of 'subtraction' from the real plenitude of the posited object. But, specifically, modalization *also* means constructing the object as fragmented, or mutilated, or possibly not there at all (Chapter 5); the fetishistic ambivalence which underlies the figure of the curtain also operates on a wider scale: anything that blocks and frustrates vision, by the same token, intensifies the desirability of its object. One important aspect of control over the phantasy object is precisely this kind of *playing* with its disappearance.

Generative discourse, on the other hand, is above all concerned with the autonomously productive capacity of language (as defined by Kristeva, Ricardou, and others – see Chapter 1). To the extent that it is governed by the play of the signifier, it can be said to construct its subject in the symbolic order, in its relation to the Other. *In itself*, therefore, it is related to the imaginary, and hence visual representation, only in a negative sense: it simply makes representation impossible. But, when it occurs in a text which constantly oscillates between it and visual discourse, it acquires, as a result of these juxtapositions, a new and very different function. It now has an effect *on the visible* as this is presented in adjacent sequences of visual discourse. The effect is, simply, to obliterate it – temporarily: it breaks into the phantasized image, in a series of repeated interruptions which deprive the visible of its imaginary stasis and plenitude. In so doing, however, it actually enhances its position as object of desire, by introducing the necessary element of lack into the phantasy, and constructing the visible as a *textually* lost object. In other words, visual discourse already presents the object of vision as diegetically incomplete, lost, fragmented, etc. (Chapter 2), but the disruptive activity of generative discourse then works to accentuate the lack in, and the 'lostness' of, the object.

This lack is a manifestation of the Other, and so is in principle far more radical than the manufactured, flirtatious disappearances of the object in visual discourse. However, in the specific conditions of Simon's 'oscillating' texts, it loses some of its force, and is never able to establish itself − the reflection in the pool, as discussed above, always re-forms. And because of its precarious position, the lack created by generative discourse is more closely aligned with the disappearances of visual discourse than it would be otherwise; so that, in practice (and arguably as a further instance of the interpenetration of symbolic and imaginary), it communicates with and actually *reinforces* the latter. The opposition of the two discourses is thus partially neutralized, at a point of indeterminacy where one kind of textual disruption of the visible becomes indistinguishable from the other.

Moreover, it is precisely this same shared textual effect that *both* attacks the visible as object of representation *and* simultaneously constructs it as object of desire. In this situation, the antagonism of the two discourses is, inevitably, fundamentally ambivalent: not only because they share some common textual procedures (fragmenting, introducing lack, etc.), but in particular because the two *conflicting* attitudes towards the visible turn out to be both produced within precisely this area of overlap, by the *same* features of discourse. That is, rather than a clear-cut opposition of two entirely separate discourses − one promoting the visible and the other negating it − the text presents us with the co-existence of two contradictory effects arising from one discursive feature which is common to two otherwise antagonistic discourses.

This in turn affects the *theoretical* status of generative discourse. I referred earlier to the way in which, in 'La fiction mot à mot', Simon presents his novels as above all anti-representational, and to this end emphasizes their purely textual elements − because in theory this generative discourse functions as a conscious strategy against representation, countering the reader's attempts to visualize a diegetic reality. But if it is also, on a different level, complicit in the production of the visible as an object of desire − i.e. is to some extent appropriated by and made to serve the purposes of the visible − then it cannot be seen simply as an instrument for the dismantling of representation.

The basic ambivalence of the opposition between the two discourses is itself, in a rather different sense, *generative*: it means that the other textual oppositions which to some extent derive from it are bound to be equally volatile. (The status of history as marking out the space of the real, i.e. that which by definition cannot be signified − see Chapter 6 − *is* fixed and static, but that is precisely because it remains outside the whole problematic of representation, textuality and the visible.) This is clear in the case of fetishism as opposed to verbal censorship, as discussed in Chapter 5, but also, and perhaps especially, in the opposition of the pictorial and the citational, and the question of what occupies the positions of 'same' and 'other' in relation to the text (Chapter 4). In all of these there is a significant amount of interplay and cross-over; all of them are as it were contaminated by the ambivalence of the underlying opposition between visual and generative discourse.

Thus Simon's texts offer us a configuration of tensions and polarities which are closely interwoven and, at the same time, extremely fluid and mobile. As he says himself in *La Bataille de Pharsale*, 'on doit se figurer l'ensemble du système comme un mobile se déformant sans cesse autour de quelque rares points fixes' (186).[7] At the root of this mobility is the deeply ambivalent position of the visible. The interaction of the two discourses in the concrete materiality of the text produces the visible as lacking, as never fully present, or as lost: and that is why it arouses such intense desire − the moment at which the mirage disappears is the essential moment of its staging as lost object of desire. The result is a text in which, on the one hand, the visible can never be fully and stably represented; while, on the other hand, the attempt to represent it can never be abandoned.

NOTES

A note immediately after a quotation − or series of very short quotations − in French simply gives a translation of the passage or passages in question, for the benefit of non-French-speaking readers. Translations are my own unless otherwise stated.

Introduction

1 'The fact remains that Claude Simon is always giving us these referents ... So we must believe that Simon accords greater importance to referents than do the other novelists at this meeting.'
2 To explain both these shifts as marking the beginning and end of the 'influence' on Simon of the theoretical work of the Nouveau Roman group, and of Jean Ricardou in particular, as is sometimes suggested, is too superficial. For one thing, Ricardou's first article on Simon appeared as early as 1963. More importantly, it begs the question of why Simon was influenced in the first place, and of the connection between personal relationships and writing texts, which can hardly be as direct and straightforward as this would imply.
3 'You cannot "see", in any way at all, the door you are talking about. Jean Ricardou has quite rightly pointed out that, contrary to the widespread cliché, one "sees" nothing when one reads (except printed or handwritten characters). As he has said, it is not vision, but intellection, which is something quite different.'
4 'a certain logic internal to the text, specific to the text, proceeding both from its music (rhythm, assonances, the cadence of the sentence) and from its material (vocabulary, "figures", tropes − because our language was not formed arbitrarily) ... enriching and, in itself, generative of fiction'
5 'And, on closing the book, the reader can actually ... "grasp the whole visual field all at once".'
6 'this passage is evidence that every kind of reading as well as every kind of writing must accept and try to think through, in the case of each text, the contradictory tension between the referential and the literal'
7 Duncan 1985: vii.
8 Thus Stuart Sykes introduces his survey of Simon criticism by saying,

174

'work on Claude Simon can arguably be divided into two broad categories on either side of the years 1969–70' (1985: 140).

9 Merleau-Ponty's notes on Simon have been published as 'Cinq notes sur Claude Simon' (1961); he also used to cite Simon's novels in his lectures.

10 'man in the world as pure gaze fascinated by images' / 'To this art, everything is transparence; it has reduced the being of that which is to this transparence to representation, to this "representability" / 'a perception which treats the real *as* illustration or drawing'

11 'the parallelism of this fictional discourse with the phenomenological discourse of Merleau-Ponty' / 'Can we speak, in connection with the fictional discourse, of a spontaneous, untutored and tragic phenomenology of perception?' / 'The relations between things and beings ... as lacking any meaning other than that of being governed by a necessity which escapes the *agents*' / 'phenomenological consciousness in relation to a *full* world revealed in *profiles*'

12 'we further believe that this way of seeing which determines this way of showing, is very profoundly determined by the ethical intuition, which itself comes from experience; or rather, the two are in this case one and the same'

13 'hence fascinated and frustrated at the same time, and in such a way that the fascination and the frustration mutually exacerbate each other'

14 'But all the novel is trying to say is a way of saying things as they are, that is, as they appear.'

15 'The movements of the look construct a building of lines whose sentences are like the written traces, the shadow cast on the paper, lines of force of the discourse, two-dimensional architecture ... The formula "camera-pen" could be applied literally to the look which speaks here.'

16 'System of a subversion of expression' / 'the traditional devices of expression' / 'the modern text' / 'means of production' / 'productive metaphor', 'productive pun', 'productive fragment', 'productive word'.

17 'In this switching, the metaphor is *structural* (it orders the cells of the text) but also *transitional* (like a canal lock, it allows passage from one to the other)' / 'the pun can also function like a switch. All it takes is for the similarity of some of their signifieds to enable two distant fictional cells to be connected.'

18 'the fanatics of expression who reduce language to an instrumental next-to-nothing' / 'It is apparently good taste, even nowadays, to consider Claude Simon's work solely as a libertarian burgeoning of the lyrical and the sensuous.'

19 'As soon as the reassuring, and complicit, formulæ of expression and representation are abolished, we have to confront a huge influx of possibilities.'

20 As, for instance, in Alastair Duncan's article 'Claude Simon: la crise de la représentation' (1981), and the conclusion to the 1975 paper by Gérard Roubichou, 'Aspects de la phrase simonienne': 'la textualité y fonde la représentation qui à son tour y fonde la textualité ... sa "production"'

scripturale est *aussi* romanesque' (1975: 209, author's italics). ['textuality founds representation which in its turn founds textuality ... its scriptural "production" is *also* fictional']

21 'With *Triptyque*, the Simonian novel takes a new step forward and can be said to accede to that place that the previous works had continually aspired to and approached without being able to reach it. Eliminating the "dross" that is still to be found in *Histoire* and *Les Corps conducteurs*, it establishes its scriptural continuity even more firmly, committing itself unreservedly this time to referential discontinuity.'

22 'The psychoanalytical monument has to be traversed, not by-passed, like the magnificent streets of a very large town, streets through which one can play, dream, etc.: it is a fiction.'

23 'Separare, séparer, ici se termine en se parere (*sic*), s'engendrer soi-même ... Ici c'est de sa partition que le sujet procède à sa parturition' (1966: 843). ['Separare, to separate, here ends up as se parere, to give birth to oneself ... Here the subject proceeds from its partition to its parturition.']

24 Thus J.-B. Fages writes, of Lacan's style: 'Une performance aussi soutenue n'est pas le fait ou le seul fait d'une nature seconde, comme qui dirait: Lacan est ainsi fabriqué. Car l'auteur, loin de se prendre à ses propres pièges rhétoriques, montre à tout instant que son écriture est piégée ... Lacan est à lire d'abord – et peut-être surtout – par ses formes signifiantes plutôt que par ses contenus signifiés' (1971: 82–3). ['Such a sustained performance is not, or not only, the result of a second nature, as to say: Lacan is made that way. For the author, far from falling into his own traps, constantly shows us that his writing is full of traps ... Lacan is to be read in the first place – and perhaps above all – through his signifying forms rather than his signified contents.']

25 See Derrida 1975.

26 'No current attempt to achieve that end has yet come close to a generally applicable language of pure percepts ... There can be no question that efforts of this sort are worth pursuing. But their result is a language that – like those employed in the sciences – embodies a host of expectations about nature and fails to function the moment those expectations are violated ... No language thus restricted to reporting a world fully known in advance can produce mere neutral and objective reports on "the given". Philosophical investigation has not yet provided even a hint of what a language able to do that would be like' (1962: 126).

27 Simon himself, in his interview with Ludovic Janvier in *Entretiens* 31 (Janvier 1972: 17) says that *Gulliver* is a failure.

28 'We have witnessed an interesting phenomenon – a dialectic of continuity and discontinuity. The producer has argued in terms of continuity, he does not discern any break in his evolution ... while the critics adopt the point of view of discontinuity.'

29 'After an initial phase of very overt realism using the technique of point of view, the technique of flashback, etc., already including some formal

elements but which have not yet developed very far, the tendency as from *La Bataille de Pharsale* is towards a more and more accentuated formalization.'

30 For instance, in Maxim Silverman's recent article (1985); and in the same volume, Alastair Duncan's comment that 'Not until *La Bataille de Pharsale*, however, does any novel as a whole give the impression of being formed from juxtaposed fragments floating free of any containing consciousness' (1985: 77).

31 'that state of disturbance ... in which representation is distorted, decomposes and poses, with the subject, the question of its otherness'

32 Stuart Sykes, for instance, opens his discussion of the novel with the comment that 'Many of Claude Simon's most faithful readers will have received *Les Géorgiques* with something dangerously close to a sigh of relief. This huge, and hugely enjoyable novel seems to indicate a return on Simon's part to a conception of writing he abandoned in 1969, a conception in which it is not illegal to refer to an extra-textual reality which the intelligent reader might possibly recognize, or to allow the odd *adjectif de valeur* to intrude into the script, or to depart from a preoccupation with the act of writing and aim at literature instead. In short, *Les Géorgiques* displays a concern with getting away from the devastating circularity of the *nouveau roman* in its more recent manifestations' (1983: 80).

33 Britton 1984.

34 'the curtness of a mere report' / 'endowing it with more persuasiveness, more credibility, by noting several of those details, those "things seen" which every good journalist knows to be the best guarantees of the authenticity of a piece of reporting'

1. The theoretical context

1 'Du réalisme artistique', 1921, reprinted in Todorov 1965: 98–108. See also the commentary on Jakobson's position by Philippe Hamon (1982: 120–3).

2 'illusion of mimesis' / 'dependent as are all illusions on an extremely variable relation between sender and receiver ... Historical evolution plays a decisive role here ... we must take into account this relation which varies according to individuals, groups and periods, and does not therefore depend solely on the narrative text.'

3 In 'Discours du récit', *Figures III*, 1972. See also Moshe Ron's comment on the two contradictory accounts of Robinson Crusoe's first period of time on the island: 'This did not seem to bother those of Defoe's contemporary readers who took the book for a true historical account' (1981: 18).

4 The term 'representation' has always carried a strong bias towards the *pictorial*. Foucault, tracing the historical origins of the term in French

classical philosophy, makes the point that in the *Logique de Port-Royal*, the first example given of a representation is, precisely, a picture (1966: 78–9).

5 Cf. Foucault's comment on the 'invisibility' of language in the classical conception: 'Il est en tout cas devenu si transparent à la représentation que son être cesse de faire problème' 1966: 93. ['It has in any case become so transparent to representation that its existence ceases to be a problem.']

6 'the notion of showing, like that of imitation or narrative representation (and more so, because of its naïvely visual character) is itself completely illusory ... no narrative can "show" or "imitate" the story it is telling. It can only tell it.'

7 'The Logical Status of Fictional Discourse', in *Expression and Meaning* (1979). Moshe Ron's article, cited above, is also illuminating in this context.

8 'This system, put into practice over forty years in both Rome and Paris, had borne fruit. After having spent about two thousand francs a year since his return from Rome, Pons kept hidden away a collection of masterpieces of all kinds, the catalogue of which reached the astounding number of 1907.'

9 'It was clear from the stairway, lit by sash windows giving onto a small courtyard, that apart from the owner and Mr Fraisier, the other tenants were manual workers. The muddy steps bore the sign of each trade, offering to the view offcuts of copper, broken buttons, trinkets made of gauze and wickerwork.'

10 As Moshe Ron argues (1981: 22). The notion of literary representation can be, and has been, arrived at via a variety of philosophical routes, a thorough and scrupulous investigation of which is given in Christopher Prendergast's *The Order of Mimesis* (1986). My concern here is rather with the end-result: representation considered simply as a literary convention, a particular and recognizable discourse which behaves in certain ways in certain texts.

11 See for instance Macherey: 'le livre ... est construit *à partir* de l'illusion que donne un langage informe, mais par rapport à ce mythe il prend *position* en même temps qu'il prend forme; il en est la révélation' (1966: 80). ['the book ... is constructed *on the basis of* the illusion given by formless language, but in relation to this myth it takes up a *position* at the same time as it takes on form; it is its revelation']

12 Prendergast (1986) offers an additional answer, although one that can also be seen as a (rather different) kind of pleasure: he first of all shows how all existing models of mimesis rest, explicitly or implicitly, on a basis of socially constructed 'knowledge', and then argues for the rehabilitation of mimesis on precisely these grounds; i.e. the fact that it is a social product does not necessarily mean, even in an unequal and divided society, that it is simply the product of a monolithic oppressive dominant ideology; rather, it is a form of 'negotiation' of reality which enables us to 'deal

with the need to make sense of how we live' (232). Drawing on Wittgenstein's language games and Ricœur's notion of 'configuration', Prendergast stresses the connections between literature and other social discourses. At the same time, however, I would wish to retain some emphasis on the specifically *escapist* pleasures of fiction: phantasy is certainly one of the ways in which we make sense of our world, but it provides other kinds of gratification as well.

13 Fredric Jameson stresses the problems associated with this overcoming of the barriers between author and reader, and notes that it is by no means always achieved: 'Thus in literature, the detectable presence of self-dramatizing, and most often, self-pitying, fantasies is enough to cause a withdrawal from the implied contract of reading' (1977: 340). Metz, on the other hand, takes a more optimistic view: when such identification *does* occur, it provides a kind of special bonus of pleasure, not to be had in one's own phantasies, precisely because it comes from 'outside': 'when chance permits this to a sufficient degree, the satisfaction − the feeling of a little miracle, as in the state of shared amorous passion − derives from a sort of *effect*, rare by nature, which can be defined as the temporary rupture of a quite ordinary solitude. This is the specific joy of receiving from the external world images that are usually internal' (1982: 135−6).

14 The concept of disavowal, which Freud elaborates in connection with fetishism (see Chapter 5 below), would provide another way of theorizing the ambiguous co-existence of belief and disbelief. A. C. Pugh comments on the status of representation in these terms, as follows: 'we might simply say that the unreal reality of the image is a source of pleasure that derives from a denial that representation perpetuates, celebrates ... and denies' (1985: 66−7).

15 Christian Metz applies the conclusions of Freud's article to narrative film, and describes the day-dream as 'a pseudo-belief, a consented-to simulation' (1982: 135); many of the points he makes on the similarities between day-dreaming and the reception of film also in fact apply to reading fiction: all three activities presuppose a subject who is awake, but the conditions in which they occur bring them unusually close to the dream state of true illusion: physical inactivity and solitude, 'a relative lowering of wakefulness' (134) which is arguably even more true for reading − 'A Book at Bedtime', etc. − than watching a film.

16 Foucault's analysis of the painting 'Les Suivantes' is a subtle demonstration of the fact that however hard it seems to be trying to do so, a representation *cannot*, by definition, include its subject and object (1966: 31).

17 'way of narrating which consists in simultaneously saying as much about it as possible, and saying it as little as possible'

18 'With internal focalization, the focus coincides with a character, who then becomes the fictional "subject" of all the perceptions.'

19 For instance, in his article on Robbe-Grillet, (1969: 69−90).

20 'presentation as phantasy' / 'the conflictual topology of variants of equal status dissolves into a reassuring atopia: in which none of the variants now claims to struggle against any other, none of them any longer lays claim to the real, which is thus removed and preserved'

21 Jonathan Culler makes this point as follows: 'The convention that in a text the narrator speaks to his readers acts as support to interpretive operations which deal with the odd or apparently insignificant ... But even when there is no narrator who describes himself we can explain almost any aspect of the text by postulating a narrator whose character the elements in question are designed to reflect or reveal. Thus, Robbe-Grillet's *La Jalousie* may be recuperated, as Bruce Morrissette has done, by postulating an obsessed narrator with paranoiac suspicions so as to explain certain fixations of description' (1975: 200).

22 'In the space thereby defined, the signified in its role as support for a signifier disappears, the meaning effect deriving solely from the relations set up between signifying elements distributed on one and the same surface, from their combinations, which may be more or less obvious but are in any case innumerable. Any piece of writing, any text, must now be conceived of not as the expression of a spectacle, a sector of an external reality, but as part, and an active part, of the text as a whole, ceaselessly writing itself.'

23 See for instance Jean-Louis Baudry's 'Linguistique et production textuelle', in *Tel Quel's Théorie d'ensemble*, 1968 (Baudry 1968: 351–64).

24 'We will define the text as a *translinguistic* machine redistributing the order of the language ... the text is thus a *productivity* ... The semiology with which we are concerned considers the text as a *production and/or a transformation*, and so will seek to formalize its *structuration* rather than its structure.'

25 The attack on representation was seen as having a significance beyond the field of purely literary activity. Representation is an essential feature of bourgeois ideology, underpinning idealist conceptions of truth, identity, origin and language as the communication of a pre-existing reality, as 'exchange-value': to subvert representation is therefore to undermine bourgeois ideology. The theorists of textual productivity vary considerably in the literalness with which they interpret this notion of 'subversion' (as they do also in the seriousness of their Marxism), but Kristeva and Baudry at least seem to have a remarkably optimistic view of its *political* efficacy. Baudry, for instance, writes: 'La théorie du texte comme production doit permettre de comprendre que l'homme dispose d'une infinité potentielle dans sa pratique. En ce point se trouve totalement renversée la dualité de la réalité et du langage et l'idée même de réalité. Celle-ci n'étant jamais qu'un système jamais fixé ni totalement observable (pas plus que le code) de transformations opérées par la pratique (nous entendons aussi évidemment la pratique théorique, la connaissance qu'on ne peut pas isoler des autres pratiques, qu'elles soient économiques, sociales ou plus

spécifiquement poétiques)' (1968: 363). ['The theory of the text as production should enable us to understand that man is capable of potential infinity in his practice. At this point the duality of language and reality and the very idea of reality are overturned completely. The latter is never anything more than a system – never fixed or totally observable (any more than the code is) – of transformations carried out by practice (by which we also of course mean theoretical practice, the knowledge that cannot be isolated from the other practices, whether they are economic, social or, more specifically, poetic.'] Nevertheless, the critique of representation in its relation to ideology makes some cogent points, and the theory remains effective in *problematizing* representation and posing an alternative to it; it has enlarged and sharpened the focus of subsequent critical attention to the purely scriptural dimension of texts in general.

26 Although it does not exhaust it – linguistic reflexivity can be taken as the equivalent of Jakobson's 'poetic function' (1963: 218–19).

27 Cf. Bakhtin 1981.

28 'Let us call a variant's ability to claim access to the real its *power*.'

29 In fact, despite Ricardou's ferocious opposition to the referential illusion, there are traces in his writing of a lingering privilege attaching to the real; in the 'transmuted narrative' for instance, the real is 'captured' by a painting, but: 'Inversement, si la mutation se fait d'une représentation vers des événements supposés réels, il s'agit d'une *libération*' (112, author's italics): reality 'liberates'. ['Conversely, if the mutation takes place from a representation to events assumed to be real, it is a *liberation*.']

30 'The parts of the analysis which are blank or vague will act as traces signalling the text's escape; for although the text is constrained by a form, this form is not unified, architectural, finite: it is the fragment, the section, the network cut up or obliterated, it is all the movements, all the inflexions of a huge *fading*, which ensures that the messages overlap but also that they are lost.'

31 'La différance, c'est ce qui fait que le mouvement de la signification n'est possible que si chaque élément dit "présent", apparaissant sur la scène de la présence, se rapporte à autre chose que lui-même, gardant en lui la marque de l'élément passé et se laissant déjà creuser par la marque de son rapport à l'élément futur, la trace ... constituant ce qu'on appelle le présent par ce rapport même à ce qui n'est pas lui' (Derrida, 1968: 51). ['*Differance* is what makes the movement of meaning impossible unless each element said to be "present", appearing on the scene of presence, relates to something other than itself, retaining in itself the mark of the past element and already being hollowed out by the mark of its relation to the future element, the trace ... constituting what we call the present by this very relation to that which is not it.']

32 The *Tel Quel* group as a whole draw on Freud as much as on Marx; Derrida links his 'différance' with various Freudian concepts ('Spur', 'Bahnung', 'Niederschrift', 'Nachträglichkeit' and 'Aufschub' 1968: 57–8)

for instance, and Kristeva speaks of 'l'apport magistral ... de Freud qui, le premier, s'est penché sur le travail constitutif de la signification antérieur au sens produit et/ou au discours représentatif' (1968: 89). ['The masterly contribution ... of Freud, who was the first to pay attention to the constitutive work of signification, prior to the produced meaning and/or representational discourse.']

33 'any reading's ... irrepressible desire: to achieve a coherent organized figure' / 'The multiplicity of fragments is then read in the form of a scattered mosaic, which must be put back together again.'

34 'To identify a *mise en abyme* in a mechanism like this is to discover a sequence which can fulfil two conditions: on the one hand, it must demonstrate sufficient cohesion to arrive, despite its fragmentation, at a fairly solid localization; on the other hand, it must bring together a convincing number of analogies with other incontrovertible aspects of the book.'

35 'Reading however is not a matter of stopping the chain of systems, or founding a truth, a legality of the text ... it is a matter of activating these systems, not according to their finite number, but according to their plurality ... I pass through, I cross over, I articulate, I unleash, I do not count. Forgetting meanings ... is an affirmative value, a way of affirming the irresponsibility of the text, the pluralism of the systems.'

36 'productive work, dialectically producing its producer and its product'

37 As Barthes puts it: 'L'Auteur lui-même – déité quelque peu vétuste de l'ancienne critique – peut, ou pourra un jour constituer un texte comme les autres: il suffira de renoncer à faire de sa personne le sujet, la butée, l'origine, l'autorité, le Père, d'où dériverait son œuvre, par une voie d'*expression*; il suffira de le considérer lui-même comme un être de papier ... l'entreprise critique ... consistera alors à *retourner* la figure documentaire de l'auteur en figure romanesque, irrepérable, irresponsable, prise dans le pluriel de son propre texte' (1970: 217, author's italics). ['The Author himself – that rather timeworn deity of traditional criticism – can, or could one day become a text like any other: it will just be a question of ceasing to equate him as a person with the subject, the aim, the origin, the authority, the Father, from whence his work would derive, as *expression*; it will just be a question of seeing him as himself a creature of paper ... the critical enterprise ... will then consist in *turning around* the documentary figure of the author, into a fictional, unidentifiable, irresponsible figure, caught in the plurality of his own text.']

38 Kristeva in her discussion of the Bakhtinian 'carnival' presents a similar position: 'Dans le carnaval le sujet est anéanti: là s'accomplit la structure de l'auteur comme anonymat qui crée et se voit créer, comme homme et comme masque' (1967: 462). ['In the carnival the subject is destroyed: it achieves the structure of the author as anonymity that creates and sees itself create, as man and as mask.']

39 'Subjectivity is an image of plenitude with which I supposedly burden

the text, but which is fake, is nothing but the trail left by all the codes that go to make me up.'

40 Although he is sometimes distinctly evasive about it, not to say confused: in the 1977 interview with Claud Duverlie, for instance, he defines 'the basic ambiguity of language' as the fact that, rather mysteriously, 'it's only in being concerned with and speaking best about itself that language begins *also* to speak about something other than itself' (Duverlie 1977: 49).

41 See for instance Dällenbach 1975 and 1977.

42 'Claude Simon at work ... is not the same as the Claude Simon of everyday life, but rather that character whom we bring into being by our labour and who leaves us as soon as we get up from our table.'

43 'and they (the four men — which, counting him, made five) standing there, appearing suddenly out of the void to which they were to return almost immediately after a brief, violent and meteoric existence ...'

44 'slightly incredible, slightly unreal'

45 'meteoric existence in which he had seen them act and behave like creatures of flesh and blood'

46 This alternative will be discussed in more detail in Chapter 3.

47 'and later he will seem to see them, immobilized or preserved as though in a photograph, in that sort of greyish congealed material that is the past'

48 'broken-down weapons ... a stationary racing car ... an unexploded shell ... demolished guns'

49 'Yes. It was ... Listen: like one of those ads for English beer, you know? The courtyard of the old inn with its walls of dark red brick and light-coloured mortar ... while the group of horsemen adopts the classic pose: hips jutting, one booted leg thrust forward, one arm akimbo with the riding crop in its hand while the other lifts a tankard of golden ale towards a first-floor window where a face that belongs in a pastel can be seen, half glimpsed behind the curtain ...'

50 'Yes: except for the fact that there was none of all that there except the brick walls, and they were dirty' / 'I don't even know if he had a drink, I don't think so' / 'a dead man (or a woman, or a child) or a lorry, or a burnt-out car'

51 'an apparition, an instant, whisked away into nothingness as furiously as it had appeared' / 'the Italian (that is the fleeting apparitions: extracted for a few brief instants from the darkness by the passing lights which sculptured him ...)'

52 'the long exhalation of the lungs beginning to function again' / 'the crackling, the yellow flame dragging out from the shadows the quixotic profile leaning over the cigarette already stuck between his lips, as though the lanky bean-pole carcass visible a moment, harshly sculptured by the fragile light, tensed up completely in order to breathe in, to fill itself with the scent of the ephemeral flower flickering yellow in the darkness'

53 The alternating rhythm of the mirage suggests a possible link with ideas in psychoanalysis; Leclaire defines 'la caractéristique majeur de ce qu'on

appelle un sujet' (1968: 131) as, precisely, 'd'être cette fonction alternative susceptible d'engendrer tour à tour son annulation et l'effacement de cette annulation même' and speaks of 'cette pulsation, ou oscillation fondamentale' (133). ['the major characteristic of what we call a subject' / 'to be that alternating function capable of generating in turn its annihilation and the obliteration of that very annihilation' / 'this pulsation, or fundamental oscillation']

54 'the readable is articulated onto the visible' / 'self-hero-looking' / 'is the exact equivalent of the vanishing point of the illusionist scenographic painting invented by the Renaissance'

55 Although they were originally published in 1959, 1956 and 1958 respectively.

56 'all the genres in which someone addresses someone, assumes the position of speaker and organizes what he says in the personal category'

57 He in fact contradicts himself on the specific point of the aorist, which in the first article was distinguished from the perfect in that its referent was independent of the speech act: 'le parfait appartient au système linguistique du discours, car le repère temporel du parfait est le moment du discours, alors que *le repère de l'aoriste est le moment de l'événement*' (244, my italics) ['the perfect belongs to the linguistic system of discourse, because the temporal point of reference of the perfect is the moment of discourse, whereas the temporal point of reference of the aorist is the moment of the event']: while in 'De la subjectivité . . .' he argues that *all* tenses are determined with reference to the present moment of the speech act, and concludes: 'Le temps linguistique est *sui-référentiel*. En dernière analyse la temporalité humaine avec tout son appareil linguistique dévoile la subjectivité inhérente à l'exercice même du langage' (263, author's italics). ['Linguistic time is *self-referential*. In the final analysis human temporality with all its linguistic apparatus reveals the subjectivity inherent in the very use of language.']

58 'It is in and through language that man constitutes himself as *subject*; because language alone is the basis in reality, in *its* reality which is that of being, of the concept of "ego".' / 'we believe that this "subjectivity", whether it is posited in phenomenology or in psychology, it makes no difference, is nothing but the emergence into being of a fundamental property of language. He is "ego" who says "ego".'

59 'A polarity which is in itself very particular, moreover, presenting a type of opposition the equivalent of which is not encountered anywhere outside language. This polarity does not mean equality or symmetry: "ego" is always in a transcendent position with regard to "tu"; nevertheless, neither of the two terms is conceivable without the other; they are complementary, but in terms of an "inside/outside" opposition, and at the same time they are reversible.'

60 Jakobson uses, in an apparently similar sense, the term 'protagoniste de l'énonciation' (1963: 181).

61 Todorov earlier in the same article uses Benveniste's 'histoire'/'discours' distinction which, as I have said, is dropped from the more general formulation, but does so in a significantly different sense; 'histoire', in his tacit redefinition, is not a linguistic category at all, but rather equivalent to the Russian Formalist 'fabula' or, as he says, 'histoire, dans ce sens qu'elle évoque une certaine réalité, des événements qui se seraient passés, des personnages qui, de ce point de vue, se confondent avec ceux de la vie réelle' (1966: 126) ['histoire, in the sense that it evokes a certain reality, events which have happened, characters which, from this point of view, merge with those of real life']; this allows him to adopt the position implicit in 'De la subjectivité ...', namely that language as a whole is subjective. The confusion between the two senses of 'histoire' has persisted, as Genette notes in his exposition of the terminological overlaps of narratology (1983: 10).

62 'Every utterance is, as we know, both a statement and an enunciation. As statement it relates to the subject of the statement and thus remains objective. As enunciation, it relates to the subject of the enunciation and retains a subjective aspect since in every case it represents an act performed by this subject. All sentences contain these two aspects but in varying degrees; there are some parts of speech whose only function is to transmit this subjectivity (personal and demonstrative pronouns, verb tenses, certain verbs; cf. E. Benveniste: 'De la subjectivité dans le langage', in *Problèmes de linguistique générale*), others are above all concerned with objective reality.'

63 'Start again, start from zero.'

64 Except for a passage near the end (207–8), as Karin Holter points out (1975: 374), where the personal style, which she defines as a 'Voix jusque-là "outrée", valorisée et valorisante' ['Voice which up to now has been "excessive", valorized and valorizing'], reappears.

65 Françoise van Rossum-Guyon suggests a connection: 'Avec ... la dispersion de l'instance narrative sur toute la surface du texte dans *Les Corps conducteurs* et *Triptyque*, toute re-présentation s'abolit' (1975: 105) ['With ... the dispersion of the narrative instance over the whole surface of the text in *Les Corps conducteurs* and *Triptyque*, all re-presentation is abolished.']

66 'idle fancy' / 'unfalsifiable' / 'In even the most austere narrative, someone is speaking to me, telling me a story.'

67 'When I open a book, it is so that the author will *speak to me*.'

68 'Language as an activity manifested in instances of discourse which are characterized as such by specific features.'

69 'Language is in man's nature: he has not invented it ... We can never get back as far as man separated from language ... What we find in the world is speaking man, and language teaches us the very definition of man.'

70 'And indeed what Freud's discovery brings us back to is the enormity of this order that we have entered, into which we are, so to speak, born a

second time, leaving the state rightly designated *infans*, without speech: that is, the symbolic order constituted by language, and the moment of universal concrete discourse and of all the channels it opens up, in which we have to find a place for ourselves.'

71 'It is in this doubling of the subject of speech that the unconscious as such comes to be articulated.'

72 'is implemented by any intervention of the signifier: notably, from the subject of enunciation to the subject of the statement'

73 Although if this implies that the *sujet d'énonciation* is *outside* language, and unconscious, Lacan's use of the term clearly differs from Benveniste's. While I prefer Lacan's formulation of the relation of subject and language as one of division, it seems to me possible, and useful, to retain 'sujet d'énonciation' in the sense of the language-producing subject *in so far as* it is manifested in the text — because 'sujet d'énoncé' is *any* noun occupying the syntactic position of subject of the sentence.

74 'want-to-be' / 'the drama of the subject in the word'

75 'language alone is the basis in reality, in *its* reality which is that of being, of the concept of "ego"'

76 'individual discourse, in which each speaker takes over the whole language for his own purposes' / 'Language is so organized that it enables each speaker to *appropriate* the whole language in the act of referring to himself as *I*.'

77 'this fundamental distinction between the true subject of the unconscious and the ego as constituted in its nucleus by a series of alienating identifications' (Sheridan 1977a: 128) / 'It is because it staves off this moment of lack that an image assumes the position of supporting the whole cost of desire: projection, function of the imaginary.'

78 'that it is in the chain of the signifier that the meaning "insists" but that none of its elements "consists" in the signification of which it is at the moment capable' (Sheridan 1977a: 153)

79 'a translinguistic machine which redistributes the order of language'

80 Fredric Jameson comments pertinently on the *political* ambiguities of the symbolic order: 'Insofar as the Lacanian version generates a rhetoric of its own which celebrates submission to the Law, and indeed, the subordination of the subject to the Symbolic Order, conservative overtones and indeed the possibility of a conservative misappropriation of this clearly anti-Utopian scheme are unavoidable. On the other hand, if we recall that for Lacan "submission to the Law" designates, not repression, but rather something quite different, namely alienation — in the ambiguous sense that Hegel, as opposed to Marx, conceives of this phenomenon — then the more tragic character of Lacan's thought, and the dialectical possibilities inherent in it, become evident' (1977: 373).

81 'the irreparable disorder of the lived with the artificial order of language'

2. Vision and textuality

1 Contrasting description in the traditional and the modern (i.e. his) novel,
he says: 'Enfin, elle faisait voir les choses et voilà qu'elle semble maintenant les détruire, comme si son acharnement à en discourir ne visait qu'à
en brouiller les lignes, à les rendre incompréhensibles, à les faire disparaître
totalement' (1963: 159–60). ['Finally, it used to show how things were
and now it seems to destroy them, as though its determination to talk
about them were only in order to blur their outlines, to make them incomprehensible, to make them disappear completely.']

2 In his first published novel, we already find the famous description of
the tomato:

> Un quartier de tomate en vérité sans défaut, découpé à la machine
> dans un fruit d'une symétrie parfaite. Le chair périphérique, com-
> pacte et homogène, d'un beau rouge de chimie, et régulièrement
> épaisse entre une bande de peau luisante et la loge où sont rangés
> les pépins, jaunes, bien calibrés, maintenus en place par une mince
> couche de gelée verdâtre le long d'un renflement du cœur. Celui-ci,
> d'un rose atténué légèrement granuleux, débute, du côté de la
> dépression inférieure, par un faisceau de veines blanches, dont
> l'une se prolonge jusque vers les pépins – d'une façon peut-être
> un peu incertaine.
>
> Tout en haut, un accident à peine visible s'est produit: un coin
> de pelure, décollé de la chair sur un millimètre ou deux, se soulève
> imperceptiblement   (*Les Gommes*: 151).

['A quarter of a tomato, truly faultless, machine-cut from a perfectly symmetrical fruit. The peripheral flesh, compact and homogeneous, is a nice chemical red, and of a regular thickness between
a strip of shiny skin and the chamber where the pips are kept –
yellow, evenly graded, held in place by a thin layer of greenish
jelly beside a swelling of the heart. The latter, of a subdued slightly
granular pink, starts off, at the side of the lower depression, with
a bundle of white veins, one of which continues as far as the pips –
in a perhaps rather uncertain fashion.

Right at the top, a barely visible accident has occurred: one
corner of the skin, detached from the flesh for one or two milli-
metres, sticks up imperceptibly.']

Here, as Stephen Heath comments, 'instead of a notation of the real,
there is a process of writing ... the tomato is no more than an itinerary
of the writing' (1972: 113–14); to which one might add that Robbe-
Grillet's syntax works to transform the tomato from a natural into an
artificial object: 'la loge où *sont rangés* les pépins, jaunes, *bien calibrés,
maintenus en place* par ...' as though someone had designed it to fulfil
a particular function – which is indeed the case in so far as it is a *textual*
object. The end result of the descriptive activity is to *prevent* us from
'seeing' the tomato.

3 'Those incompetent heavyweights planted or rather rooted in the middle of the ring mountains of meat exchanging blows that would fell an ox stupid eyes sniffing as they shake their heads sending drops of blood onto the starched shirtfronts and minks in the front rows until one of them without warning without moving a step suddenly collapses in a heap the referee rushing over raising the winner's arm the winner's legs seeming then to come to life and go through the motions of dancing a joyous jig moving apparently of their own accord while, the gaze still vacant in the terrifying martyred face, he goes on peacefully licking up the two trickles of red snot descending from his nostrils.'

4 'Della Francesca's warriors battering each other senseless with slow gestures "telegraphed" as they say in boxing slang like those incompetent heavyweights'

5 'violent obscene uncontrollable leaping stampeding just for a moment then everything (the gilding the old queens the rouged scarecrow the paintings the portrait) separating disintegrating at top speed blurring fading absorbed drunk as though by the fabric of the greyish empty screen'

6 Cf. Georges Raillard's comment on *Femmes*, the text Simon wrote on the basis of Miró's paintings: 'Chez Miró le chromatisme tend à l'érotisme, chez Simon l'érotisme s'accomplit en chromatisme' (1975: 77). ['With Miró colouring reaches towards eroticism, with Simon eroticism happens in colour.']

7 'And I seemed to be there, be seeing it: green shade with women in coloured print dresses ... the horses' coats and the women's dresses, and the fawn leather of the boots making bright splashes (mahogany, mauve, pink, yellow) against the green depths of foliage' / 'And again I seemed to be seeing it: standing out against the inimitable green of the opulent chestnut trees, almost black, the jockeys go past ... their multicoloured helmets one after another in the dappled sunlight, like this: Yellow, blue hoops and cap – the green black background of the chestnut trees – Black, blue St Andrew's cross and white cap – the green black wall of the chestnut trees ...'

8 'But there were no stands, no elegant crowd to watch us.'

9 Irène Tschinka comments that the occurrence of erotic passages in Simon's writing 'relève moins d'un rapport à un référent que d'une certaine production phantasmatique' (1975: 262) ['has less to do with a relation to a referent than with a certain kind of production of phantasy']; and Alastair Duncan refers to 'le paradoxe central de *La Route des Flandres*: d'une part, un grand effet de réel, et surtout de perception visuelle; d'autre part, la brusque mise en cause de cet effet' (1981: 1194). ['the central paradox of *La Route des Flandres*: on the one hand, a strong reality effect, particularly in terms of visual perception; on the other hand, the sudden questioning of this effect']

10 'Iglesia going past without looking at her' / 'like the scented rippling wake of her own flesh'

11 'and finally Corinne standing up nonchalantly, walking unhurriedly – her vaporous and indecent red dress fluttering, swinging above her legs – towards the stands'

12 The connection between film and phantasy has already been mentioned in Chapter 1, note 15, p. 179.

13 'the most womanly woman I had ever seen' / 'fabricated ... on the basis of a single brief vision' / 'the girl in the barn – an apparition – seeming to disappear, although they went on looking at her ... dissolving'

14 'he seemed to see her still ... or rather to feel her, to perceive her as a sort of lasting, unreal imprint, left not so much on his retina (he'd seen her so little, so indistinctly) as, so to speak, in himself: a warm, white thing ... a sort of apparition not lit by that lamp but luminescent ... not a woman but the very idea, the symbol of all women'

15 The endless irritating chattering of Sabine in *L'Herbe* is the most obvious example, echoed however in *Histoire* in the woman in the restaurant who has 'le même trop-plein de bijoux, de fards, de paroles ... essayant de remplacer l'éclat de leur peau, de leur chair, de leurs yeux par des éclats de voix' (170). ['the same excess of jewellery, cosmetics, words ... trying to replace the brightness of their skin, their flesh, their eyes, with the shrillness of their voices'.] *Histoire* also opens with the evocation of the old women's voices, sinister ghosts from the past, 'mystérieuses et geignardes' ['mysterious and moaning'], and *La Route des Flandres* with a piece of women's language, written this time: Sabine's letter to De Reixach which annoys and embarrasses Georges so much. It is only in *Les Géorgiques* that women's language is presented in its specific difference as having a positive value of transgression of the male law: LSM's brother has disgraced the family and no-one is allowed to mention his name, but the *women* do, 'lui dont il était même défendu maintenant de prononcer le nom (sauf peut-être, quelquefois, les femmes entre elles, à la veillée, à voix basse)' (420). ['he whose name it was now forbidden to mention (except perhaps, occasionally, the women amongst themselves, in the evenings, whispering).'] See Britton 1985: 98–9.

16 'They went on talking but I couldn't understand I tried but I couldn't I could understand each word but I didn't manage to follow ... women's talk like when I was a child those medical notices or those advertisements women's diseases something mysterious delicate and a little terrifying which I knew I would always be excluded from.'

17 'All I am for you is a soldier's whore something like what you see drawn in chalk or with a nail on barracks walls.'

18 'The old king whose face is covered in wrinkles looks through a slit in the curtain at the two lovers entwined.'

19 'an object whose value depends solely on its indefinable difference from a lost model' / 'the *objet a* is thus indeed the cause of desire, its irremediable absence generates the eternity of desire, its ceaseless flight' / 'And the enigmas that desire seems to pose for a "natural philosophy" –

its frenzy mocking the abyss of the infinite ... these amount to no other derangement of instinct than that of being caught in the rails – eternally stretching forth towards the *desire for something else* – of metonymy' (Sheridan 1977a: 166–7) / 'which aim rather to insist, to repeat themselves, enigmatic, than to be saturated, fulfilled or sutured'

20 'The convergent bundle of their parallel rows fleeing away sucked by perspective towards an imaginary point beyond the opposite wall' / 'the convergent rows of bricks sucked up over there beyond the corner wall, beyond the other houses, the suburbs, the hills, rushing motionless and dizzying towards the same invisible non-existent and imaginary point'

21 'they (the rows of bricks) were lost, sank away, disappeared in the dark converging on that imaginary point at infinity where everything joins up fuses annihilates itself' / 'Able once again to make out the lines formed by the rows of bricks converging on the vanishing point ... saying if the only solution was for me to run away.'

22 Deguy defines it in rather similar terms as a 'regard insatiable': 'jamais le *visible* ne peut venir le combler' (1962: 1010, author's italics). ['an insatiable gaze' / 'the *visible* will never be able to satisfy it fully']

23 'I could see it or at least the last branches lit up by the lamp ... the more distant branches more and more weakly lit less and less distinct glimpsed then merely guessed at then completely invisible.'

24 'There's got to be something that I can't see.'

25 'the vast earth the fabulous sumptuous colourful inexhaustible world'

26 See Caminade 1975: 150–2.

27 '[the look] bears witness to the separation (castration) on which vision is based, but which it endlessly attempts to ignore' (MacCabe 1976: 15).

28 'are vertical and horizontal only because man himself is only ever in a vertical or horizontal position'

29 'the function that is found at the heart of the institution of the subject in the visible. What determines me, at the most profound level, in the visible, is the gaze that is outside' (Sheridan 1977b: 106)

30 'of all the objects in which the subject may recognise his dependence in the register of desire, the gaze is specified as unapprehensible' (Sheridan 1977b: 83)

31 'le mauvais œil, c'est le *fascinum*, c'est ce qui a pour effet d'arrêter le mouvement et littéralement de tuer la vie' (Lacan 1973: 107) ['the evil eye is the *fascinum*, it is that which has the effect of arresting movement and, literally, of killing life' (Sheridan 1977b: 118)]

32 'Le regard ne se présente à nous que sous la forme d'une étrange contingence, symbolique de ce que nous trouvons à l'horizon et comme butée de notre expérience, à savoir le manque constitutif de l'angoisse de la castration' (1973: 69). ['The gaze is presented to us only in the form of a strange contingency, symbolic of what we find on the horizon, as the thrust of our experience, namely, the lack that constitutes castration anxiety' (Sheridan 1977b: 73).]

33 'this *belong to me* aspect of representations, so reminiscent of property' (Sheridan 1977b: 81).

34 Jacqueline Rose comments: 'Lacan ... challenges what he calls the idealizing presumption whereby the subject assumes it "can see itself seeing itself", persistently referring back to its own subjectivity a "look" which manifestly pre-exists its intervention as subject' (1981: 152).

35 'the gaze is that underside of consciousness' (Sheridan 1977b: 83)

36 'Let O be the position occupied by the eye of the observer ... and OF the straight line which joins this point to the window F.'

37 'And, in order to arrive at a complete idea of the set of relations, we must also consider the line OF in its direction FO; that is, another observer (male or female) O located at F ... and observing the first observer (who thus, from being the subject, becomes the object — and who therefore can continue to be designated by the letter O).'

38 Rose explains this as follows: 'Thus the subject of representation is not only the subject of that geometrical perspective whereby it reproduces objects as images: it is also represent*ed* in that process, illuminated by the light emitted by the object of its own look, and thereby registered simultaneously as *object* of representation' (1981: 153). To which one could add that it is the light that accounts for this: Lacan points out that a blind man could quite well, by means of touch and threads, etc., position himself as 'geometric' subject of representation: what is specific to vision, therefore, is the light which travels from what is seen back to the eye, which becomes its receptacle and so, in a sense, its object.

39 'careful to observe not only the window but also to imagine the spectacle that he might himself provide for a look from the outside, whether of the female observer hidden behind the reflection on the window pane or that of anyone else who could observe him, either at the present time, or later, O thus being nothing but a simple point contained within any other field of vision sweeping across the square'

40 'I see only from one point, but in my existence I am looked at from all sides' (Sheridan 1977b: 72).

41 'as he can, for instance, glimpse his own image reflected in a mirror in a shop'

42 'the object on which depends the phantasy from which the subject is suspended in an essential vacillation is the gaze' (Sheridan 1977b: 83)

43 'told me mummy was looking down at me from heaven'

44 'He held a letter in his hand, he looked up at me.'

45 'the motionless and watchful eye of his patient killer finger on the trigger seeing so to speak what I could see the other way round or me the other and he the right way'

46 'the Simonian obsession with the totalizing Look'

47 'that's to say that both together me following him and the other one watching him get nearer we possessed the mystery in its entirety (the killer knowing what was going to happen to him and me knowing what had

happened to him, that's to say before and after, that's to say like the two halves of a divided orange which fit together perfectly'

48 'but I didn't see them properly, all I could see ... like a sort of target, a landmark, was that bony back'

49 'he should have had a mirror with several facets, then he could have seen himself'

50 'Blind Orion walking towards the rising sun'

51 With Claud Duverlie: Duverlie 1977: 52.

52 'the gigantic body of Orion walking to meet it fades, seems to dissolve in the light, and disappears' / 'One of his arms stretched out in front of him, groping in the void, Orion moves forward' / 'sick man ... the palms of his hands stretched out in front of him to protect him'

53 Thus Lucien Dällenbach comments on 'l'insistance [dans *Les Corps conducteurs*] du sectionnement, de la castration ... qui correspondent, en se rencontrant, à la fragmentation et à l'articulation' (1975: 20). ['the insistence (in *Les Corps conducteurs*) on cutting up, on castration ... which corresponds, as it encounters it, to the fragmentation and articulation']

54 'Everything suggests however that he will never attain his goal.'

55 Duverlie 1977: 52.

56 'pale gigantic body swaying, shaky, unbalanced by the whirling of the sword that he swung with outstretched arms around his head'

57 'URINE–SALIVA–BLOOD'

58 'Ear which can see'

59 'moving through the blinding light, surrounded by that sickening aura of unreality and carnival dawns'

60 'it seems that a grey gleam of light is beginning to filter between the side of one of the windows and the edge of the carelessly drawn ... velvet curtain which blocks it out (blinds it)' / 'One of his arms stretched out in front of him, groping in the void, Orion is still moving on.'

61 'Le rideau' is a highly charged element in all Simon's texts, discussed at greater length in Chapter 5.

62 'the sunrise' / 'the violent wind' / 'the plane rises' / 'the line of the horizon' / 'the ocean ... spreads out like a canvas'

63 As can be read into Stephen Heath's analysis of a fragment from *La Route des Flandres*: 'l'orifice de cette matrice le creuset originel qu'il lui semblait voir dans les entrailles du monde' (42). ['the orifice of this womb the original crucible that he seemed to see in the bowels of the earth'] Heath comments: 'The discovery is that of an absence, *orifice* ... as centre and origin, *le creuset originel*: it is pertinent to note in a text the activity of which is as great as that of Simon's the possibility of the passage from *orifice* to *creuset* via the homonymous *creuser*, with its repetition of *orifice* in *creux*, that gives the intended relation *absence–origin*' (1972: 165). Origin, then, as absence or equally as blindness: 'origine aveugle' as a further transformation of 'Orion aveugle'. The text offers explicit support

for this reading in so far as what leads up to the piece just quoted is: 'faisant penser à ces organismes marins et carnivores aveugles mais pourvus de lèvres, de cils: l'orifice de cette matrice ...' (42). ['made him think of those marine organisms carnivorous blind but equipped with lips, with hairs: the orifice of this womb'] – so that in '*org*anismes ... *aveugles*' we find a clear echo, yet again, of the figure of Orion, and another juxtaposition of blindness with vision: 'qu'il lui semblait voir'.

64 'carried along motionless on this seat so I could see words sequence of words stretching out inscribed on the kilometers of time of air I mean like those notices or bulletins whose text files past in wobbling golden letters on those luminous screens'

65 See 'L'instance de la lettre dans l'inconscient ou la raison depuis Freud', in *Ecrits* (1966).

66 'euphoria of narrative' / 'contestation of narrative'

67 'Thus every narrative is constrained by the subtle, wily, sometimes very abstruse game between the euphoric and the contestatory' / 'the site of a permanent conflict' / 'the battle of the sentence'

68 'bring to life the shimmering luminous pictures by means of the fleeting, the incantatory magic of language'

69 'Wack came in ... saying The dogs have eaten the mud, I'd never heard the expression, I seemed to see the dogs, sort of mythical hellish creatures'

70 'name (memel) which made one think of 'Mamelle' [Nipple] with something icy about the way it looked (the two blank e's perhaps) black town crowned with snow beside a pallid frozen lake inhabited by Slavonic women with flaxen hair heavy breasts (the double l of 'mamelle' suggesting the sight of twin shapes swinging) and snowy'

71 'it seems that a sort of silent crashing can be heard, like the advance of an invisible glacier' / 'Pursuing its slow progress the grimy snowy mass moves relentlessly on'

72 'a room representing the basilica with three naves In the parts of the tub where the water reflected the dark leaves of the bay trees you could see more of them piled up on the bottom black–green brown slimy rotting the most recent still reddish sepia stuck together in clumps thin films of time of dead summer'

73 'or rather creased: old skin of this old world this old monster Creased pliscenian or whatever Pliocene Probably nothing to do with it just words which sound the same plesiosaurus'

74 'when the visible world becomes in some sense separate from you ... objects no longer identifiable with the verbal symbols whereby we possess them, making them part of us'

75 'the mind (or rather: still the eye, but no longer only the eye, and not yet the mind: that area of our brain through which the sort of seam passes, the hasty and crude tacking that links the unnameable with the named ...)

76 'after all any kind of knowledge merely leads to another kind of knowledge and words only lead to other words'

77 'In front of a photograph of a film star an enormous magnifying glass is placed so that the passer-by can see her eye enlarged out of all proportion, spreading across almost the whole width of her face, like the eye of a cyclops.'

78 'the thin membrane of the retina upon which the images of the world settle, on which they slide past, taking each other's place'

79 '*On* qui se diversifie ... sans jamais se loger définitivement', as Holter calls it (1975: 373). ['the "on" that takes various forms ... without ever being definitively situated.'] At the same conference Françoise van Rossum-Guyon, replying to a question about the 'dispersion' of the subject in Simon's earlier texts, comments pertinently on the distinction: 'il y a donc déjà amorce de dissolution de la personne, mais demeure une instance narrative, un sujet, qui se cherche justement, qui est problématique. En parlant de cet on anonyme diffusé à l'intérieur du texte de *Triptyque* il n'y a effectivement plus de sujet' (115). ['So there is already the beginning of a dissolution of character, but a narrative instance remains, a subject, who is, precisely, in search of himself, who is problematic. In the case of this anonymous "on" diffused in the text of *Triptyque* there is in effect no longer any subject.']

80 This point is developed in Chapter 3.

81 See above, note 34.

82 'All you can say is that there is *looking*.'

83 As Karin Holter argued in her paper on Simon at the Colloque de Cerisy, 'il faudrait souligner aussi, et surtout, combien ces *degrés* de différence de tensions [entre le référent et le littéral] *orientent* et *décident* en fait de tout le reste; c'est-à-dire à quel point le fonctionnement du même procédé,. chez des écrivains différents ou dans des textes différents du même écrivain, varie et se définit par rapport à la place qu'occupe sur cet axe référentiel–littéral l'écrivain ou le texte particulier' (1975: 272). ['one should also, and above all, emphasize how much these *degrees* of difference of tension (between the referential and the literal) *orientate* and in fact *determine* all the rest; that is, the extent to which the same device, used by different writers or in different texts by the same writer, varies and is defined in terms of the point at which the particular writer or text is situated on this referential–literal axis'] The altered status of the visual in the formalist novels is a case in point.

84 'Under the arch of the bridge the shadow is completely black. In the sky, the clouds, no longer pulled along by the wind, turn slowly from blond to salmon pink, then to a rose pink which soon remains only as traces in the grey which invades them at the same time as their shapes also change infinitely slowly. The sky green for a while gradually grows dull, ends up periwinkle blue.'

85 'the dazzling tender apotheosis of the diamond-bright dawn' / 'the

194

sparkling enchantment, the icy blazing, like diamonds, the colour of almonds and roses'
86 Cf. Barthes 1970: 27.

3. The mirror and the letter: modalities of the subject

1 'The hero is therefore an important element in the *readability* of a narrative, and the reader must be able to identify him without any doubt; a whole series of devices ... are usually used to emphasize his identity. In so far as he organizes the ideological space of the narrative, he inserts it into the cultural system shared by author and reader outside the text, and thereby constitutes an important disambiguating factor.'

2 Nathalie Sarraute writes in *L'Ere du soupçon*: 'Il (le personnage du roman) était très richement pourvu, comblé de biens de toute sorte, entouré de soins minutieux; rien ne lui manquait depuis les boucles d'argent de sa culotte jusqu'à la loupe veinée au bout de son nez. Il a, peu à peu, tout perdu: ses ancêtres, sa maison soigneusement bâtie, bourrée de la case au grenier d'objets de toute espèce, jusqu'aux plus menus colifichets, ses propriétés et ses titres de rente, ses vêtements, son corps, son visage, et, surtout, ce bien précieux entre tous, son caractère qui n'appartenait qu'à lui, et souvent jusqu'à son nom' (*L'Ere du soupçon*: 71–2). ['He (the character of a novel) was very generously endowed, showered with all sorts of possessions, surrounded by meticulous care; he lacked for nothing, from the silver buckles on his breeches to the veins in the wen on the end of his nose. Little by little, he has lost everything: his ancestors, his carefully built house, stuffed from cellar to attic with objects of all kinds, right down to the smallest knick-knacks, his properties and his government bonds, his clothes, his body, his face, and, above all, this most precious possession of all, his character which was his alone, and often even his name.']

3 'able as it were to see himself ... as though he were a spectator'

4 'Then he saw himself, that is to say years later' / 'erupting without even having been invited ... – then once again oblivion, nothingness' / 'pathetic character who can be seen bustling about, ridiculous and pompous, over there, far away, as though seen through the wrong end of a spyglass'

5 'looking at the microscopic and startled double of himself'

6 'the student (he who had been the student)'

7 'that part of himself which was in the form of a gangling American ... carrying on a conversation with that other part of himself which was in the form of a bald man'

8 'his skin no longer constituted a covering, a separation between the external universe and himself but seemed to contain, indistinguishably and as the inseparable parts of the same whole, the metallic sky ... people, smells, and his own bones'

9 'seeing herself, able to see the pale dress running across the screen of memory; the bright patch followed by the brush of the projector hurtling down the green hillside'

10 'everything stopped frozen time frozen I suppose if someone had taken a photo then, you could have seen us both distinct standing face to face in front of the side of that railway carriage'

11 'the dark light of the window' / 'the blue-green depths of the mirror unchanging, virginal and cold –, and he remembering: "... Until I realized"'

12 'looking in a piece of mirror hung over a canvas bucket full of icy water at our dirty-grey-faces' / 'then I moved the mirror away, my or rather that stupefied face swinging flying away as though sucked up by the shadowy brown depths of the barn, disappearing with the lightning speed that the smallest change of angle transmits to reflected images'

13 'then moving forward in the mirror, shakily, the inglorious ghost of the human race in crumpled pyjamas, dragging his feet, and from whose navel hangs the plaited cotton ribbon, limp and whitish, which holds up his trousers as though he still retained, anæmic, clumsily cut off with jagged ends, some visceral bond, colourless in the dark, torn from the pale belly of the night'

14 'my double still shaky as he emerged from the maternal darkness, fragile, dirty, protesting and miserable'

15 'the fact of a real *specific prematurity of birth* in man' (Sheridan 1977a: 4)

16 'This jubilant assumption of his specular image by the child at the *infans* stage, still sunk in his motor incapacity and nursling dependence' (Sheridan 1977a: 2).

17 'caught up in the lure of spatial identification' (Sheridan 1977a: 4)

18 There is of course a different sense in which one can apply the *metaphor* of the mirror to Simon's novels, and that is in relation to the structure of the texts themselves: the *mise en abyme*, which Simon uses frequently, and which he sees as setting up a play of reflections within the text: 'L'idée que le roman doit être un jeu de miroirs internes'. ['the idea that the novel must be a play of internal mirrors'] This remark is quoted at the opening of Lucien Dällenbach's paper on Simon at the Colloque de Cerisy (Dällenbach 1975: 151–71). His paper, entitled 'Mise en abyme et redoublement spéculaire chez Claude Simon', traces the evolution of the device through Simon's novels, from unity to multiplicity, from being first a means of centring and organising the structure as a whole to finally, with *Triptyque*, producing a decentred 'réflexivité permanente à l'intérieur même de structures aporistiques' (169). ['permanent reflexivity within aporistic structures'] It would follow from this that the earlier stages of the development would be closer to the psychoanalytic function of the imaginary. Sylvère Lotringer, however, in his paper in the same collection (Lotringer 1975: 313–33), takes the example of the jigsaw puzzle as *mise en abyme* in *Triptyque* – which Dällenbach interprets as a sort of post-structuralist

critique of the sign (166) — as the definitive image of the text as *solvable* puzzle, as recuperable meaning, and therefore also as fulfilling the function of the mirror image. He says: 'L'image visée par le puzzle sollicite l'*imaginaire* du lecteur, c'est-à-dire sa fonction intégrative, captatrice, spéculaire. Elle l'invite à saturer les manques, à suturer les coupures. A recouvrir d'un voile de vraisemblance un fantasme d'ordre' (316). ['The image that the jigsaw puzzle aims at sollicits the reader's *imaginary*, that is to say his capacity to integrate, to capture: his specular capacity. It invites him to fill in the gaps, to join up the breaks. To cover a phantasy of order with a veil of realism.']

19 The mirror stage involves not only identification with one's mirror image, but also with one's 'semblable' — for the child, another child of the same age. ('Parallèlement à la reconnaissance de soi dans le miroir, on observe chez l'enfant un comportement typique à l'égard de son homologue en âge. L'enfant mis en présence d'un autre l'observe curieusement, l'imite en tous ses gestes ... et on reconnaît ici l'instance de l'imaginaire, de la relation duelle, de la confusion entre soi et autre', Lemaire 1977: 271. ['As a parallel to the recognition of oneself in the mirror, we also observe in the child a characteristic behaviour pattern vis-a-vis another child of the same age. One child placed in the presence of another will observe it with curiosity, imitate all its gestures ... and we recognize here the agency of the imaginary, of the dual relation, the confusion between self and other.']) On this point, Simon provides an illustration of the confusion of subject and other which in some ways is so exemplary as to be almost a caricature. In *Les Géorgiques*, the cavalrymen get lost in a snowstorm; and the subject, who has already been defined as simply one of the cavalrymen, asks himself whether he is in fact himself or another cavalryman: 'un cavalier (l'un ou l'autre) prend tout à coup conscience qu'il n'a plus devant lui la croupe du cheval qui le précédait ... il continue ... et un moment plus tard ... cela recommence, c'est-à-dire un autre cheval et un autre cavalier arrêtés (mais peut-être est-ce le même type et le même cheval, ou peut-être que le cavalier arrêté c'est maintenant lui, et que c'est lui aussi qui, à son tour, émet des bruits bizarres, misérables) et un cheval et un cavalier passant sans s'arrêter, et le cavalier arrêté (peut-être lui après tout?) se remet en marche' (*Les Géorgiques* 97–8). ['a rider (one or the other) suddenly realizes that he no longer has in front of him the rump of the preceding horse ... he goes on ... and a moment later ... it starts again, that is another horse and another rider who have stopped (but perhaps it's the same man and the same horse, or perhaps the rider who stopped is now him, and it's also him making, in turn, these strange miserable noises) and a horse and a rider going past without stopping, and the rider who stopped (perhaps him after all?) moves off again'] Once again, however, there are significant differences from the psychoanalytical account. The end result of the process is not an achieved identification but rather a loss of ego, the generalized obliteration of any identity: a 'désagrégation ... (qui) ne peut être décrite que de façon fragmentaire

à l'image du phénomène de fragmentation lui-même' (97). ['disintegration ... [which] can only be described in a fragmentary fashion in accordance with the phenomenon of fragmentation itself'] Like the snow, wind and darkness in the scene described, the text too wipes out all traces of individual difference.

20 'leaving the room, finding herself (she will remember having found herself) a moment later in the bathroom'

21 'her face (as though it had been someone else's face, looking at her)' / 'still standing there alone, face to face with this fashion model's face which looked at her unsympathetically, absent'

22 'exactly back to back on each side of the partition wall'

23 'that oil engineer, I'm sure she's his mistress'

24 'still facing that same hard look, cold, too calm – her own – which continued to stare at her without blinking, without any obvious emotion, from the other side of the mirror, from the exact place in which the old woman was probably standing'

25 'still fascinated by her reflection in the mirror ... calm careful distant as though she were enclosed out of reach in the grey background of the mirror'

26 'without taking her eyes off her reflection'

27 This idea of women's fascination with their image in the mirror, which is at odds with the widespread view that visual perception is less affectively charged for women than it is for men (e.g. Luce Irigaray in *Speculum de l'autre femme*, 1974, and elsewhere), is perhaps derived from the way in which Simon presents women as essentially objects of men's vision (see Chapter 2); as though from being seen by men in the first place, the images of women thus constituted then become available to women themselves, and the women's fascination with them is arrived at by extrapolation from the male gaze.

28 'Since his large hand is completely concealing the object it is impossible to know whether he is kissing his own reflected image or the naked woman'

29 'those which you can see or rather in which you can see yourself at the barber's'

30 'and probably because of my drunkenness, impossible to be visually conscious of anything except that mirror and what was reflected in it my gaze clinging onto it so to speak like a drunk clings onto a lamp-post as onto the only fixed point in a vague invisible colourless universe'

31 Ludovic Janvier interprets the place of the mirror in Simon's work along similar lines; he comments that since 'l'homme est privé de lui-même, c'est ce que l'œil du miroir servira à révéler, lui montrant qu'il n'est qu'une présence vide et gesticulante' (1964: 105). ['man is deprived of himself, that is what the mirror's eye will serve to reveal to him, showing him that he is nothing but an empty gesticulating presence']

32 Rose translates this as follows: 'For the Other, the place of discourse, ... is not yet so long as it has not spread right into the specular relation

in its purest moment: in the gesture with which the child in front of the mirror, turning to the one who is holding it, appeals with its look to the witness who decants, verifying it, the recognition of the image, of the jubilant assumption, where indeed *it already was.*'

33 See Britton 1985 for more detailed discussion of this.

34 'This problematic of the subject's identity ... with Simon is always expressed in a relationship of fascinated imitation and emulation of an 'ancestor' or member of the family (in some cases by adoption or marriage) who plays the role of the forerunner.'

35 'For a moment I could see him like that his arm raised brandishing that useless derisory weapon like an equestrian statue in a hereditary gesture probably transmitted to him by generations of swordsmen, dark silhouette against the light which drained him of colour as though his horse and he together had been cast in one and the same material, a grey metal, the sun gleaming a moment on the naked blade then the whole thing − man horse and sword − crashing down all at once.'

36 'arsenal of puns and spoonerisms supposed to liberate him by the magic of the word from maternal beliefs and the lessons of the catechism'

37 'after a moment he said Your mother has written to me'

38 'nothing but an old mailbag'

39 'He had a letter in his hand, he looked up at me then at the letter again then again me'

40 'the antique old phallus ... something to be written − or described − in Latin'

41 'The sound gives birth to me' / 'the lesson gives birth to me'

42 'Then O looks quickly at the thin face whose eyes, hidden by a reflection on the glasses, he cannot see'

43 'He waited, patient or rather resigned, his head slightly bent, the lenses of his glasses in that position like two moons reflecting the jumble of papers on his desk lit by the lamp'

44 'Le registre du signifiant s'institue de ce qu'un signifiant représente un sujet pour un autre signifiant. C'est la structure de toutes les formations de l'Inconscient et c'est aussi ce qui explique la division originaire du sujet. Le signifiant se produisant au lieu de l'Autre (le symbolique), y fait surgir le sujet mais c'est aussi au prix de le figer. Ce qu'il y avait là de prêt à parler, disparaît de n'être plus qu'un signifiant.' (Lacan, 'Discussion de l'article de S. Leclaire et J. Laplanche: l'inconscient, une étude psychanalytique', *L'Inconscient*, Desclée de Brouwer, 1966, quoted Lemaire 1977: 126.) ['The register of the signifier is instituted by a signifier representing a subject for another signifier. This is the structure of all the formations of the unconscious and it is also what explains the originating division of the subject. The signifier producing itself in the place of the Other (the symbolic), makes the subject emerge there but it is also at the cost of immobilizing him. What there was there ready to speak, disappears through being nothing more than a signifier.']

45 'COIFFURE (Barber) written diagonally across the shutters of the shop opposite rising from left to right the curves or the uprights of the letters vertical but the bars of the Fs and the Es slanting ... reflecting in the mirror ... so that onto the first two letters of the inscription were superimposed, transparent, the three chests ... the word SALON above the head wearing the dark-red beret the scarlet patch of the bodice just below the I and the F, the second F and the U crossing through the face of the person leaning on the counter, front view (*me*?), the word MESSIEURS painted horizontally in smaller letters ...'

46 'a relentless regularity O-R-I-O-N separated by shifting intervals of time and space' / 'for instance now O bank dropping quickly away R to reveal an I enclosure surrounded by barbed wire O meadow with two cows' / 'the word never being visible all at once me already not the same somewhere else several hundred yards further on already older by several seconds O-R-I-O-N'

47 'the major determination conferred on the subject by the trajectory of a signifier'

48 See Chapter 1.

49 As I have argued in Britton 1984: 426.

50 'it must be over quickly you probably don't suffer for long'

51 'Start again, start from zero'

52 Heath interprets this as a mark of absence and of the sign as simultaneously presence and absence: 'At the centre of *La Bataille de Pharsale* is placed the cipher O, mark of absence, marking now man now woman, assuming the function of the writing ('O écrit'), and that may be read here, after Lacan, as 'l'atome O du signe, du signe en tant d'abord qu'il connote la présence *ou* l'absence ...' (1972: 156). ['the atom O of the sign, of the sign firstly in so far as it connotes presence *or* absence']

53 'bisector' / 'the line OT hypotenuse of the right-angled triangle whose vertex is at O's feet'

54 'one must imagine the system as a whole as a mobile continually re-forming its shape around a very few fixed points'

55 'for instance the intersection of the line OO' and the trajectory of the pigeon's flight, or again of the itineraries of two journeys, or again the name PHARSALUS figuring both in a collection of Latin texts for schoolboys and on a sign post by a road in Thessalia'

56 'O is translating a Latin text'

57 'another (male or female) observer O'

58 'O sees the body leaning over her ... the arms supported by the hands flat on the sheet on each side of O's shoulders bent, so that the shaggy chest is lowered, the yellow hairs first brush against the points of O's breasts, which stiffen'

59 'O writes: Yellow and then black the time it takes to flicker an eyelid and then yellow again'

60 As Ricardou comments, 'Au terme du texte, ou de toute spire de sa

circularité, celui qui prend la plume ne saurait être un écrivain qui s'apprête à représenter ce qu'il voit ou exprimer ce qu'il sent. O dépourvu d'identité par le travail du texte, c'est, pris dans la trame et produit de son produit, un scripteur (1971: 155). ['At the end of the text, or of any one spiral of its circularity, he who takes up the pen could not be a writer preparing himself to represent what he sees or express what he feels. O stripped of identity by the work of the text is, caught in the fabric and product of his product, a scriptor.']

61 'legs', 'the male nurse', 'a naked young woman' / 'The doctor tells him to take down his trousers.'
62 See Roman Jakobson: 'Les embrayeurs, les catégories verbales et le verbe russe' (1963: 176—96).
63 Miller defines 'le rapport du sujet à la chaîne de son discours; on verra qu'il y figure comme l'élément qui manque, sous l'espèce d'un tenant-lieu (1966) ['the subject's relation to the chain of his discourse; we will see that he figures as the missing element, in the form of a stand-in'] and Lemaire explains the 'rapport' further as 'celui d'un manque à une struc-ture (le symbolique), manque qui n'est pas totalement exclu de la structure néanmoins, puisqu'il est "représenté" sous forme d'un tenant-lieu' (122). ['that of a lack in a structure (the symbolic), a lack which is nevertheless not totally excluded from the structure, since it is "represented" in the form of a stand-in']
64 As already discussed in Chapter 2, p. 65.
65 A marginal exception is 'soi' which contrasts with 'lui' or 'elle'.
66 'Then they understand that they have been ambushed and that nearly all of them are going to die. Immediately after writing this sentence he realizes that it is almost incomprehensible for anyone who has not been in a similar situation and he lifts his hand from the paper. Between the base of the thumb and that of the index finger the network of wrinkles, flabby then crinkled, surrounds the handle of the pen in near-parallel curves'
67 'He writes telling the Committee of Public Security that someone is trying to murder him and that several of his officers who for operational reasons were riding ahead of him along roads which he was to take were ambushed and killed'
68 'He recounts in a novel the circumstances and the way in which things developed'
69 I have analysed this in more detail in Britton 1984.
70 'They can feel, on their tongues and against the roof of their mouths, tiny crystals which crunch in their teeth and melt immediately'
71 'What they have swallowed, in their stomachs like a block of cold stone. They stand with their backs against the wall of the carriage, hunched in their coats, silent and taciturn.'
72 'You can see the monotonous countryside move slowly past'
73 'and it must have been there that I saw him for the first time ... staring at him through that sort of half sleep, that sort of brown slime in which

I was so to speak trapped ... and more guessing at him than seeing him: that is to say ... three-quarters covered in mud – Georges wondering without exactly wondering'

74 This question has been raised in Chapter 1, p. 42.

75 'And I wondered' / 'Then he realized' / 'Because I knew perfectly well that ...'

4. Words and pictures: the text and its other

1 I take 'pictorial to include film images but not the various allusions to theatre, circus, etc. Françoise van Rossum-Guyon's article (1975) gives a careful analysis of all four types. See also Duverlie 1981 for a detailed examination of the function of paintings in Simon's later works.

2 'some of the spectators ... back view looking into a boxing ring at an invisible spectacle hidden by a white cloud with jagged edges inside which can be read the words DO YOU KNOW HE'S ESCAPED DARLING I'M AFRAID HE'S AFTER YOU'

3 'towards the spectator' / 'without actually seeing it, looking in reality at a spectacle inside her head' / 'perhaps the shape the colour of the words she has just spoken' / 'as though they appeared to her not printed and enclosed in bubbles but rising out of nothingness ... like those magic lantern pictures'

4 'semiological complementarity' / 'the text then appears as over-coded ... and can effect redundancies of meaning'

5 'according to the principle that Art is truer than Life'

6 'So one could define realist discourse as a paraphrasable discourse. Very often the readable is articulated onto the visible, and the visible can conversely be identified with the readable, the tellable'.

7 'the photograph or the postcard in the Nouveau Roman'

8 'might lead us to believe that the presentation as spectacle is nothing other than a figuration of the narrative in so far as this both institutes and denounces the fiction (and thereby, indirectly, reality) ... So we could talk about partial *mises en abyme* here, in Jean Ricardou's terms.'

9 'the deliberate coldness detailing stereotyped anatomies'

10 'the convention is that two intersecting straight lines signify – not represent – the existence of a plane'

11 'a royal blue tunic with a high red collar ... decorated with epaulettes with gold tassels' / 'the colouring has been taken further. Not content with painting in the powerful ruddy face ... the artist, advancing further, has dressed the shoulders in a royal blue tunic ... [the] hands which the artist has so to speak gloved in human skin, also slightly reddish.'

12 'something like one of those old tobacco-coloured paintings' / 'ghostly in the clouds of vapid steam, like some Pre-Raphaelite allegory of the vulnerable fragile flesh' / 'like a pathetic parody, a pathetic replica of all the Perseuses, the Goliaths, the Leonidases, the cohort of warriors congealed in tarry paintings in museums'

13 'the scene … unfolding like this: characters, a group of characters sitting peacefully beneath the big chestnut tree, as in one of those Impressionist paintings'

14 He defines it as a *'segment double*, superposition d'une scène (les événements supposés réels) et de sa propre mise en abyme (les événements considérés maintenant comme représentés). La procédure s'apparente donc au fonctionnement d'une écluse: le segment fictif appartient d'abord à une séquence puis à une autre. Ou, si l'on préfère, il y a une rétroaction: les éléments supposés encore réels étaient peut-être *déjà* représentés' (1973: 111–12, author's italics). ['double segment, the superimposition of a scene (the events taken as real) and its own *mise en abyme* (the events now considered as represented). The procedure is thus rather like the operation of a lock: the fictional segment belongs first to one sequence and then to another. Or, alternatively, it can be seen as a retroaction: the events taken as still real were perhaps *already* represented.']

15 In a different sense, *Les Corps conducteurs* and *Triptyque* were in reality generated from a sequence of real pictures: principally Rauschenberg's 'Charlene' in *Les Corps conducteurs*, and paintings by Dubuffet, Delvaux and Bacon in *Triptyque* (as is clear from Claud Duverlie's interview with Simon: Duverlie 1977). This fact is not, however, deducible from the texts themselves.

16 'the valet rushing up at the sound of the shot, his clothes thrown on anyhow'

17 Thus Tom Bishop, for instance, describes them as 'tremplins pour une réaction en chaîne dans un espace intérieur' (1972: 33) ['springboards for chain reactions in an internal space'] and Serge Doubrovsky defines 'le déroulement du livre' as 'une combinatoire d'instantanés (1972: 61) ['the development of the book' / 'a combinatory of snap shots'].

18 'rustling' / 'continuing to slide slowly'

19 As Jean Rousset points out, this also involves eliminating the distinction between description and narration: 'on y voit l'acte descriptif se pervertir d'assez curieuse façon. Il s'agit en fait, à travers l'animation de l'image, de sa mise en récit; en d'autres termes, la description est narrativisée' (1981: 1207). ['the act of description is seen to undergo a rather curious perversion. As it becomes animated, the image is in fact presented as a narrative; in other words, description is narrativized'] The article as a whole provides a detailed analysis of the treatment of these paintings in *La Bataille de Pharsale*.

20 'the players now silhouetted against the setting sun the dust under their feet rising up in a golden cloud, opaque patches where the paint – or the mosaic – has come off its backing in large flakes'

21 'and I no longer on the outside, spectator watching the elegant savage condottieri … but now in the very centre of this mælstrom: the space, the air itself whirling round' / 'the eddies of thick air immobilized … in the same opaque stuff, solidified, spread by the paint brush … and swirling endlessly inside the pompous gilded frames and me in the centre'

22 'As the head of the column approaches the butterfly takes off again, flutters a moment, undecided, as though drunk, then disappears to the right out of the rectangle of the photograph.'

23 'As with great effort the soldiers begin to overcome the force of the current they catch sight of a considerable number of canoes full of armed Indians' / 'the figure 35 followed by the word CENTAVOS is engraved in the sky no doubt coloured by the light of the sunset.'

24 As Dällenbach comments (1975: 168).

25 This is actually rather unfair to van Rossum-Guyon, who herself stresses differences in temporal organization and relative simplicity and complexity: see especially van Rossum-Guyon 1975: 105.

26 That is, the illusory stability and harmony of pictures is ironically juxtaposed with the chaos and disintegration of both narrative and history; so, for instance, 'in Georges's narration, canonical forms of artistic representation are frequently designed to provide aesthetic *garde fous* to contain the explosive discontinuity and fragmentation of wartime events' (106): but, with the introduction of the painterly apparition of the girl in the barn, 'The telos of the great march of history is here ironically assigned to a luminous image of femininity; since neither history nor the image may be isolated from each other, the scene bringing them forcefully together in this context radically undermines the aesthetic alibi' (ibid.).

27 'because this thing absorbs sight like a gulf in which vision is engulfed, a dizzying distance, an abyss into which the fickle look plunges and never reaches anything at the bottom'

28 'this winged arrow / Which vibrates, flies and does not fly! ... Achilles striding motionless!'

29 'fixed, frozen, motionless (like the different luminous arrows which made up the sign lighting up and going out in turn)'

30 Jean Rousset's article on *La Bataille de Pharsale* (1981) explores the different aspects of this 'contradiction féconde', and gives numerous examples of its textual manifestations.

31 'the sooty trace left by the face in the course of its several changes of position restoring to the event its thickness, postulating ... the double sequence of past and future moments, the double series, from the same angle and in the same setting, of positions occupied respectively by the various characters before and after'

32 Although in more general terms, as van Rossum-Guyon quite correctly points out, the distinction is neutralized by the kind of anti-representational inversion described above: 'l'on sait que dans les romans de Simon les photographies s'animent, alors qu'au contraire la plupart des images filmiques se figent' (1975: 93). ['In Simon's novels, as we know, photographs come to life, whereas conversely most of the film images are still.']

33 'one of those snapshots, one of those flat slices cut out from inside duration' / 'so to speak deny time'

34 'advertisement for an English make of beer'

35 'distorted like those pictures which you have to look at in a mirror in order to restore their true dimensions and discover what they represent'

36 'her face appearing through the glass of tears ... in the bathroom mirror, coming up to the surface through green depths, blurred, as though it were liquid, dissolved in the diamond-like transparence of tears, gradually emerging from them – like the image that the photographer brings into focus on his screen.'

37 'stuck together ... invisible in the half of the tub that was full of sky ... but on the other side of the jagged outline of the top of the ivy bush you could see our images'

38 'so that I could so to speak see him twice' / 'staring at the artist painting him (perhaps himself in a mirror)'

39 'that burning yet calm conviction that He existed in some place where one day she would go to join him, the other side, a vaguely oriental paradise' / 'enormous enlargement' / 'he looked as though he were hovering hanging weightless and smiling like one of those apparitions surrounded by a halo of light ... seeing him always present the unforgettable image floating ethereal and wreathed in mist'

40 'portraits of ancestors' / 'abundant exhibition or rather collection of ancestors, or rather sires' / 'male begetters' / 'leaving no trace except the arrogant series of portraits or photographs'

41 'immobilized or preserved as though in a photograph, in that sort of greyish congealed matter that is past time'

42 'Ce que la Photographie reproduit à l'infini n'a eu lieu qu'une fois ... elle est le Particulier absolu, la Contingence souveraine' (1980: 15). ['What the Photograph reproduces *ad infinitum* has taken place only once ... it is the absolutely Particular, sovereign Contingency.']

43 'Le nom du noème de la Photographie sera donc: "*Ça-a-été*", ou encore: "l'Intraitable" ... il a été là, et cependant tout de suite séparé; il a été absolument, irrécusablement présent, et cependent déjà différé' (1980: 120–1). ['The name of the Photograph's noeme is thus: "*This-has-been*", or again: "the Uncompromising" ... it has been there, and yet immediately cut off; it has been absolutely, indisputably present, and yet already deferred.']

44 'for those men and women who, years later, looked at the photograph, the fact of knowing that almost all of them had died, that those same bodies with their nonchalant, affected and ridiculous poses, were all destined ... soon to rot away ... conferred on them a sort of second virginity'

45 'thinking about all those enigmatic, rigid, solemn dead people who from within their gilt frames fixed their descendants with a thoughtful, distant eye' / 'that absence, the presence of that absence'

46 Minich-Brewer stresses the productive *antagonism* of this relation – 'the corrosive power of the encounter between the pictorial (or picturesque representation) and writing' (1985: 105) – while, as I have mentioned above, situating it in a rather narrower context.

47 'and perhaps one o'clock in the afternoon' / 'and about midday'
48 'series of cards ... on the back of which the same missive continued, begun on the first one, then because there was no more space continued on a second one, and so on'
49 Ricardou's demonstration of how textual description transforms its object into a series of sequential relations (1967: 91–111) is still the best account of this.
50 As van Rossum-Guyon puts it: 'la narration restitue au temps, que la mise en spectacle a pour effet de figer dans l'anachronisme et l'immobilité, sa présence et son dynamisme. Le texte instaure en effet une durée propre avec son rythme, ses ruptures et ses continuités inédites' (1975: 105). ['the narration restores to time, which has been frozen into anachronism and immobility by the effect of the presentation as spectacle, its presence and its dynamism. In fact the text institutes its own time-scale with its rhythm, with new breaks and continuities.']
51 'painting is surface, simultaneity, writing is linearity, duration' (in the 1972 interview with Ludovic Janvier).
52 'that, is, starting from the top right-hand corner (the part that can be most clearly seen) and going downwards and to the left, a network of lines extends, light brown lines edged with black framing broad dark brown diamond shapes each of which has a spot of the same light brown in its centre, neither the network nor the diamonds offering the regularity that would be possessed by straight lines intersecting on a flat surface: on the contrary each of the diamonds more or less asymmetrical and pulled out in different directions'
53 See Holter 1982 for an interesting discussion of this point.
54 'a church in which the faithful would gradually be able to learn truths and discover harmonies, the master plan of the whole'
55 'they beat the carpets ... from which emanated a sort of subtle and faint perfume of withered things (the bouquets of bleached roses, the faded garlands entwined with insipid ornamental flourishes) while the pendants of the chandelier, suddenly disturbed, shaken by the draughts, clinked against each other in a waterfall of light, crystalline tinklings, like those reedy tunes that accompany the movements, the pirouettes, bows and curtseys of mechanical figures dressed as marquises and shepherdesses like those that could be seen, graceful and melancholy, in the form of pieces of Dresden china'
56 'odour of wilted bouquets ... the discreet fragrance ... of withered days'
57 'golden sun' / 'garlands' / 'dining-room clock'
58 'as though ... it had known, the graceful century, and its graceful shameless marchionesses, and its marquises with their powdered wigs, cynical, libertine, encyclopaedic and despairing, that they were soon going to have their heads cut off'
59 I have discussed this question in more detail in Britton 1984.

60 'But he did not talk about them either. Perhaps because he also refused to look up at the windows that remained lit until late at night. Perhaps because he had decided not to mention them, at least at this stage of his narrative. Not that he was unaware at the time of the presence of those sorts of people. He knew that they existed somewhere, that is as one knows (abstractly) something learnt from newspaper articles or books, without forming an exact idea of their reality.'

61 'the huge ovation which lasted several minutes When it repeats itself for the second time nothing more than farce And how many times now'

62 'all the voluptuous memories which he carried away from her house allowed him to imagine the ardent or languishing postures which she might assume with other men'

63 'The last thing I want is to string together more words and more and more words. Haven't you finally had enough of it too?'

64 'the old illiterate peasant ... imbued through and through with a super-stitious faith'

65 'grabbing ... the piece of paper which he holds in both hands, grasping it as though it had been not a simple piece of paper but an enemy, an adversary which he must control and dominate ... the eagle-like face marked at that moment with an inexpressible defensive despair'

66 Ralph Sarkonak makes this point in his discussion of Simon's 'middle period' novels: 'l'opacification du langage' means that 'la façon dont le signe est appréhendé est *étrange*, puisqu'elle sort de la norme représenté par le langage dénotatif'. (1986: 44) ['The sign is apprehended as *strange*, because it does not fall within the norm of denotative language']. Jean Duffy (1983) also examines various different kinds of defamiliarization (not including writing) in Simon's work.

67 'with each time the same bewilderment, the same apprehension, before going up to her room, feeling around in a drawer for the case, her broken nails scrabbling at its clasp until she managed to open it, taking out of the worn velvet lining one of those pairs of metal-rimmed spectacles, its bridge adorned with a piece of yellowing cambric bound up in black thread, unfolding the ear-pieces, placing them carefully behind her ears, shutting the case, finally deciding (resigning herself) to break the wax seal, going over to the window, her lips moving silently as between the flabby eye-lids her pupils slid slowly from left to right, returned quickly to the left to set off again in the opposite direction, her eye-lids dropping a little lower each time, frowning, her lips continuing to form the words one after another'

68 'pressing on the pencil with all his strength, tracing deep furrows not on but in the page of the notebook, as though the paper, the fragile, dangerous, intangible support of signs, abstractions, had to be confronted and mastered by means of a violent physical effort'

69 'pressing down strongly on the point to cut into the marble, the point skidding sometimes so that most of the letters have that clumsy jerky look'

70 'the letters sometimes too big, sometimes almost missed out, scribbled, as though his strength were failing him' / 'the lines distended, diverging, the corrections, crossings out and interpolations proliferating'

71 'UNION FOR PROG' / 'the incomprehensible traces of an incoherent language'

72 'on the grainy gnawed stone the inscription, the epitaph, the visitor stooping to read (or rather to make out the slight hollows in the stone ...) the words ... reading at the pace of his finger following the sequence of letters MARIE ANNE ... then scratching the stone with his finger-nail, flaking off the the yellow scales of lichen, saying HASSEL ..., the end of the name completely worn away, the stone splintered at that point, the characters becoming legible again a bit further on'

73 'finally offering the visitor no more than an enigmatic skeleton of language with the calloused flesh of shreds of vowels, shreds of diphthongs, sticking to it in places'

74 'or at least consciousness of your death' / 'May the gods give you not death, which is the punishment reserved for all, but after your fateful destiny, the consciousness of your death.'

75 Ralph Sarkonak refers to this as Simon's 'mimétisme verbal' (1986: 47).

76 'and again in black on the green background ... the remarks certified by a hand-written signature ...'

77 'There were also the initials BΠT repeated three times in varying sizes ΔMP and also the letters Δ and Π inscribed in the angle formed by the top half of the huge Σ whose bottom corner contained in tiny figures the date 1966.'

78 Loubère argues along similar lines that the presence of a foreign word makes the reader pause, and 'The pause, therefore, draws insistent attention to the work performed by a word, any word, in constituting the text' (Loubère 1982: 187). She also makes the point that the materiality of the foreign words is emphasized by the way they are referred to in the matrix text, citing this description of Latin words from *Histoire*: 'les mots semblables à ces coupes, ces peignes, ces aiguilles, ces bracelets de bronze ou de cuivre verdis, un peu rongés, maix aux contours précis, ciselés' (120). ['the words like those goblets, those combs, those needles, those bracelets made of bronze or greenish copper, a little worn, but with precise, chiselled outlines']

5. The unseen and the unsaid

1 'she – with her body hidden beneath the corset's stiff whalebone, the stiff rustling skirts, her serene face coated in respectable creams and respectable veils of powder – like one of those high blank walls facing onto a street, impenetrable, haughty, secret, so that all you can see are the tops of clumps of laurels or camelias inviolable flowers motionless in the stiff dark greenery and behind which you hear (you think you hear) sounds like fountains, like bird-song'

2 'through the slit in a curtain the two lovers entwined'

3 In this passage Lacan also invokes the curtain as literary figure, referring to three famous examples in Racine, Stendhal and Shakespeare: 'le mouvement où se traduit la présence d'Agrippine au Conseil de l'Empire, ou le regard de Madame de Chasteller sur le passage de Lucien Leuwen ... Polonius que je frappe ...' (1966: 167). ['the movement which signals Agrippine's presence at the Imperial Council, or Madame de Chasteller watching Lucien Leuwen go past ... Polonius whom I strike']

4 'Curtain! It is an image, finally, of meaning as such, which to be discovered must be unveiled.'

5 'Georges looked as well ... but probably not quickly enough, for at one of the upstairs windows of the house he was just in time to see the curtain falling back into place, one of those cheap lace curtains, the sort that are sold at fairs, with a pattern showing a peacock with a long drooping tail framed in a diamond shape whose slanting sides went up in steps because of the mesh of the lace, the peacock's tail swaying once or twice, then stopping.'

6 In *Illusions perdues*, for instance, there is the important description of Lucien's first visit to the theatre in Paris.

7 'makes it clear that if one wishes to deceive a man, what one presents to him is the painting of a veil, that is to say, something that incites him to ask what is behind it' (Sheridan: 1977b: 112).

8 Ann Jefferson makes a similar point in her discussion of the hero's mistaken judgements about other people: 'Such misapprehensions constitute a significant element in the poetics of fiction, not only in providing a *telos* for the narrative, but also in the creation of realism. The revelation of the hidden life at its source makes fiction appear in some way more real than history or chronicle, because fiction reveals what is secret ... Just as in narrative what comes last is regarded as the truth, so in characters, what is secret is held to be most *real* ... Appearance, rumour and deception give way to *facts*, *truth*, and *reality* in direct proportion to the inventiveness of fiction. Novels invert the truth values of history so that appearances must always be regarded as deceptive or mysterious and secrets as truthful. The visible is described in terms of masks in order to provide a realist motivation for that most fictional domain of fiction: the hidden life at its source' (1980: 91–2, author's italics).

9 'the desire to know the truth ... He knew that the reality of the situation, which he would have given his life to reconstruct exactly, could be read behind that window streaked with light.'

10 'the whole peacock palpitating together with the curtain its arched neck curving into an S-shape ... the curtain continuing to oscillate after she had let it fall palpitating like a living creature like the life concealed behind it'

11 'the net curtain ... breathing gently like a stomach'

12 As Christian Metz comments in a somewhat similar context (cinematic

framing techniques, i.e. placing limits on the visible): 'It can be observed once again that the defence against desire itself becomes erotic, as the defence against anxiety itself becomes anxiogenic; for an analogous reason: what arises "against" an effect also arises "in" it and is not easily separated from it, even if that is its aim' (1982: 70–1).

13 'the curtain covered with gaudy advertisements, rediscovered each time with the same impatience and the same reassuring satisfaction, for if it intervened, blocked, deferred pleasure, it was at the same time the guarantee, the promise that, behind its blind opacity, somewhere, ready at a moment's notice to glitter in the crackling of the projector, were the expected visions of cavalcades, kisses and fights'

14 'the reflection in the half-closed window pane still two-thirds filled with the corner of the building and one-third with the sky, the large mesh of the net curtain behind the glass more visible in the dark grey part than in the stripe filled with pale blue, the swollen shape of the cloud worming its way from one pane to the other contorting itself so to speak across the uneven surface of the glass, sliding and disappearing, the reflected image of the corner façade, balconies, windows, also sinuous, like those reflections in water'

15 'the drawn curtain only lets in a softened light. O sees the body leaning over her'

16 Laplanche and Pontalis define disavowal as a 'mode de défense consistant en un refus par le sujet de reconnaître la réalité d'une perception traumatisante, essentiellement celle de l'absence de pénis chez la femme' (1967: 115). ['mode of defence consisting in a refusal by the subject to recognize the reality of a traumatic perception, essentially the perception that the woman has no penis'] As Freud says, 'It is not true that, after the child has made his observation of the woman, he has preserved un-altered his belief that women have a phallus. He has retained that belief, but he has also given it up. In the conflict between the weight of the unwelcome perception and the force of his counter-wish, a compromise has been reached, as is only possible under the dominance of the un-conscious laws of thought – the primary processes' ('Fetishism', vol. 21: 154).

17 'her peaceful and banal nakedness so lacking in mystery that from it there emanated a sort of second-degree mystery hidden beyond the visible, the tangible, this terrifying enigma, insoluble, dizzying'

18 'But motionless. The mesh of the curtain motionless as well' / 'Perhaps the curtain behind the right-hand pane had moved slightly or the wind?' / 'the net curtain absolutely motionless as well'

19 'her hand over it hiding it then revealing it then covering it up again running quickly to the bed Let me see I said Oh let me see'

20 'observing the first observer ... through the mesh of the net curtain'

21 I have discussed the question of the exchange of looks in Chapter 2.

22 'a gaze imagined by me in the field of the Other' (Sheridan 1977b: 84)

23 That there is an element of anxiety and almost of threat as well as titillation in the supposition that one is the object of the other's look comes across more clearly when the other in question, the figure behind the curtain, is not a woman. Thus when in *Les Géorgiques* 'O' is in the streets of Barcelona and sees 's'écarter un rideau laissant entrevoir la moitié d'un de ces visages épais, harassés, dont pendant quelques instants les yeux légèrement bridés … contemplaient … le bruyant défilé, puis … disparaissait derrière le rideau' (337) ['a curtain move aside showing a glimpse of half of one of those heavy, exhausted faces, whose slightly slanting eyes … contemplated for a few moments … the noisy procession, then … vanished behind the curtain'], the brevity of the glimpse and the fact that only half the face is seen are reminiscent of the vision of the woman behind the curtain (particularly the version given in *Le Palace*, for instance), but the overall impact is frightening rather than erotic: the sinister Russian agent master-minding the Spanish communists. Here to be the object of the half-hidden look is simply to be vulnerable, to be exposed to the power and hostility of others.

24 'Isn't the most erotic part of a body *the place where the garment gapes open*?' / 'In perversion (which is the regime of textual pleasure) … it is intermittence, as psychoanalysis rightly says, which is erotic' / 'what is seductive is this shimmering itself, or in other words: the staging of an appearance–disappearance'

25 'seeing her then, just for a fraction of a second' / 'the naked body [which] … was not wholly visible, jammed tightly between the two verticals and even partly masked by the left side of the rectangle formed by the window which split the right thigh exactly in two'

26 Freud remarks that 'Affection and hostility in the treatment of the fetish – which run parallel with the disavowal and the acknowledgement of castration – are mixed in unequal proportions in different cases' (vol. 21: 157), and sees a parallel to fetishism in 'the Chinese custom of mutilating the female foot and then revering it like a fetish after it has been mutilated' (ibid.).

27 'one of those weird erections of disparate objects one on top of the other … which seem to balance weightlessly on the juggler's finger'

28 'But how was it, how was it? Merely an instant, the space of scarcely a fraction of a second. Then she drew the curtain, removing herself, erasing herself, effacing herself' / 'glimpsed, she too emerging from nothingness and the next moment returning for ever to nothingness'

29 'the vanished apparition remaining there probably as the result of a persistence in the retina, its very brevity giving it … this prolongation of existence, so that he seemed to be still continuing to see her'

30 'sequence of simple images'

31 'the old curtain draped against the wall as a backcloth'

32 'the unnameable' / 'the named' / 'not saying but feeling'

33 'the first example in Simon's texts of a radically non-representational, non-narrative, and above all non-visual writing'

34 'like a retarded adolescent, gauche and so to speak virginal'

35 'another woman' / 'the same part of her body, although used, if the
expression may be allowed, in the opposite direction'

36 'or again seeing in the gap between the drapes that closed the entrance ...
(spread out with the quiet indifference or rather obviousness of an object,
or rather an entity, in the midst of that setting of kitchen furniture, guitars
with no strings and faded old carpets hung up to form partitions, so that
they cooked, slept and made love in the shadow of garlands of flowers
and yellowed leaves swaying against reddish backgrounds, like a
temporary and dusty encampment of crimson and faded laurels) ... a
fragment (between the two parallels or the acute angle of the opening),
a section: black and white: a hip, the bar of shade between the thighs,
the hollow of a waist breathing: something strange: that matt texture,
that lustre, that guessed-at warmth, the inoffensive and terrifying
immobility of a trap.'

37 'for a moment I could see or rather glimpse mummy's face'

38 'the motionless rush of purple waves the spots of blood the leaves'

39 'trampling on the garlands of roses on the carpet'

40 'festooned pillows'

41 'brushing against the little black knob and immediately below it standing
out against the white of the pillows'

42 'like a knife blade seen from the front the nose too like a knife blade'

43 'glimpse mummy's face ... in a triangle delimited by the bent arm the
inlaid wooden pediment at the foot of the bed and the right-hand upright'

44 'the screen is no longer that which masks, but the temple in which is
represented, derealized, the real as image'

45 'by virtue of the light which had outlined in sinuous moving Chinese
shadows the sinuous contour of the raised arm, the breast, the hip and
the thigh undulating, stretching, swelling on the cloth which was then
suddenly drawn across' / 'the green–black Chinese shadows projected
onto the curtain'

46 'they suddenly flew off ... a snowy palpitating curtain run through with
multiple eddying currents ... like a moving curtain behind which, in the
bar mirror, he seemed to see it, intact, its craggy bloated architecture
rearing up ... the shivering veil of pigeons rippling, sagging, falling back,
finally subsiding, the blank cold wall of the bank reappearing again,
geometrical, square ... and in front of it, her painted face smiling at him,
and he wondering how long she had been sitting there ... her heavy young
flesh like a mysterious seething, a secret'

47 Apart from a brief mention on page 289.

48 'with no more substance than that curtain on which we thought we saw
the lace peacock stir palpitate breathe imagining dreaming about what
was behind it probably without even having seen the face cut in half the
hand which had let it drop watching passionately the slight movement
caused by the draught'

49 'disappointing secret that consists in the certainty of the absence of any secret and any mystery'

50 'the power of fascination which the famous "peacock curtain" possesses in *La Route des Flandres*' / 'emblematic metaphor of a book obsessed by un-covering and concerned with everything that signifies, it invites us precisely to look behind and to examine, in order to bring it to light, the quotient of invisibility that is retained in the visible'

51 'then a few more drops, then, after a long while, another – then no more'

52 'spread of variations on the same haunting question: ¿QUIEN ASESINO A SANTIAGO?'

53 See Britton 1984.

54 'In Simon's writing, no desire to put an end to meaning, but, on the contrary, an implicit recognition that one can never put an end to it, in so far as Simon's semantic regime is, fundamentally, that of the enigma.'

55 'reconstitute ... the whole story'

56 'like the surface of a painting obscured by varnish and dirt, which a restorer would reveal one patch at a time – trying out different cleaning agents, experimenting with them on small areas here and there'

57 With reference to *Histoire*, T. H. Jones points out that the actual structural principle which generates the novel, and which Simon represents pictorially as a series of 'waves' alternately present in the text and submerged beneath it (see 'La fiction mot à mot': 94), implies a kind of repression or unseen/unsaid: 'According to this conception, the readable text of a narrative becomes an explicit alternative for the "invisible", suppressed text of what is neither said nor read. Moreover, as the readable text evolves to become one term on what might be considered an axis of expression and suppression, it tends increasingly to suggest the existence of its unexpressed counterterm and thus reflects a potential for meaning never explicitly stated' (Jones 1981: 110).

58 'she wouldn't find in them any diary, or memoirs, or yellowing letters, or anything like that'

59 'the kind of ideas (keeping a diary, writing the story of her own life) that could not possibly even cross the mind of the woman who had kept them'

60 'he did not talk about the processions, or the insidious and deadly newspaper headlines, or the rivalry between the different barracks with their different patrons' / 'passing by without seeing them (in any case he did not talk about them – or perhaps they were among ... those things that he had decided once and for all not to see any more' / 'But he did not talk about them either'

61 'perhaps he also thinks that ... the necessities of syntactical construction will bring out relations of cause and effect' / 'There will however be gaps in his story, obscure parts, even inconsistencies.'

62 'his adventure (or rather the adventure that he (O) was now trying to recount) was like one of those novels in which the narrator who has been carrying out the investigation turns out to be not the murderer, as in some sophisticated versions, but the actual corpse'

63 'drowning the reader in a profusion of irrelevant details whose accumulation serves to cover up the hidden link in the chain, the missing information'

64 The connection between the two levels is in fact already present in Freud's original formulation of censorship: see vol. 4: 142.

65 'so heavily censored that some of their pages ... were almost entirely blank'

66 '"You mean: why has no-one ever talked about him? Well, that's the point: exactly!"'

67 'of whom, later, no trace must remain, not even a locket, or a letter, or a document proving that he had lived (except these two simple words: my brother, when his possessions had to be shared out, and that notice, those three columns of print that bore witness to his existence only by virtue of the judgement that deprived him of it), he whose very name it was now forbidden to utter'

68 'rigidly closed over his secret, with that thin grimace perhaps still twitching at his lips' / 'writing ... with his mouth so to speak twisted, twitched to one side by a grimace that was both mocking and nervous'

69 'Saying that jealousy is like ... like ... Remembering the place: roughly in the top third of a right-hand page.'

70 E.g. pp. 38, 84, 90, 168.

71 'jealousy where was it right hand page at the top'

72 'LEAPS FROM FOURTH FLO' / 'TAKES HER OWN LIFE LEAPING FROM'

73 'occulted scene of the drowning at night'

74 Cf. S. Lotringer's paper (1975: 325). Lotringer, it should be said, would not accept the notion of censorship in the reductive sense of *a* meaning 'in disguise' and therefore in principle recuperable: in his view, *Triptyque* 'ne s'offre plus à une activité balisée, banalisée de déchiffrement, au décryptage d'un sens préalablement encodé ... le texte exige le *sacrifice* de la communication, de tous ses pôles et ses rôles' (331, author's italics). ['is no longer open to a guided, routinized activity of deciphering, of decoding a previously encoded meaning ... the text demands that communication be *sacrificed*, in all its polarities and all its roles'] But the *mechanisms* that he demonstrates, and defines in Derridean terms of supplementarity, repetition and dissemination, are not dissimilar to those of the Freudian unconscious; it is only the finality of meaning, meaning as solution and closure, that is contested. This position is certainly tenable in general terms, but his own phrase: 'scène occultée de la noyade nocturne' would seem to imply that on this occasion at least the reader can and does recover a determinate hidden meaning.

75 'Rambuteau conveniences were called 'pistières' [instead of 'pissotières', i.e. urinals] Probably as a child he had not heard the o and the pronunciation had stayed with him.'

76 'In particular the quotation from Proust in which a character calls the

Rambuteau conveniences 'pistières' enables us to interpret the letter 'O' (emphasized by its unwarranted disappearance, since in Poe the purloined "letter" is hidden by carefully leaving it on view) as bearing a "trail" [piste].'

77 See Chapter 2, p. 58.

78 'So let us track it down where it throws us off the scent.'

79 'widower [veuf] limping word truncated left hanging so to speak cut off unnaturally like the English *half* half sectioned *cut off* cut from something missing suddenly in the mouth the lips pronouncing VF continuing to go fff like the rustling sound of the air torn by the swift glittering deadly sweep of a blade' (The italicized words are in English in the original.)

80 'poor old Charles: such naïvety where women were concerned'

81 'that same agitation, that same slightly shameful excitement, the awareness that a prohibition had been disobeyed' / 'the word libidinous its consonance rather pink, rather soft, pleated so to speak by the repetition of the same syllables and evocative sounds (bed, prick, cock)'

82 'scented with the heavy sensuality that seems to emanate from that language from the names the words themselves'

83 'crucial secret' / 'The excitement, the sort of fever, the crude, violent Latin words whose disorientating, so to speak exotic, appearance and uncertain meaning charged them with an ambiguous, multiple power.'

84 'læta proximat rosa serta renudata crinibusque dissolutis running up crowned with roses joyful completely naked beneath her hair falling loose mane fleece that I could feel in my hand the hairs silky and rough at the same time escaping from me rippling undulating'

85 'what had I sought in her hoped for pursued even on to her body into her body words sounds as mad as him with his illusory sheets of paper covered with spidery black scribbling words that our lips pronounced in order to deceive ourselves live a life of sounds with no more reality no more substance than that curtain on which we thought we saw the lace peacock stir'

86 In connection with this passage, among others, Pat O'Kane gives an interesting interpretation of the woman's body as text, in '*La Route des Flandres*: Reader's Rout(e)?' (1985: 50−60).

87 'one of them, then another, suddenly breaks off, giving way (like a curtain opening onto another curtain) to the same chirping' / 'strident chant ... weaves a sort of second layer of silence'

88 'implicit recognition ... that one can never put an end to [meaning]' / 'semantic regime of the enigma' / 'obsession with meaning and with depth'

89 'rising to burst at the surface like bubbles empty like bubbles and nothing else Clear to him who does not seek to go into it deeply'

90 'as though in all surfaces, appearing to be other than what they are, there is a sort of fold, a shimmering of shadow which gives the impression of a play of depth, while it is nothing but the symptom of the surface folding

back on itself ... We thus witness a reversal of the imaginary model of knowledge. Whereas for the whole of metaphysical thought it is the surface which hides the depth, here depth will be nothing more than an illusory effect of the surface which makes it impossible to consider it for itself.'

91 'Inside the window, against the glass, their hems falling behind the photographs, two lace curtains patterned with garlands of leaves surrounding a bird are parted in symmetrical curves. Whether because they are dirty, or have been dyed, or even turned yellow by the sun, they are the colour of piss. The square mesh of the lace gives the designs zigzag outlines like stairs. Despite being fragmented and telescoped by the folds, the bird is recognizable as a peacock with a long drooping tail.'

6. The invisibility of history

1 This is recognized by most of his earlier critics. Thus Ludovic Janvier, for instance, finds that his initial impression of the corpus up to 1962 'nous amène rapidement à constater qu'il s'agit sans doute d'une problématique de l'individu dans l'Histoire, et cet aspect se révèle de façon privilégiée dans la première œuvre: *Le Tricheur*, sans jamais s'estomper par la suite ... à travers lui il est possible, dès maintenant, d'apercevoir toute l'œuvre en perspective' (1964: 90). ['quickly leads us to observe that it is probably concerned with the problematic of the individual in History; this aspect is particularly prominent in the first work, *Le Tricheur*, and never fades thereafter ... through it we can, right from the start, put the whole corpus in perspective']

2 'pitiless, arrogant and mysterious History'

3 'this cold Olympian advance, this slow glacier on the move since the beginning of time, grinding, crushing everything'

4 Janvier sees the evolution of the concept of history slightly differently, but arrives at the same conclusion for *Le Palace*: 'L'histoire a subi la même évolution: de spectaculaire et cruelle qu'elle était, en passant par le riche écroulement de *La Route des Flandres*, elle est devenue indifférente, anonyme, laissant le personnage apercevoir tragiquement sa totale inutilité. A l'absolu anonymat, l'absolue dérision' (1964: 102). ['History has undergone the same evolution: from being spectacular and cruel, by way of the richly collapsing *La Route des Flandres*, it has become indifferent, anonymous, giving the character a tragic perception of his total uselessness. Absolute anonymity goes together with absolute futility.']

5 'and, as always, acting (History) with its terrifying excess, its incredible heavy humour'

6 'Laws perhaps (an order or rather a regulation impossible to detect but as imprescriptible, as mathematical in its nature as the laws governing the spirals of sea-shells).'

7 'And he was just getting down to it when History (or destiny – or what else? the inner logic of matter? its implacable mechanisms?) decided otherwise.'

8 'History, futility, fatality'

9 'to endure History (not to be resigned to it: to endure it) is to make it'

10 'the world stopped frozen crumbling gutting itself collapsing bit by bit like an abandoned, unusable building, given over to the incoherent, casual, impersonal and destructive work of time'

11 'It will be evident that Claude Simon's political position, a *paralysed* position more common than one might believe, is likely to be uncomfortable.'

12 'proliferating and rigorous disorder'

13 'Nobody makes History, you can't see it, any more than you can see the grass growing.'

14 'the real as encounter – the encounter in so far as it may be missed, in so far as it is essentially the missed encounter' (Sheridan 1977b: 55)

15 'emptying itself in a tiny unceasing and futile hæmorrhage ... an invisible fissure in the very centre of her body' / 'thin stealthy hissing of a leak, that sort of invisible permanent hæmorrhage'

16 'There was probably something that he hadn't been able to see, that had escaped him, and perhaps then he too could get into, settle down in, wangle himself a place in that tangential, edible, optimistic derivative of metaphysics named carp or History.'

17 'looking out of the window with an expression of charitable disgust' / 'There's got to be a knack to it.'

18 'things happening, like the movements of land that has been slowly and stealthily undermined, in sudden jerks' / 'in a sequence of sudden mutations'

19 This is exactly the same kind of image of history that Deguy finds in *La Route des Flandres* and *Le Palace*, and which he defines as 'grand guignol, grande charade animée' (1962: 1026) ['a Punch and Judy show, a great living charade'], and, earlier, as 'l'histoire des hommes comme fleuve de pus, océan charnier, putréfaction sans commencement ni fin' (1024). ['the history of man as river of pus, oceanic charnel-house, putrefaction with no beginning or end'] He, too, identifies a fundamental causal connection between history and vision (1026–7), but in his view the causality works the other way round: that is, the privileging of vision (and, even more so, the particular structure of Simon's vision) is the *consequence* of the failure to invest history with any positive meaning, the result of the 'horror' with which history is consequently regarded: 'l'œil qui regarde est un œil *agrandi d'horreur* depuis l'origine, l'origine criminelle d'où ne cesse de couler le fleuve sanglant de l'Histoire; œil vidé par et pour l'horreur' (1025, author's italics). ['The eye that looks is an eye *widened in horror* since the beginning, since the criminal origin whence the bloody river of History constantly flows; an eye emptied by and for horror.'] I have already argued (see Introduction) that Deguy derives the 'representability' of Simon's real from too limited a base, excluding the elements of pleasure and phantasy that also, and in my view more centrally, determine it, and this is why I disagree with the formulation he gives; but the

observable *interdependence* of the two major textual concerns, vision and history, is an important common factor in both his position and mine.

20 'History ... turning to parody, clowning: one of those films shown speeded up, with its crowds, its ataxic characters with their incoherent gestures, unfinished – or finished too soon'

21 Individual, and also individualist: as Janvier says of the hero of Simon's earliest novel, *Le Tricheur*: 'De la nostalgie de l'histoire à faire, il en arrive au classique constat individualiste de l'histoire subie ... (dans l'œuvre tout entière) il y sera toujours question de cet individu problématique que le flux des événements finit par entraîner avec lui. Le rapport individu–histoire informe pour toujours la recherche, et nous allons semble-t-il toujours au-devant de la même réponse' (1964: 91). ['From nostalgia for history as act, he arrives at the classic individualist position of history passively endured ... (in the whole work) it will always be a question of this problematic individual who is in the end swept along by the flux of events. The relation between individual and history always orientates the search, and we always seem to come up against the same answer.']

22 'The goddess Reason Virtue'

23 See Randi Birn's article (1981) for a detailed discussion of these.

24 'the consequence of the ancestral fear of hunger and death'

25 'their abundance of interminable patient demonstrations, their look of evening class textbooks'

26 'the other Bible which ... had nourished his adolescence'

27 'those things that he had decided once and for all not to see any more'

28 'a tearful Swiss morality which he would never have been able to know if his fortune, his rank, had not provided him with the means, that is the leisure and the ability to read' / 'so that now all he could do was look or rather avoid looking ... at the rabble scattering in all directions'

29 'what (... the idyllic tearful reign of Reason and Virtue) his readings had given him a glimpse of' / 'something in which he had believed and in which he could now see no sense'

30 'lacking reality, like smoke when you smoke in the dark, when you can't see it, and so just something burning ... escapes from your mouth, your nose, with no real existence'

31 David Carroll endorses the interpretation of history as lack, arguing that Simon's novels demonstrate 'the failure of history to institute itself as an entirely progressive, continuous process and ... the dissemination of this failure or lack throughout history' (1982: 39). But elsewhere he equates this with a radical *critical* position, saying, for instance: '*The Palace* is not the simple alternative to "optimistic visions" of history, but rather a radical investigation and critique of history and fiction as modes of representation of the past that in no way attempts to do away with history, to transcend it, or to ignore it' (111). He arrives at this view by tying history in to the general issue of representation ('Irresolvable contradiction, loss, repetition and conflict within history are the origin and the end of representation', 110), and then arguing very cogently that Simon is deconstructing

representation − thereby allowing 'history' to be carried along in the momentum of this positive move towards 'open' forms: 'the "crisis of representation" thematized and practiced (*sic*) in *The Palace* necessitates that history and fiction be conceived as open rather than closed processes or forms' (111). But in fact it is an over-simplification to equate history and representation in this way; the work Simon carries out on representation is not − as I have argued throughout this book − consistent or total, and moreover the countervailing representational impulse is closely linked to the epistemological status of the visible which I have posited above as the major factor determining Simon's attitude to History. The liberating critical deconstruction of representation co-exists with a substantive and far less sophisticated despair in the face of the unintelligibility of history. Simon's repeated references to 'l'Histoire' as a mysterious impersonal force which men cannot comprehend or intervene in − and which in that sense is far from 'open' − are difficult to reconcile with a consistently practised operation of deconstruction.

32 Thus A. B. Cobban, for instance, writes: 'While ... attention was concentrated on a mechanical universe and its laws, interest in the individual had naturally declined ... he ... had come to be regarded as just a result, the product of the action of a set of mechanical laws on a material so purely passive, so lacking in qualities, and so undifferentiated, that it could hardly be said to exist at all' (1929: 32).

33 As when they say: 'What is abandoned is the whole claim and approach of knowledge: to comprehend the given as such; not merely to determine the abstract spatio-temporal relations of the fact which allow them just to be grasped, but on the contrary to conceive them as the superficies, as mediated conceptual moments which come to fulfilment only in the development of their social, historical, and human significance' (1979: 26).

34 See for instance Cobban 1929: 32, for a discussion of this.

35 'Now we're getting there: History ... Like the Immaculate Conception: a sparkling and uplifting vision traditionally reserved for simple souls and cranks, the good conscience of the informer and the *philosophe*.'

36 Presumably because of the incident in the *Confessions* where he blames a servant for the theft of a ribbon which he has in fact stolen himself.

37 Thus Marx argues that 'the distinction should always be made between the material transformation of the economic conditions of production which can be determined with the precision of natural science, and the legal, political, religious, aesthetic or philosophical − in short, ideological − forms in which men become conscious of this conflict and fight it out. Just as our opinion of an individual is not based on what he thinks of himself, so can we not judge of such a period of transformation by its own consciousness; on the contrary, this consciousness must rather be explained from the contradictions of material life, from the existing conflict between the social forces of production and the relations of production' (from the Preface to *A Contribution to the Critique of*

Political Economy, 1859, translated by T. B. Bottomore and quoted in Bottomore and Rubel 1956: 68).

38 Cf. Marx's comment that '*History* does *nothing*; it "does *not* possess immense riches", it "does *not* fight battles". It is *men*, real living men, who possess things and fight battles. It is not "history" which uses men as a means of achieving — as if it were an individual person — *its* own ends. History is *nothing* but the activity of men in pursuit of their ends' (*Die heilige Familie, Marx—Engels Gesamtausgabe*, vol. I section 3, p. 265, translated T. B. Bottomore, quoted in Bottomore and Rubel 1956: 78).

39 'places perennially reserved for this purpose ... those plains, those two or three rivers which Europe has grown accustomed to use as its lists, as natural drains'

40 'But it was the same roads, the same frozen ponds, the same silent forests that had been traversed again and again by successive hordes of looters, arsonists and murderers, first of all coming from the depths of Asia, and then iron-clad men with red beards ... and later armies with nothing but rags round their feet, and then still others, and always the same valleys ... simply because it was the best route going from East to West.'

41 In his chapter 'Errance et question' (1964: 27—36), Ludovic Janvier makes the point that 'errance' is a characteristic feature of many *nouveaux romans*: Jacques Revel in Bleston, Wallas in *Les Gommes*, etc. In the case of Simon's novels, Janvier sees it as a kind of derisory counterpoint to the 'universel acheminement' ['universal moving on'] of history (29), in which 'tout ce monde marche à la fois convaincu et sans conviction, et personne n'arrive jamais nulle part sinon à la mort, ou dans le lit d'une femme facile qu'il faudra quitter pour repartir, ou encore à la conscience de l'universelle dérision' (29). ['all these people walk, both convinced and lacking conviction, and no-one ever arrives anywhere except at death, or in the bed of a loose woman who will have to be left behind when they set off again, or else at a realization of universal futility']

42 'come straight from the depths of Asia, of the ages, emerging just as they are now from the entrails of the world' / 'the immemorial laws of wandering'

43 'those civilians who persisted in incomprehensible fashion in wandering around trailing a broken suitcase or one of those children's carts loaded with vague bundles'

44 'these terrible migrating multitudes endlessly swirling round the surface of the earth wandering from East to West dragging themselves from holy place to holy place'

45 'chased like an animal' / 'the hunted beast'

46 'wandering in three dimensions, as though forced to fly aimlessly ... as though some torment were forcing them to wander like this without going anywhere'

47 'that interminable roaming ... from one side to the other of the Europe that he had defied, crossed and re-crossed in all directions, forever

setting off on journeys back and forth that forever brought him back to the same places'

48 'perhaps they were going round in circles in the city searching for the enemy who could not be found, that thing that had no name, no face, no appearance, doomed to wander endlessly like the Jew in the legend who could find no rest, like the flocks of anxious, plaintive, savage birds that you see fluttering interminably and moaning above something invisible, some carcass, some dying beast, some monster'

49 'placed, we thought, by right and in fact, outside what we had been taught ... to consider as the livestock of History' / 'History is not, as the textbooks would have us believe, a discontinuous series of dates, treaties and spectacular jingling battles (comparable ... to the other kinds of scourge manifesting themselves sporadically at well-defined times, places and dates ...) but on the contrary without limits, and not only in time (never stopping, slowing down or breaking off, non-stop, like cinema performances ...) but also in its effects'

50 'as though it (History) stopped there, as though the long sequence of chapters ... the long sequence of pictures that illustrated them ... had been written, sculpted, painted, engraved with that sole aim in mind, that sole ending, that apotheosis; the grey expanses of land, dismal, formless, with no trace of humanity'

51 'projected, as it were out of History, or abandoned to something which existed beyond all measure ... the state (time, space, cold) the world must have been in at the time of the cavemen, the mammoths, the bison'

52 'go back at top speed through the space of several centuries' / 'forgotten by history' / 'populations themselves still in a wild state, a primitive state'

53 'rejected by geography, like some container ... into which everything that other countries had gradually and painfully expelled over the centuries had slid down, come to rest, piled up'

54 'the name that had swung the fatal vote'

55 'the three orgasms, the three ejaculations of male semen through which the name had been preserved until it reached her'

56 'still bore the name no-one now answered to' / 'no longer anything, therefore, later on, from the day she married: a sound, a mere combination of letters which on the map or the sign at a cross-roads now indicated nothing more than the location of a hamlet and of the ruined chateau long since sold'

57 'the famous name, the coat-of-arms, were no longer to be seen except, as though in mockery, improperly used on the lable of a cheap aperitif sold in groceries'

58 'in very ancient times'

59 'basic and brutal actions like murder, barter or coitus'

60 'the complicated, subtle mechanism of exchanges and metamorphoses whereby the invisible air itself mutates through a series of transformations'

61 'mercenary everyday reality'

62 'because there two cigarettes can be traded for a bowl of soup' / 'now like starving beasts' / 'as though the summer, time, History, were themselves rotting, decomposing' / 'haggling in whispers ... over their pathetic treasures'

63 'transmute, that is make them undergo the operation which consists in converting raw, rough matter into something ... convenient to stock and buy' / 'the next operation consisting in a second transmutation of all that into watermarked paper decorated with financial or commercial deities'

64 'as though the same model with the thoughtful, pitiless and sceptical mask posing for the same painter had got one outfit after another from a theatrical costumier, reincarnations, sporadic reappearances repeated across centuries in the same calm, perfidious and weary pose, in front of allegorical backgrounds of swords, trophies, galleons, ears of corn and scales'

65 'the slow, inexorable notion of time' / 'a sort of umbilical cord leading symbolically to a woman, to the warm dark womb from which all life comes and for which the flesh yearns, the nostalgic groaning flesh haunted by the desire, and more than the desire the need, and more than the need the necessity to return to it, to die there once again'

66 'As if, sitting there as time stood still beside Rose who was dead ... he found himself taken back to a kind of fœtal state, curled up in the painful and torturing (so they say) tranquillity of a life inside the womb'

67 'not of the same blood but of the same milk as him' / 'so to speak like another brother. That is, more than a sister: not of the same blood but of the same milk as them, with whom they were as one'

68 'as an acknowledgement, a debt, a payment in return for the milk they had sucked'

69 'a fœtus with too big a head wrapped up in newsprint, nothing but a little macrocephalus prematurely deceased because the doctors couldn't agree and thrown into the sewers in a shroud of words'

70 'the enthusiastic army of the foreign correspondants of the liberal press'

71 'History will tell us, at some later date, what humanity lost the other day in a few minutes, the heritage of several centuries, in the bombing of the most precious library in the world, all this is infinitely sad, your old father'

72 'scribblings with no real existence other than that attributed to them by a mind itself without real existence in order to represent things imagined by it and perhaps also lacking existence'

73 'The 16 Ventose of year III he enters the Committee of Public Security. From Milan he organizes the ceremonial for the emperor's visit to the kingdom of Italy. In the midst of the Terror he is elected Secretary to the Convention and rescues a royalist woman who will become his second wife.'

74 'He sees black spots in front of his eyes' / 'he is a giant'

75 Benveniste 1966: 238. He specifically states that this covers fiction as well as factual writing, saying à propos of an example he takes from Balzac:

'Bien entendu l'énonciation historique des événements est indépendante de leur vérité "objective". Seul compte le dessein "historique" de l'écrivain' (240). ['Of course the historic enunciation of events is independent of their "objective" truth. All that counts is the "historic" intention of the writer.'] The French language, of course, allows in the term 'histoire' a fruitful ambiguity between history and narrative.

76 'an original hole which would never be able to regain its substance because its substance has never been anything but that of a hole'. The difference between repression and foreclosure is explained via the image of a piece of cloth: 'Si nous imaginons l'expérience comme une pièce d'étoffe constituée de fils entrecroisés, nous pourrions dire que le refoulement y serait figuré par quelque accroc ou déchirure, toujours reprisable, alors que la forclusion y serait figurée par quelque béance due au tissu lui-même, bref un trou originel, etc.' ('A propos de l'épisode psychotique que présenta l'homme aux loups', *La psychanalyse* no. 4, 1957; quoted in Lemaire 1977: 341). ['If we imagine experience as a piece of cloth made up of interwoven threads, we could say that repression would be like a snag or tear, which could always be repaired, whereas foreclosure would be a kind of gap intrinsic to the cloth itself, in short, an original hole.']

77 'a certain limit, which is known as the real' (Sheridan 1977b: 49).

7. Fiction word by word

1 'retrace the veins of meaning'
2 'through the actual progression of the writing'
3 'Claude Simon at work' / 'the Claude Simon of everyday life' / 'You must be able to abandon the picture you would like to paint in favour of the one that is painting *itself*.'
4 'as the surface of the water closes over a pebble, the reflected landscape for a moment broken, shattered, split up into an incoherent multitude of splinters, of entangled scraps of sky and trees (that is to say, no longer the sky, the trees, but mixed-up patches of blue, green, black), re-forming, the blue, the green, the black regrouping, so to speak coagulating, sorting themselves out, still undulating a little like dangerous snakes, then becoming motionless, and so all that remains is the polished surface, treacherous, serene and mysterious, and in it the peaceful opulence of the branches, the sky, the slow peaceful clouds, all in order, nothing now but this lacquered impenetrable surface'
5 'sentences ... infinitely reassuring, as smooth, as polished, as glazed and as insubstantial as the shimmering reflections on the surface of the water'
6 'the watering-place where we had to break the ice'
7 'the system as a whole should be pictured as a mobile constantly changing shape around a few fixed points'

BIBLIOGRAPHY

(Place of publication is Paris or London unless otherwise stated.)

1. Works by Claude Simon

The following editions have been used for purposes of reference:

Le Sacre du printemps, Calmann-Lévy, 1954

Le Vent, Editions de Minuit, 1957

L'Herbe, Editions de Minuit, 1958

La Route des Flandres, Editions de Minuit, 1960

Le Palace, Editions de Minuit, 1962

Histoire, Editions de Minuit, 1967; reprinted Gallimard, 'Folio', no. 388, 1973
    (page references are to the Folio edition)

La Bataille de Pharsale, Editions de Minuit, 1969

Orion aveugle, Skira, Geneva, 'Les sentiers de la création, no. 8, 1970

Les Corps conducteurs, Editions de Minuit, 1971

'La fiction mot à mot', in *Nouveau Roman: hier, aujourd'hui*, Colloque au
    Centre Culturel International de Cerisy-la-Salle, 1971; published by
    the Union Générale d'Editions, 2 vols, Collection 10/18, 1972, vol.
    1, 73–97

Triptyque, Editions de Minuit, 1973

Leçon de choses, Editions de Minuit, 1975

Les Géorgiques, Editions de Minuit, 1981

2. General

T. W. Adorno and M. Horkheimer: *Dialectic of Enlightenment*. Translated
    by John Cunningham, Verso Editions, 1979

Mikhail Bakhtin: *The Dialogic Imagination*, University of Texas Press,
    Austin, 1981

Honoré de Balzac: *Le Cousin Pons*, Gallimard, Collection Folio, 1973

Roland Barthes: *S/Z*, Editions du Seuil, 1970

    Le Plaisir du texte, Editions du Seuil, 1973

    La Chambre claire, Gallimard, 1980

    'L'effet de réel', in *Littérature et réalité*, Editions du Seuil, 1982, 81–90

Bibliography

Jean-Louis Baudry: 'Ecriture, fiction, idéologie', in *Théorie d'ensemble*, Editions du Seuil, 1968, 127–47

'Linguistique et production textuelle', ibid., 351–64

Emile Benveniste: *Problèmes de linguistique générale*, Gallimard, 1966

Olga Bernal: *Alain Robbe-Grillet: le roman de l'absence*, Editions du Seuil, 1964

Randi Birn: 'The Road to Creativity: Eighteenth Century Parody in *The Flanders Road*', in *Orion Blinded*, ed. Birn and Gould, 1981, 87–104

Randi Birn and K. Gould, ed.: *Orion Blinded: Essays on Claude Simon*, Bucknell University Press, Lewisburg, 1981

Tom Bishop: 'La vue d'Orion ou le processus de la création', in *Entretiens sur les Lettres et les Arts*, 31, 1972–3, 20–40

T. B. Bottomore and Maximilien Rubel, ed.: *Karl Marx: Selected Writings in Sociology and Social Philosophy*, Penguin Books, Harmondsworth, 1956

Malcolm Bowie: 'Lacan', in *Structuralism and Since*, ed. John Sturrock, Oxford University Press, Oxford, 1979

Celia Britton: 'Diversity of Discourse in Claude Simon's *Les Géorgiques*', in *French Studies* 38, 1984, 423–42

'*The Georgics*: the Limits of History', in *The Review of Contemporary Fiction* 5, 1985, 95–9

'Claude Simon's Generation Game: the Family and the Text', in *Claude Simon: New Directions*, ed. Duncan, 1985, 19–29

Pierre Caminade: 'Le mouvement métaphorique dans *L'Herbe*', in *Claude Simon: analyse, théorie*, ed. Ricardou, 1975, 348–63

David Carroll: *The Subject in Question*, University of Chicago Press, Chicago, 1982

A. B. Cobban: *Edmund Burke and the Revolt Against the Eighteenth Century*, Allen and Unwin, 1929

Jonathan Culler: *Structuralist Poetics*, Routledge and Kegan Paul, 1975

Lucien Dällenbach: 'Mise en abyme et redoublement spéculaire chez Claude Simon', in *Claude Simon: analyse, théorie*, ed. Ricardou, 1975, 151–71

Le Récit spéculaire, Editions du Seuil, 1977

'Le tissu de mémoire', in Claude Simon, *La Route des Flandres*, Editions de Minuit, Collection Double, 1982, 299–316

Michel Deguy: 'Claude Simon et la représentation', in *Critique* 18, 1962, 1009–32

Jacques Derrida: 'La différance', in *Théorie d'ensemble*, Editions du Seuil, 1968, 41–66

'Le facteur de la vérité', *Yale French Studies* no. 52, 1975

Serge Doubrovsky: 'Notes sur la genèse d'une écriture', in *Entretiens sur les Lettres et les Arts* 31, 1972, 51–64

'Preface' to *Orion Blinded*, ed. Birn and Gould, 1981, 11–16

Jean Duffy: 'Art as Defamiliarization in the Theory and Practice of Claude Simon', in *Romance Studies* 2, 1983, 108–23

Bibliography

Alastair Duncan: 'Claude Simon: la crise de la représentation', in *Critique* 1981, 1181–1200

  (ed.) *Claude Simon: New Directions*, Scottish Academic Press, Edinburgh, 1985

Claud Duverlie: 'The Crossing of the Image', in *Diacritics* 7, 1977, 47–58

  'Pictures for Writing: Premises for a Graphopictology', in *Orion Blinded*, ed. Birn and Gould, 1981, 200–17

Umberto Eco: *Opera aperta*, Bompiani, Milan, 1962. French translation: *L'Œuvre ouverte*, Editions du Seuil, 1965. References are to the French translation.

Jean-Baptiste Fages: *Comprendre Jacques Lacan*, Privat, 1971

Michel Foucault: *Les Mots et les choses*, Gallimard, 1966

Sigmund Freud: *The Complete Psychological Works*, 24 vols, The Hogarth Press and the Institute of Psychoanalysis, 1953–74. Translated from the German under the general editorship of James Strachey in collaboration with Anna Freud.

Colette Gaudin: 'Niveaux de lisibilité dans *Leçon de choses* de Claude Simon', in *Romanic Review* 68, 1977, 175–96

Gérard Genette: 'Vertige fixé', *Figures I*, 1969: 69–90

  'Discours du récit', *Figures III*, Editions du Seuil, 1972

  Nouveau Discours du récit, Editions du Seuil, 1983

Philippe Hamon: 'Un discours contraint', in *Littérature et réalité*, ed. G. Genette et T. Todorov, Editions du Seuil, 1982

Stephen Heath: *The Nouveau Roman*, Elek, 1972

  Questions of Cinema, Macmillan, 1981

Karin Holter: 'La Constance difficile', in *Claude Simon: analyse et théorie*, ed. Ricardou, 1975, 368–75

  'Simon Citing Simon: a Few Examples of Limited Intertextuality', in *Orion Blinded*, ed. Birn and Gould, 1981, 133–47

Luce Irigaray: *Speculum de l'autre femme*, Editions de Minuit, 1974

Rosemary Jackson: *Fantasy: the Literature of Subversion*, Methuen, 1981

Roman Jakobson: *Essais de linguistique générale*, Editions de Minuit, 1963

  'Du réalisme artistique', orig. 1921, reprinted in *Théorie de la littérature*, ed. Todorov, Editions du Seuil, 1965, 98–108

Fredric Jameson: 'Imaginary and Symbolic in Lacan: Marxism, Psycho-analytical Criticism and the Problem of the Subject', in *Yale French Studies* 55/56, 1977, 338–95

Ludovic Janvier: 'Réponses de Claude Simon à quelques questions écrites de Ludovic Janvier', interview with Simon in *Entretiens sur les Lettres et les Arts* 31, 1972, 15–19

  Une Parole exigeante: le nouveau roman, Editions de Minuit, 1964

Ann Jefferson: *The Nouveau Roman and the Poetics of Fiction*, Cambridge University Press, 1980

T. H. Jones: '*Histoire*: the Narrative as a Bio-Graph', in Birn and Gould, ed., *Orion Blinded*, 1981, 105–16

Bibliography

Julia Kristeva: 'Bakhtine, le mot, le dialogue et le roman', in *Critique* 239, 1967, 438–65

'La sémiologie: science critique et/ou critique de la science', in *Théorie d'ensemble*, Editions du Seuil, 1968, 80–93

Thomas S. Kuhn: *The Structure of Scientific Revolutions*, The University of Chicago Press, Chicago, 1962

Jacques Lacan: *Ecrits*, Editions du Seuil, 1966. An English translation of some of the chapters of this is available in Sheridan 1977a.

Le Séminaire XI: Les quatre concepts fondamentaux de la psychanalyse, Editions du Seuil, 1973, translated Sheridan 1977b

J. Laplanche and J.-B. Pontalis: *Vocabulaire de la psychanalyse*, PUF, 1967

Serge Leclaire: 'Notes sur l'objet de la psychanalyse', in *Cahiers pour l'analyse*, no. 2, 1966

Psychanalyser, Editions du Seuil, 1968

Jacques Leenhardt: 'Claude Simon: l'écriture de la ressemblance', in *Claude Simon: analyse, théorie*, ed. Ricardou, 1975, 119–50

Anika Lemaire: *Jacques Lacan*, Pierre Margada, Brussels, 1977

Sylvère Lotringer: 'Cryptique', in *Claude Simon: analyse, théorie*, ed. Ricardou, 1975, 313–33

J. Loubère: 'The Generative Function of Translation' in *Orion Blinded*, ed. Birn and Gould, 1981, 184–99

Colin MacCabe: 'Theory and Film: Principles of Realism and Pleasure', in *Screen* 17, iii, 1976, 7–27

Pierre Macherey: *Pour une théorie de la production littéraire*, Maspéro, 1966

Maurice Merleau-Ponty: 'Cinq notes sur Claude Simon', in *Médiations* 4, 1961–2, 5–10

Christian Metz: *Psychoanalysis and Cinema*, Macmillan, 1982

J. A. Miller: 'La suture', *Cahiers pour l'analyse* no. 1, Paris, 1966. Translated by J. Rose in *Screen* 18 (1977/8), 24–34

Maria Minich-Brewer: 'Claude Simon: The Critical Properties of Painting', in *The Review of Contemporary Fiction* 5, no. 1, 1985, 104–9

Pat O'Kane: '*La Route des Flandres*: Reader's Rout(e)?', in *Claude Simon: New Directions*, ed. Duncan, 1985, 54–60

Christopher Prendergast: *The Order of Mimesis*, Cambridge University Press, Cambridge, 1986

Marcel Proust, *A la Recherche du temps perdu*, 3 vols, Pléiade, 1954

A. C. Pugh: 'Invitation à une lecture polyvalente' in *Claude Simon: analyse, théorie*, ed. Ricardou, 1975, 387–94

'From Drawing, to Painting, to Text: Claude Simon's Allegory of Representation and Reading in the Prologue to *The Georgics*', in *The Review of Contemporary Fiction* 5, 1985, 56–71

Georges Raillard: 'Femmes: Claude Simon dans les marges de Miro' in *Claude Simon: analyse, théorie*, ed. Ricardou, 1975, 73–87

Jean Ricardou: 'Un ordre dans le débâcle', in *Critique* 163, 1960, 1011–24

'La bataille de la phrase', in *Pour une théorie du nouveau roman*, Editions du Seuil, 1971

Bibliography

Le Nouveau Roman, Editions du Seuil, 1973

(ed.) *Claude Simon: analyse, théorie*, Centre Culturel International de Cerisy-la-Salle, 1974; published by the Union Générale de l'Edition, Collection 10/18, 1975

Alain Robbe-Grillet: *Les Gommes*, Editions de Minuit, 1953

Pour un nouveau roman, Editions de Minuit, 1963

Moshe Ron: 'Free Indirect Discourse, Mimetic Language Games and the Subject of Fiction', in *Poetics Today*, 2:2, 1981

Jacquelin Rose: 'The Imaginary', in *The Talking Cure*, ed. C. MacCabe, Macmillan, 1981, 132–61

Françoise van Rossum-Guyon: 'La mise en spectacle chez Claude Simon', in *Claude Simon: analyse, théorie*, ed. Ricardou, 1975, 88–106

Gérard Roubichou: *Lecture de l'Herbe de Claude Simon*, L'Age d'Homme, Lausanne, 1976

'*Histoire* or the Serial Novel', in *Orion Blinded*, ed. Birn and Gould, 1981, 173–83

Jean Rousset: 'La guerre en peinture', in *Critique* 37, 1981, 1201–10

Ralph Sarkonak: *Claude Simon: les carrefours du texte*, Editions Paratexte, Toronto, 1986

Nathalie Sarraute: *L'Ere du soupçon*, Gallimard, Collection Idées, 1956

John Searle: *Expression and Meaning*, Cambridge University Press, Cambridge, 1979

Alan Sheridan (trans.): *Ecrits: a Selection*, Tavistock, 1977a

The Four Fundamental Concepts of Psychoanalysis, The Hogarth Press, 1977b

Maxim Silvermann: 'Fiction as Process: the Later Novels of Claude Simon' in *Claude Simon: New Directions*, ed. Duncan, 1985, 61–74

Stuart Sykes: '*Les Géorgiques*: "une reconversion totale"?', in *Romance Studies* 2, 1983, 80–9

'*Parmi les aveugles le borgne est roi*. A Personal Survey of Simon Criticism', in *Claude Simon: New Directions*, ed. Duncan, 1985, 140–55

Tzvetan Todorov, ed.: *Théorie de la littérature*, Editions du Seuil, 1965

'Les catégories du récit littéraire', in *Communications* 8, 1966, 125–51

Irène Tschinka: 'La fabrique du corps ou la corrida du hors-corps' in *Claude Simon: analyse et théorie*, ed. Ricardou, 1975, 395–9

Jean-Claude Vareille: 'What We Learn from an Open Window', in *The Review of Contemporary Fiction* 5, 1985, 114–27

Index

229

Index

Index

Searle, John, 20–2
Sheridan, Alan, 164
signifier, 26, 30, 40, 42, 59, 60, 80, 81,
    82, 83, 85, 88, 91, 107, 112, 130,
    134, 135, 136, 137–8, 156, 171
signifying chain, 39, 41, 42, 82, 85, 89,
    134, 135, 139
Silverman, Maxim, 177 n. 30
Stendhal, 116, 129, 209 n. 3
structuralism, 1, 5, 26, 36
subject, 9, 11, 15, 23, 29–30, 31, 33,
    48, 52–4, 64, 68, 70–1, 74, 76, 78,
    85, 86, 89, 102–3, 120–1, 129,
    145, 170, 171; of perception, 6,
    64–5, 66, 69, 78, 148–9; of
    representation, 23–5, 33–5, 41,
    60, 61, 64, 68–9, 81, 85, 90, 96,
    102, 117
subject-in-language, 34, 35–40, 64, 65,
    66, 68, 76, 78–85, 90, 132, 171
sujet de l'énonciation, 30, 36–7, 40,
    41, 64, 71, 85, 86, 87, 88, 90; *de
    l'énoncé*, 30, 36–7, 40
Sykes, Stuart, 174 n. 8, 177 n. 32
symbolic order, 40, 42, 74, 75–9,

80–1, 89, 90, 105, 112, 145, 161,
    162, 164, 170, 171, 172

Tel Quel, 26, 28, 181 n. 32
Todorov, Tzvetan, 36, 185 n. 61
Triptyque, 5, 8, 10, 15, 16, 33, 37, 38,
    50, 65, 75, 86, 90, 97, 101, 105,
    128, 134, 138, 139
Tschinka, Irène, 10, 188 n. 9

unconscious, 12, 13, 19, 22, 23, 40,
    125, 132, 166, 169

Vareille, Jean-Claude, 98, 99
Vent, Le, 2, 13, 16, 37, 44, 160
vision, 1, 3–5, 17, 20, 31, 32, 34,
    44–9, 50–2, 54–7, 60–4, 66–7,
    77, 78, 80, 84, 93, 98, 104, 114–16,
    117–19, 121–2, 123, 126, 128, 130,
    131–2, 136, 141, 144, 145, 146,
    149–50, 151, 154, 157, 158–9, 167,
    168
visual discourse, 37, 47–8, 57, 60–1,
    63, 65, 66–7, 69, 165, 168, 169–73
voyeurism, 49–50

women's language, 49, 189 n. 15

Cambridge Studies in French

General editor: MALCOLM BOWIE

234